D0906674

Pseudo-Science and Society in Nineteenth-Century America

Pseudo-Science and Society in Nineteenth-Century America

ARTHUR WROBEL, Editor

THE UNIVERSITY PRESS OF KENTUCKY

Scholarly publisher for the Commonwealth,
serving Bellarmine College, Berea College, Centre College of Kentucky, Eastern Kentucky University, The Filson Club, Georgetown College, Kentucky Historical Society, Kentucky State University, Morehead State University, Murray State University, Northern Kentucky University, Transylvania University, University of Kentucky, University of Louisville, and Western Kentucky University.

Editorial and Sales Offices: Lexington, Kentucky 40506-0024

Library of Congress Cataloging-in-Publication Data

Pseudo-science and society in nineteenth-century America.

Bibliography: p.
Includes index.
1. Therapeutic systems—United States—History—19th century. 2. Quacks and quackery—United States—History—19th century. 3. United States—Social life and customs—History—19th century. I. Wrobel, Arthur, 1940- .

R733.P78 1987 615.5 87-12464
ISBN 0-8131-1632-5

Contents

Acknowledgments

I wish to thank friends and colleagues who cheerfully read the various drafts of my contributions to this volume and made helpful suggestions with tact: Lance Olsen, Joseph A. Bryant, Jr., and Rush Welter. Taylor Stoehr shared with me a wealth of valuable information and minimized errors and oversights with his incisively critical readings. The volume also benefited immeasurably from the care with which Howard Kerr read the entire manuscript and gave of his knowledge and critical insights. Whatever errors remain, however, are my responsibility.

My dissertation director at the University of North Carolina, C. Carroll Hollis, not only introduced me to the subject of the nineteenth-century pseudo-sciences, and phrenology in particular, but nurtured me both as a mentor and as a friend. I also wish to acknowledge my appreciation and debt to S.B.W., who saw me through the long foreground that led to this book, and to my wife, Maureen, for her patience and love.

Arthur Wrobel

ARTHUR WROBEL

1. Introduction

Recent studies about the nineteenth-century pseudo-sciences—primarily phrenology, mesmerism, spirtualism, hydropathy, and homoeopathy—have assumed a new character. Instead of being polemics by either partisans or opponents, or mere journalistic histories recounting the sensational and eccentric, these studies range from the popular and biographical to the intellectually esoteric. They are also interpretive. Scholars are discovering that these disciplines were warmly received during their heyday, not only among the uninformed and credulous but also among the respectable and educated, and that the diffusion and practice of these disciplines intertwined with all the major medical, cultural, and philosophical revolutions in nineteenth-century America.

On the surface, these pseudo-sciences have apparent differences. Homoeopathy and hydropathy, for instance, were medical sects, while spiritualism, mesmerism, and phrenology explored uncharted avenues of knowledge. Such differences, however, should not be overemphasized. Of greater significance are the remarkable number of premises, methodologies, and teleological assumptions they shared and that placed them squarely in the midst of major currents of nineteenth-century thought. Their doctrines complemented the national belief that America occupied a special place in mankind's history; denied the distinction between body and mind, the material and the spiritual; gave credence to the message delivered by reformers that health and happiness are accessible to men; and presented a unified view of knowledge and human nature that seemingly accounted for the structure of nature and man's place within it. Rationalistic, egalitarian, and utilitarian, they struck familiar and reassuring chords that were pleasing to the ears of Americans.

The essays in this volume reflect the richness and diversity that research in these disciplines offers. They illuminate and in some instances alter our understanding of some major nineteenth-century American cultural configurations. And they suggest how several of these sciences survived the profound revolution in scientific methodology at the turn of the last century and extended well into our own—some intact, others in modified form, and others as renascent influences on disciplines currently held as "true" sciences. Most of the essays in this volume also have bearing on the seemingly insoluble debate over demarcation, the criteria that differentiate "true" science from "pseudo" science.

Science, as formalist critics assert, must be consistent to be true; but for scholars who approach it from the perspective of the history of science, the problem is compounded. Taylor Stoehr's essay provides fuel for historicist externalists who take into account the degree to which the politics, cultural milieu, or ideology of a given era determines or influences judgments as to whether a discipline is proper science or not. In tracing the colorful career and intellectual peregrinations of a pseudo-scientist par excellence, one Robert Collyer, Stoehr leaves us wondering whether arguments about demarcation should not take into account changing concepts of the scientist and his discipline. Collyer's case reminds us that discovery is a precarious affair; the ability to ask the right questions or recognize the proper application often distinguishes a scientist from a pseudo-scientist. In short, the fineness of the line separating science from pseudo-science very nearly gives the whole demarcation debate, as one scholar maintains, mere emotive value.

Also, this distinction often becomes obvious only in retrospect. As John Greenway shows, the many nostrums and mechanical devices that filled catalogues and newspapers in the last quarter of the nineteenth century shared the same premises and even the language of legitimate research programs. At a time when the medical community was unable to account for seeming electrotherapeutic cures and the properties and nature of electricity were still unknown, the gulf separating commercial electric gadgets claiming to cure everything from nervous exhaustion to constipation from those sanctioned by the medical establishment was negligible. Greenway also underscores the point implicitly made in several ensuing essays in this volume: after pseudo-scientific explanations proved inadequate, researchers were forced into new ways of thinking about the etiology of disease and pursued new areas of research.

During their heyday, nevertheless, all the pseudo-sciences explored in this volume amassed an impressive list of testimonial successes. While questions can be raised about the legitimacy of their cures or the experiences they professed to unfold, we know that a large segment of the American population did believe in their efficacy. Given the state of contemporary scientific theory and practice, all these disciplines could even lay fair claim to being legitimate sciences. Their methodological underpinnings were securely grounded in scientific induction, or Baconianism. Empirical rather than speculative, reasoning from experimentation and observations rather than a priori arguments, Baconianism universally came to be regarded—according to Edward Everett, editor of the *North American Review* and a Unitarian minister—as "the true philosophy."[1]

For some of the newer sectarian medical movements, induction was a relatively straightforward matter of observing the effects of certain drugs or procedures. In many ways, homoeopathy and hydropathy seemed to have greater claims to empiricism than did orthodox medicine, which was comprised of a motley admixture of folk wisdom and intuitive approaches to healing.

In attempting to understand the living organism in light of its own laws, Samuel Hahnemann, the German founder of homoeopathy, devised a "law of similars," which, he asserted, was a "law of nature." Imitating nature, which they claimed often cures one disease by generating a milder one with similar symptoms, homoeopaths administered medicines or curatives in infinitesimal quantities that were known to generate in a healthy person symptoms like those exhibited by the patient. In combating the less virulent, artificially induced disease, homoeopathic theory asserted, the body cured simultaneously the primary disease. The process of testing the effects of these drugs or curatives was known as "proving." In a prover's scrupulous recording of every symptom he felt after taking a dose, the homoeopaths had their strongest claim as an inductive science. For a period of forty years homoeopathy enjoyed sufficient respectability to challenge orthodox medicine as the primary system of medical care in this country.[2]

While the lore in historical annals recording cures wrought by hydrotherapeutics, especially the precedent of the Roman Thermae, formed the long foreground of hydropathy, its more immediate history and its development into a medical system can be traced to Vincent Priessnitz. Noting how native Silesian peasants successfully used cold water compresses to aid in reducing the swelling of bruises or treating tumors in cattle, Priessnitz cured himself of injuries sustained from a severe horse fall with the consumption of cold water and the use of cold compresses. By the mid-1830s, Europeans and Americans made medical hegiras to Gräfenberg in Silesia. They were fleeing the violent procedures of orthodox medicine—blistering, puking, purging, cupping, bleeding, and poisonous doses of mercury and arsenic—as well as seeking this gentle therapy for relief from a host of ailments ranging from dyspepsia and prolapsus uteri to broken bones and rheumatism. Very soon water-cure emerged in this country as a viable system of medical treatment. It attracted adherents from all classes of society. No section of the country enjoyed a monopoly on the system, but the Northeast nurtured the system's leaders, published most of its monographs and periodicals, and refined its methodology.

While homoeopathy and hydropathy largely confined themselves to the curing of bodily ailments, the other pseudo-sciences—phrenology, mesmerism, and spiritualism—used empirically derived data to carry their scientific investigations into considerably wider areas. By nineteenth-century standards their empiricism was beyond reproach. Phrenology's founder,

Franz Josef Gall, a brilliant Viennese anatomist who made revolutionary discoveries about various neurophysiological functions, also established the physiological basis of mind. His theories were soundly based on comparative anatomical studies of the brain. Gall attributed the higher mental functioning of humans over other species to humans' more highly developed cortexes. He also attributed differences in personal characteristics among humans to cortical differences. He went even further. He identified twenty-seven faculties that he felt comprised the cognitive, sensory, and emotional characteristics of a human being. He taught that these faculties are located in identifiable areas of the brain and that the contour of the cranium provided an observer with an accurate understanding of the development of those faculties.[3]

Mesmerism had equally convincing claims to science. It provided a reasoned theory based on repeated successes and experiments to account for the cure of bodily diseases by inspired individuals from Jesus to a late eighteenth-century Austrian exorcist, Father J.V. Gassner. This movement's founder, Franz Anton Mesmer (1734–1815), believed that all human bodies are subject to an invisible magnetic fluid. Physicians could cure imbalances or misalignments of this magnetic force-field by manipulating the fluid in a patient's afflicted areas, using either magnets or, with the more gifted healer, the passing of hands over the body. Mesmer's theory had just enough science to appeal to a new rationalism—his hypothesis of a universal fluid derived from Newton's electromagnetic ether—and enough spiritual overtones to appeal to latent religious needs as well. Though a Royal Commission that included Benjamin Franklin, the chemist Lavoisier, and the physician Guillotin denied the existence of animal magnetism and consequently the utility of Mesmer's therapeutics, followers of Mesmer continued to effect cures for ailments ranging from hysteria to mysterious pains.[4] By the time mesmerism blossomed in the 1830s on these shores, it had assumed a new guise having sinister and even occult overtones: it could cure ailments, but a mesmerist could also control the mind of another and even elicit clairvoyant visions.[5]

An eclectic synthesis that included mesmerism's probing of telepathy, clairvoyance, and precognition, the doctrines of the Swedish mystic Emanuel Swedenborg, and the social thought of Charles Fourier formed the next major pseudo-science to emerge in America—spiritualism.[6] A doctrine about communication between spirits of the dead and human mediums, spiritualism began in Hydesville, New York, in 1848 when two sisters, Margaret and Kate Fox, professed to have received intelligent communication, in the form of mysterious rappings, from the spirit of a murdered man. Spiritualism absorbed the Swedenborgian doctrines of the correspondence between material and spiritual realities and the existence of a hierarchical series of spiritual spheres surrounding the earth. Swedenborg did spirtualism another service when, in 1848, his spirit and that of the Greek physician Galen allegedly visited the mesmerized body of Andrew Jackson Davis, soon to be dubbed the "Poughkeepsie Seer." According to Davis, Swedenborg promised to make him a channel of divine truth and wisdom and Galen proclaimed him a clairvoyant healer. The latter prophecy had merit insofar as the nineteen-year-old Davis started healing by prescribing cures after visualizing the inner organs of patients.[7] All such occurrences appeared to verify the claims spiritualists so often made, namely that theirs was an empirical science that repeatedly proved the reality of spiritual communication and cured bodily and spiritual ills.

Encouraged by such discoveries about the relation of anatomical and physiological characteristics to the operation of the human mind, about the existence of paranormal mental activities, about reciprocal communications between the mundane and spiritual worlds, the various pseudo-scientists widened their field of inquiry. They felt about their various disciplines as Emerson did about mesmerism, that "it affirmed unity and connection between remote points, and as such was excellent criticism on the narrow and dead classification of what passed for science."[8] Their discoveries also appeared to confirm their age's certainty that mind and matter were transcendentally linked. Homoeopathy, for instance, attributed disturbances in the body to perturbations in a person's spiritual force that, in good health, animates and governs the body. Thus, homoeopathic doses were not aimed at the disease but at strengthening the spiritual force and reestablishing the harmonious interrelationship between the two spheres.[9] Similarly, Davis taught that discord in man's spiritual principle caused an ensuing material imbalance manifesting itself as disease.[10]

Speculations about the constitution of man and its relation to external meaning at this time were as understandable as they were irresistible. For the first time men seemed close to discovering empirical proof supporting ontological and teleological premises that their age inherited from eighteenth-century discourses on natural law—that system of universal and invariable laws which sustain the visible creation. The works of the pseudo-scientists regularly invoked the sacred terms of "natural law" as the proof-stone when assaying their own doctrines. Andrew Jackson Davis's "harmonial philosophy," that an eternal and immutable set of divine principles rules the universe, is but a recasting of natural law; the true initiate who discovered the spiritual and material worlds could expect to find the same principles of natural law governing both realms.[11] The premise of an intimate relationship between the human world and nature's eternal processes offered the hope that a new moral social order and unlimited personal improvement could be lawfully engineered.

Both ends of the cultural spectrum welcomed such promise. With major intellectual upheavals and rapid changes threatening the old stabilities, conservatives faced the future anxiously. More than novel and imaginative solutions, they desired some form of authority. To many of them, phrenology, spiritualism, and mesmerism had the potential to design institutions based on the finest intellectual tools available and to offer sound analyses of human nature. Utopian visionaries as well welcomed their guidance in plotting a new and permanent order comprised of enlightened institutions and people.

Ordinary people with reasons less grandiose but no less compelling listened attentively. They wished to know about the laws governing their own constitutions, to reach beyond the merely temporal and establish connection with the eternal, or simply to improve their lives by realizing greater health and the full use of all their innate faculties. As Marshall S. Legan shows in his survey of water-cure in America, hydropathy attracted all classes of society, the prominent and anonymous alike, and it surfaced in all sections of the country. Further, hydropathic theory reasserted the widespread belief that ultimately all meaningful phenomena of life, including health, are intimately related to nature's processes. The prospect of consulting science and nature rather than traditional wisdoms appealed to many in this country where egalitarianism assumed the force of an ideology and men assigned divine and regenerative qualities to nature.

Though the hopes these psuedo-sciences raised appear misguidedly extravagant, they were not atypical. In collapsing the spiritual and physical into a unity, these pseudo-sciences came to resemble any number of social and health reform movements,[12] except for one important difference: they appeared to offer corroborative inductive support, not mere visionary hopes. Their empirical pretensions placed them amid the major forces of change in the nineteenth century.

Predictably, these pseudo-sciences became embroiled in most of the age's reform movements, lending their voice to the period's restless search for new human, social, and political solutions. While their proposals were not always novel, they vigorously challenged the musty premises that they believed perpetuated injustice, disease, social unrest, and crime. For instance, Davis, among others, committed himself so powerfully to the eradication of other social evils—drunkenness, violence, racial and sexual injustice, and even war—that the spiritualist movement eventually fragmented. In his essay Robert Delp details the last years of Davis's life when he bitterly struggled to keep phenomenal spiritualism, namely rappings and communicating with the dead, from dominating his revelation of the reformatory Harmonial Philosophy.

All the pseudo-sciences also supported the women's rights movement. Those with medical pretensions contributed to the widening of women's sphere, specifically by pioneering the training of women as medical practitioners. Women's rights also won the support of spiritualism's Andrew Jackson Davis, who thundered against the duplicity of a society whose women were "insulted with flattery, deceived by false attention, enslaved by heartless promises." He urged woman to demand of men her "Rights" and "a *just* representation of her interests."

Phrenology also served as a potent ally among those desiring to widen women's sphere. The firm of Fowler and Wells on Nassau Street published major feminist tracts, entertained their authors, and endorsed the rights of women to enter not only health-related fields as practitioners but all spheres of employment—from printing to legislation, engraving to law. Its proprietors even advocated full suffrage and equal pay for equal work.[13] Phrenology's proponents with an eschatological bent applied its optimistic doctrines, that the brain's faculties could be modified through exercise and will, to just about every reform: health (including temperance, anti-tobacco, Bloomerism, water-cure, and vegetarianism), penology, education, treatment of the insane, human sexuality, religion, and even political theory, the subject of my own essay. To liberals and conservatives alike, phrenology appeared to offer a solution to the problem vexing Jacksonian America, namely how men could be made to act morally responsible with minimal external authorities to monitor their behavior. Phrenology seemed a logical authority. Besides justifying democracy as a form of government sanctioned by and consistent with the laws of nature, phrenology promised to identify man's self-governing and moral faculties and to design ways of strengthening them in preparation for enlightened self-rule.

Daring flights of pseudo-scientific thought even ventured into the area of human sexuality. Aspiz treats a subject that has been scantily studied, the actual teaching on sex, marriage, and parentage that ran through pseudo-scientific and reformist sex and marriage manuals between 1830 and 1900. In these sources he finds a pseudo-science of eugenics that bordered on a form of scientific breeding aimed at creating the cultural ideal of the well-sexed man and woman. For an age that is generally tagged as prudish and fastidious in regard to sexual matters and the transmission of sexual information, Aspiz uncovers a surprising number of recurring "laws" and "principles" on all phases of sexuality and to which conflicting parties commonly referred in arguing their positions.

The different reforms responded in kind and welcomed these powerful allies. The Grahamites not only trumpeted their brand of vegetarianism but embraced as well phrenology and mesmerism.[14] Their emphasis on dietary restraint and wholesomeness and cleanliness put them as well in sympathy with the major tenets of hydropathy. Reformers as disparate as Amelia Bloomer, the woman's rights and temperance activist, and Thomas Low Nichols and Mary Gove Nichols, followers of and criers for just about every mid-century crusade, all espoused phrenology and hydropathy. Robert Dale Owen, a labor reformer, politician, diplomat, and utopian was so impressed with spiritualism that he published *Footfalls on the Boundary of Another World* (1860), arguing that spirit communication with another world was real.[15] His enthusiasm for spiritualism never abated; in *The Debatable Land between This World and the Next* (1871) he proposed spiritualism as a mediator between faith and science.[16]

The enlightened humanitarianism those pseudo-sciences preached also caught the attention of several nineteenth-century utopian leaders. To many communitarians these new and imposing disciplines offered fresh solutions and tenable alternatives to warrant further investigation. Bronson Alcott studied physiognomy and metempsychosis, while his diagrams of mental powers which he often illustrated on a blackboard were no more than a phrenological chart.[17] As a disciple of Andrew Jackson Davis, Thomas Lake Harris dabbled in magnetic trances before commencing his career at Mountain Cove; John Humphrey Noyes of the Oneida Community consulted phrenological works before formulating his theories of Bible Communism and even Complex Marriage. Millerite Elder George Storrs's explanation, after the last day failed to materialize,[18] that he was laboring under the delusion of mesmerism did not deter other communitarians from studying mesmerism or spiritualism: Adin Ballou of Hopedale, Mary Gove and Thomas Low Nichols of Modern Times, and John Murray Spear of Kiantone.

After the failure of New Harmony, Robert Owen and his son Robert Dale Owen converted to spiritualism, while Albert Brisbane became a practitioner in the 1850s.[19]

In allying themselves with so many of the reform movements and attracting the interest of various communitarians, several of the pseudo-sciences came to absorb and then employ the rhetoric common to millennial tracts about the dawning of a new age of peace, prosperity, and Christian morality. This drift served them well—it blunted attacks of religious leaders by appearing to complement standard religious belief about the approaching Kingdom of God while simultaneously placing these disciplines in a major tributary of the age's popular cultural mainstream. Confidence that millennial glory hovered just over the horizon pervades the thought of pseudo-scientific writers, each of them as immodestly certain as O.S. Fowler that phrenology was bringing mankind closer to that blessed day: "Then shall God be honored, and man be perfectly holy and inconceivably happy, and earth be paradise."[20]

A syncretic phenomenon transpired as well among the different pseudo-sciences themselves, no doubt because of their similar teleologies and reforming passions. Mesmerism intrigued all of them, the seeming influence of mental concentration on physical actions shoring up their doctrine about the unity of spirit and matter. Even homoeopathy's founder, Hahnemann, was himself caught up in Europe's late eighteenth-century mesmeric craze and believed it represented an alternative to his own healing theory. Later Hans Gram's homoeopathic circle in New York turned to works on phrenology and mesmerism to be instructed more profoundly in the relationship between the body and soul. Homoeopaths were drawn as well to Swedenborgianism, while some Transcendentalists joined the latter in embracing homoeopathy, mesmerism, and phrenology. Orson Fowler liked to travel by railroad, believing that such journeys electrically charged his body.[21] Never very bashful about generously appropriating materials that promised fast profits, he developed "Phreno-Magnetism" and took over publication of the *Water-Cure Journal and Herald of Reforms* in 1848.[22] William Wesselhoeft, a homoeopathic physician who moved in Transcendentalist and reformist circles, espoused temperance, gymnastics, and hydropathy.[23]

But by no means was the march of the pseudo-sciences in nineteenth-century America an entirely triumphal procession. It encountered considerable numbers of critics if not downright scoffers. One was David Meredith Reese, a splenetic New York physician. With *The Humbugs of New York* (1839) he hoped to eradicate all the humbugs, both domestic and foreign, in a powerful lightning bolt of derision and invective. He accused them of practicing the pernicious doctrines of materialism and fatalism, condemning phrenology for encouraging people to accept their vices and delinquencies as merely constitutional in origin.[24] That the accidental shape of a person's head, a clergyman similarly wrote in the *Boston Investigator* in 1835, was said to determine a person's mind simply subverted religion, morals, and, certainly, free agency. "Avoid phrenologists," he thundered, "as worse than the French infidels."

Spiritualism came under attack as well, for both the support it lent to various reforms and the threat it posed to orthodox ecclesiastical authority. Clergymen looked askance at the theological liberalism spiritualism fostered—dissolving the personality of God and denying the Trinity, man's depravity, predestination, vicarious atonement, and even the final judgment. In making mediumship available to women, spiritualism granted them a form of spiritual leadership by giving them access to the very powers that had hitherto been available only to the male clergy.[25] The Protestant clergy also saw in spiritualism a heresy that deluded followers into thinking that they were as capable of divine inspiration as Christ, as well as a heretical recrudescence of demonism. Many viewed spiritual evidences as Satanic in origin. Predictably, the clergy stood aghast when Episcopal, Presbyterian, and Methodist laypersons adopted spiritualist views and the spiritualist quarterly *Shekinah* used a portrait of Jesus as the frontispiece for its first volume in 1852. When one of their own appeared to break ranks, the clergy struck back: it brought heresy charges against Charles Beecher in 1863 for holding twin beliefs in evolution and spiritualism. Exonerated and undeterred, Beecher published *Spiritual Manifestations* in

1879, in which he attempted to synthesize spiritualism, the Bible, and liberal Christianity.[26]

The response of the medical establishment to these disciplines, particularly since many of them were blossoming into competitive medical sects, was hardly sanguine, either. With good reason did the *Boston Medical and Surgical Journal* editorially grouse about the fashionable enthusiasms that kept sweeping through the ranks of orthodox physicians. It noted, rather dourly, that the very same practitioners who were currently "running after this hydropathic mummery" were last year "equally full of transcendentalism, the year before of homoeopathy, the years before of animal magnetism, Grahamism, phrenology. Next year they will be Fourierites, communists, George Sandists, etc."[27] Oliver Wendell Holmes mounted perhaps the most classic and systematic attack on homoeopathy in a two-part lecture before the Boston Society for the Diffusion of Useful Knowledge in 1842. Holmes placed homoeopathy in the company of other kindred delusions—the royal touch for scrofula, weapon salve, tar water, and the Perkins tractor. (He could have enlisted Mrs. Carlyle's concurrence. Her brief trial with homoeopathy ended in disappointment and with the wail: "Homoeopathy is an invention of the Father of Lies; I have tried it, and found it wanting.")[28] Holmes predicted that homoeopathy would shortly expire, leaving only the "ultra Homoeopathist," who will "embrace some newer and if possible equally extravagant doctrines; or he will stick to his colors and go down with his sinking doctrine."[29]

The reasons for repudiating these pseudo-sciences, however, were not any more in number or variety than those for embracing them. The *New England Magazine* in 1832 reported, on the occasion of Johann G. Spurzheim's unexpected death in Boston, that Spurzheim had had remarkable success in attracting converts to phrenology, "not only from among mere lecture-goers and literary triflers, but from the most scientific and learned in various professions: Physicians, Surgeons, and Lawyers, of great present eminence."[30] The same could have been said about the other pseudo-sciences. Innumerable public figures, whether out of curiosity, hope, or belief, submitted to phrenological examinations. Their results, more often than not, were promptly published in the *American Phrenological Journal:* P.T. Barnum, the Siamese Twins, Amelia Bloomer, Brigham Young, Andrew Carnegie, Thomas A. Edison, and Henry Ward Beecher.[31] Spiritualism had no lesser claims to the eminent. William Lloyd Garrison, George Ripley, Horace Greeley, Lydia Maria Child, William Cullen Bryant, Rufus W. Griswold, James Fenimore Cooper, George Bancroft, and John Roebling all attended seances, attracted no doubt as much by interest as bafflement. Horace Greeley's wife attended a seance to contact her dead son Pickie.[32] So pervasive was spiritualism's presence that George Templeton Strong, the New York lawyer and diarist, wryly lamented how "ex-judges of the Supreme Court, senators, clergymen, professors of physical sciences" were "lecturing and writing books" on the spiritualist phenomenon.[33] Mesmerism's advocates included Charles Dickens; Harriet Martineau, whose skepticism about mesmeric healing was dispelled in 1844 when she was successfully treated for polypous tumors and prolapsus uteri; and Margaret Fuller, who was successfully treated mesmerically for headaches and spinal curvature.[34] Daniel Webster, Henry Clay, and Sam Houston added their names to a petition asking that John Dods deliver a series of lectures in the nation's capital on mesmerism.[35] Other notables attended hydropathic spas or underwent a course of water-cure: Harriet Beecher Stowe, Catharine Beecher, Henry Wadsworth Longfellow, Francis Parkman, and Fanny Fern. In England, George Henry Lewes and George Eliot, the Carlyles, the Dickenses, T.B. Macaulay, Darwin, Huxley, Ruskin, and Tennyson all tried water-cure for varying lengths of time; Bulwer-Lytton remained its steadfast champion.[36] Noted Americans who were homoeopathically treated included: Henry Wadsworth Longfellow, William Lloyd Garrison, Julia Ward Howe, Louisa May Alcott, William Seward, Thomas Wentworth Higginson, John D. Rockefeller,[37] and Washington Irving, the subject of George Hendrick's essay. Hendrick details a little-known chapter in Irving's life when, beset by a number of health problems that interfered with his work on the massive *Life of Washington*, the writer sought but failed to find relief in homoeopathy.

These various disciplines also attracted authors who believed they found in them a creative lodestone that revealed knowledge unattainable by rational investigation or systematized knowledge about human nature. Louisa May Alcott, William Cullen Bryant, Stephen Crane, William Dean Howells, Henry Wadsworth Longfellow, and James Russell Lowell submitted to phrenological examinations, as did Walt Whitman.[38] Whitman's own highly favorable head-reading, given him by the great American phrenologist Lorenzo Niles Fowler, provided the basis for his conceptualization of the poet-prophet in *Leaves of Grass.* Phrenology also shaped much of Whitman's thinking about other subjects: education, America's millennial future, women's rights, sex, eugenics, even his mystical religious views.[39] For Edgar Allan Poe phrenology represented a psychology useful for analyzing human nature in such short stories as "The Imp of the Perverse" and "The Fall of the House of Usher." He also wrote several mesmeric spoofs.[40] Melville used phrenology for humorous purposes as well—he phrenologized the whale and favorably compared Queequeg's head to George Washington's, "cannibalistically developed," of course.[41] Mark Twain started his own study of phrenology at nineteen, submitted to head-readings on at least three occasions, and used its vocabulary and concepts throughout his career, from *The Innocents Abroad* (1869) to *What Is Man?* (1906). Though he used it at times for humorous purposes, the phrenological notion of "temperaments" shaped his self-concept, and he never gave up investigating its claims that it offered a means of character detection or psychological remedy.[42] The novels of George Eliot, Bulwer-Lytton, and Charlotte Brontë, popular on both sides of the Atlantic, show a working familiarity with phrenological terms and concepts.[43]

The vocabulary of mesmerism, phrenology, physiognomy, homoeopathy, and spiritualism, the concepts they proposed and issues they raised, are woven into the plots, characterizations, themes, and even methods of Hawthorne's fiction. The characterization of Westervelt in *The Blithedale Romance,* the homoeopathic ideas in the alchemical lore of Drs. Rappaccini, Aylmer, Grimshawe, and Dolliver, the "spiritual voyeurism" that characters such as Matthew Maule and Holgrave practice on innocent victims, and the revelation of complex psychic organizations in characters such as Hepzibah, Holgrave, and Clifford, all testify to Hawthorne's simultaneous fascination with and repulsion from the artistic and philosophical potential these disciplines held.[44]

Artists and sculptors were also cheered at the prospect of creating works of art more esthetically pleasing, analytically true, and scientifically accurate. As C. Thomas Walters shows, American artists turned to discoveries about human character in phrenology and physiognomy and to comparative anatomy to develop a range of sculptural technology and to gain conceptual inspiration.

Writers and thinkers, among them Coleridge and several American Transcendentalists—James Freeman Clarke, Frederick Hedge, and Theodore Parker—read widely in these pseudo-sciences which discoursed so knowingly about man's place in nature. Though they never found in them a decisive repudiation of Lockean epistemology or Hume's skepticism, they originally turned to these pseudo-sciences, as did many of their age, to learn about the relation of mind to body and about the unity of man's mental and spiritual life with higher or transcendent realms of being.[45]

In short, these pseudo-sciences captured the imagination of a wide spectrum of followers because of the relevance they had for disciplines ranging from medicine and art to philosophy, and for the way they resonated with major nineteenth-century cultural assumptions and aspirations. This is especially evident, Robert C. Fuller argues, in the case of mesmerism. Originally a system of bodily and mental healing that discovered a stratum of mental life just below the threshold of ordinary consciousness, mesmerism evolved into a discipline that successfully grafted a pre-scientific psychology to many current religious and philosophical beliefs. While satisfying a yearning in Americans for a non-scriptural source of spiritual enlightenment, American mesmerists simultaneously recapitulated many of the themes raised in the nation's revivalist tradition. Mesmerism also reaffirmed core American faiths—that the created universe was harmonious, that the material and spiritual realms were intimately connected, and that men could anticipate the complete transformation of their physical and spiritual beings.

Such resonances eventually contributed to and even accelerated their own decline. Erected on rather shaky scientific foundations to begin with, they teetered more and more precariously each time noisy enthusiasts added new deductions to existing structures. What once passed for refreshing philosophical adaptability soon appeared to many as grotesque ploys by shameless hucksters to stretch the fabric of their thought to fit either the age's constantly changing cultural and intellectual configurations or their own ambitions.

Except for homoeopathy, the lives of the rest of the aforementioned pseudo-sciences did not extend much beyond the turn of this century. The delicate balance each achieved during its own heyday—among science, healing, aggressive entrepreneurship, and entertainment—became upset, the latter two usurping and in time replacing the former entirely. Dabblers and professionals alike were reluctant to weigh down their enthusiasms with such leaden matters as establishing sounder methodologies, or pursuing serious experimentation that reflected better ways of testing data, or even adjusting their doctrines to accommodate new discoveries in neuro-anatomy, physiology, and chemistry. Instead, they lazily clung to a dubious Baconianism, readily succumbing to the temptation of seeking only confirmation, however specious, and ignoring contradictory or conflicting evidence. Also, in the absence of any legitimate institutional authority, proponents sought confirmation in popular rather than scientific audiences, adjusting doctrines to meet the practical requirements or sensational expectations of uneducated audiences.

The pseudo-sciences declined also because they gradually lost two of their most attractive appeals—as alternate healing therapies and as heralds of reform. As medical heresies they flourished because of the public's well-founded skepticism about the ability of traditional medicine to treat disease. But with the emergence of an improved materia medica and healing techniques, orthodox medicine regained the ascendancy, ironically profiting because it absorbed, if not appropriated outright, principles of healing from the very medical heresies it so often publicly debunked. Homoeopathic therapeutics, for instance, contributed significantly to the formation of modern medicine. Homoeopathy evolved new applications of medicinal substances and, according to its system of pharmacology, developed new drugs and medicines that orthodox medicine eventually assimilated into its own materia medica.[46] The collapse of reform during the post–Civil War period also precipitated their decline. The war's reality appeared to mock the earlier faith that individual moral regeneration was possible or that any of the newly emerging economic, urban, or political problems could be solved in any way other than legislatively or institutionally. The ancient dream of renovating man and his institutions according to the eternal laws upon which nature and society were said to rest seemed delusive.

Notes

1. George H. Daniels, *American Science in the Age of Jackson* (New York: Columbia Univ. Press, 1968), p. 63. For a complete account of American Baconianism, see chap. 3, "The Reign of Bacon in America."

2. William G. Rothstein, *American Physicians in the Nineteenth Century* (Baltimore: Johns Hopkins Univ. Press, 1972). For an account of the rise, theory, and spread of homoeopathy in nineteenth-century America, see chap. 8, "The Rise of Homoeopathy."

3. Raymond E. Fancher, *Pioneers of Psychology* (New York: Norton, 1979), pp. 43-51.

4. Thomas H. Leahey, *A History of Psychology: Main Currents in Psychological Thought* (Englewood Cliffs, N.J.: Prentice-Hall, 1980), pp. 156-59.

5. *The Occult in America,* ed. Howard Kerr and Charles L. Crow (Urbana: Univ. of Illinois Press, 1983), p. 2.

6. Ernest Isaacs, "The Fox Sisters and American Spiritualism," *The Occult in America,* p. 80.

7. R. Laurence Moore, *In Search of White Crows: Spiritualism, Parapsychology, and American Culture* (New York: Oxford Univ. Press, 1977), pp. 9-11.

8. Ralph Waldo Emerson, *The Complete Works of Ralph Waldo Emerson,* ed. Edward Waldo Emerson, 12 vols. (Boston, 1903-1904),

10:337-38. Cited in Taylor Stoehr, *Hawthorne's Mad Scientists: Pseudoscience and Social Science in Nineteenth-Century Life and Letters* (Hamden, Conn.: Archon Books, 1978), p. 25.

9. Joseph F. Kett, *The Formation of the American Medical Profession: The Role of Institutions, 1780-1860* (New Haven: Yale Univ. Press, 1968), pp. 132-34.

10. J. Stillson Judah, *The History and Philosophy of the Metaphysical Movements in America* (Philadelphia: Westminster Press, 1967), pp. 151-52.

11. Moore, *Metaphysical Movements*, p. 12.

12. Ronald G. Walters, *American Reformers: 1815-1860* (New York: Hill and Wang, 1978), p. 170.

13. Andrew Jackson Davis, *The Great Harmonia* (Boston: Sanborn, Carter, & Bazin, 1855), 2:199. Madeleine B. Stern, *Heads and Headlines: The Phrenological Fowlers* (Norman: Univ. of Oklahoma Press, 1971), pp. 165-67.

14. Kett, *American Medical Profession*, p. 125.

15. Isaacs, "*Fox Sisters*," p. 96.

16. Howard Kerr, *Mediums, and Spirit-Rappers, and Roaring Radicals: Spiritualism in American Literature, 1850-1900* (Urbana: Univ. of Illinois Press, 1973), p. 109.

17. John B. Wilson, "Phrenology and the Transcendentalists," *American Literature* 28 (May 1956): 222.

18. Stoehr, *Hawthorne's Mad Scientists*, p. 28.

19. Ibid., pp. 254-55.

20. Orson Squire Fowler, *Hereditary Descent: Its Laws and Facts Illustrated and Applied to the Improvement of Mankind* (New York: Fowler and Wells, 1843), p. 24.

21. Kett, *American Medical Profession*, pp. 141, 150, 154, 146.

22. Stern, *Heads and Headlines*, p. 51.

23. Kett, *American Medical Profession*, p. 154.

24. John D. Davies, *Phrenology: Fad and Science: A 19th-Century American Crusade* (New Haven: Yale Univ. Press, 1955), p. 69.

25. Ibid., p. 68; Moore, *White Crows*, pp. 40-69, passim; Mary Ferrell Bednarowski, "Women in Occult America," *The Occult in America*, pp. 180-82.

26. Moore, *White Crows*, pp. 44-46; Jon Butler, "Dark Ages of American Occultism," *The Occult in America*, p. 72; Kerr, *Mediums*, p. 14.

27. Kett, *American Medical Profession*, pp. 154-55.

28. Bruce Haley, *The Healthy Body and Victorian Culture* (Cambridge: Harvard Univ. Press, 1978), p. 13.

29. Martin Kaufmann, *Homeopathy in America: The Rise and Fall*

of a Medical Heresy (Baltimore: Johns Hopkins Univ. Press, 1971), pp. 35-41.

30. "The Late Dr. Spurzheim," *New England Magazine* (Jan. 1833): 40.

31. *A Phrenological Dictionary of Nineteenth-Century Americans*, compiled by Madeleine B. Stern (Westport, Conn.: Greenwood Press, 1982).

32. Kerr, *Mediums*, p. 6.

33. As quoted in Isaacs, "*Fox Sisters*," p. 79.

34. Stoehr, *Hawthorne's Mad Scientists*, pp. 23, 46.

35. Robert C. Fuller, *Mesmerism and the American Cure of Souls* (Philadelphia: Univ. of Pennsylvania Press, 1982), p. 70.

36. Harry B. Weiss and Howard R. Kemble, *The Great American Water-Cure Craze* (Trenton, N.J.: Past Times Press, 1967) pp. 182, 214-15; Haley, *Healthy Body*, p. 16.

37. John S. Haller, Jr., *American Medicine in Transition, 1840-1910* (Urbana: Univ. of Illinois Press, 1981), p. 117.

38. Stern, *Phrenological Dictionary.*

39. Ibid., pp. 99-124, passim; Harold Aspiz, "Educating the Kosmos: 'There Was a Child Went Forth,' " *American Quarterly* 18 (winter 1966): 655-66; "Unfolding the Folds," *Walt Whitman Review* 12 (Dec. 1966): 81-87; and Arthur Wrobel, "Whitman and the Phrenologists," *PMLA* 89 (Jan. 1974): 17-23.

40. Davies, *Phrenology*, pp. 120-22; Stern, *Heads and Headlines*, pp. 73-7.

41. Harold Aspiz, "Phrenologizing the Whale," *Nineteenth-Century Fiction* 23 (June 1968): 18-27; and Tyrus Hillway, "Melville's Use of Two Pseudo-Sciences," *Modern Language Notes* 64 (March 1949): 145-50.

42. Davies, *Phenology*, p. 120.

43. Alan Gribben, "Mark Twain, Phrenology and the 'Temperaments': A Study of Pseudoscientific Influence," *American Quarterly* 24 (March 1972): 45-68.

44. Stoehr, *Hawthorne's Mad Scientists*, passim.

45. Wilson, "Phrenology and the Transcendentalists," pp. 220-25, passim.

46. Harris L. Coulter, "Homoeopathic Influences in Nineteenth-Century Allopathic Therapeutics," *Journal of the American Institute of Homeopathy* 65, no. 3 (Sept. 1972): 139-81; and 65, no. 4 (Dec. 1972): 207-44.

TAYLOR STOEHR

2. Robert H. Collyer's Technology of the Soul

Back in 1958 two computer scientists could write: "There are now in the world machines that think, that learn and that create. Moreover, their ability to do these things is going to increase rapidly until—in the visible future—the range of problems they can handle will be coextensive with the range to which the human mind has been applied."

The blurb for a book published in 1983 goes further: "Are computers alive? Yes! and today they truly represent an emerging family of living species in the world—*that* is the startling argument of this landmark book."[1]

At funeral services I recently attended, the minister (of no minor sect) encouraged our faith in life after death by pointing to everyday phenomena just as miraculous as resurrection: a few drops of a liquid extracted from deep in the earth, and our car engines come to life; a flick of the switch, and our beloved president materializes before our eyes, transported thousands of miles, in full color. Why should not this clay rise again?

Others believe that science will soon do away with mortality itself; our species will not suffer by comparison with its self-repairing and reconstituting electronic cousins. A recent survey of research into the biochemistry of longevity quotes one enthusiastic fund raiser as saying, "We are either the last generation to die or the first one to live forever."[2]

I cannot recite such crudities without being reminded of the tradition, European in its origins with E.T.A. Hoffman and Mary Shelley, but most at home in America, from its early masters Poe and Hawthorne through its near burlesque in B movies a hundred years later—the gothic tradition of the mad scientist, whose Faustian *hubris* destroys the strongest bonds of kin and love, threatens the whole human community, and finally ends in despairing gnashing of teeth and, especially in modern versions, self-annihilation.

What would Hawthorne have made of these current blasphemies, new elixirs of life and machines that think? We like to regard such developments as throwbacks to the alchemical necromancers that people his stories. One can almost see them in their robes and funny hats and wands. The stalwarts of modern science are not like that; they are the anonymous researchers pictured in the ads, who promise to save our environment *and* keep the consumer economy viable. Yet is theirs not the same deadly prescription Dr. Rappaccini concocted, however much the lab coats and technology have changed? Teamwork and knowhow, the commercial assures us, will find new sources of energy, end tooth decay, and cure mortality itself. There is no ill in nature that will not yield to scientific method—that is the message.

In the following pages I am not dealing with the whole issue of mad science, the doomsday technology that has given us such lessons as DDT, Chernobyl, and Star Wars, still less with the mixed blessings to traditional human community and intelligence of those cultural Trojan horses TV and the automobile. My focus is on one man and his peculiarly revealing career in what I have called the Technology of the Soul, the nineteenth century's frantic effort to find a modern, scientific way of understanding—and controlling—individual human consciousness.

My representative pseudo-scientist's closest brush with fame grew out of the "discovery" of anesthesia in 1846. He was one of the minor claimants to the honor—and to the $100,000 reward debated in Congress—for developing a practical means of painless surgery. The chief contestants were a Boston dentist, William T.G. Morton, who demonstrated the technique in the operating room of Massachusetts General Hospital; Horace

Wells, another dentist, who had been Morton's partner and who had started things off with the idea of using laughing gas, nitrous oxide, in pulling teeth; and Charles T. Jackson, a well-known Boston scientist who gave Morton advice about how to administer the sulphuric ether he substituted for Wells's nitrous oxide. (Before any of them, Crawford W. Long, a country doctor in the Deep South, had used ether for a few operations, until his neighbors began to shun him.)

Who really deserved the credit? Was it the idea of painless surgery that counted, or the method? And which method, nitrous oxide or sulphuric ether? Or was it the public demonstration of the method? The squabble left them ruined men—Morton a pauper, Wells a chloroform addict and suicide, Jackson locked away in an asylum. Only Long, who never pushed his claim, died in obscurity rather than misery.

A generation later the medical profession was still raking these coals. In 1870 the London *Lancet* published the first "definitive" history of the controversy, attempting to settle the issue of originality once and for all.[3] After distributing praise among the principal contenders, the *Lancet* writer surprisingly came up with a new candidate, who "is to our minds the true pioneer after all—the man who ran first, and beckoned and called, however oddly, others to follow, with so much effect that a few followed at once, and many afterwards."[4]

History has not accepted the decision of the *Lancet,* though it was the foremost medical journal of its day, because the man proposed as the true pioneer was not an orthodox scientist. His case for priority rested on the most blatant quackery. Who was this man? Why was his science *pseudo* while that of Morton, Wells, and Jackson was *true?*

Robert Hanham Collyer, M.D., was an Englishman, probably born on the Channel Island of Jersey, though neither his origin nor his end is certain.[5] He had some medical training at the University of London in the mid-1830s, under Dr. John Elliotson, England's first advocate of mesmerism;[6] even before that he seems to have studied in Paris, where he met the famous prophet of phrenology Johann Gaspar Spurzheim.[7]

Collyer had a Yankee temperament. His scientific approach was that of the jack-of-all-trades; he dabbled in everything but

Fig. 2.1. Robert H. Collyer, from the title page of *Lights and Shadows of American Life* (Boston, 1843).

was too volatile for serious research. It was not surprising that the *Lancet* writer mistook him for an American, characterized by "impetuous perception, impulsive action, open nature, and unrestrainable fluency of speech."[8] Even his American admirers spoke of his "burning enthusiasm" and "dauntless energy," though he betrayed his British origins in being "somewhat peculiar in his public discourses, and somewhat eccentric in his general character."[9]

These traits might not make a good scientist, but they made an excellent pseudo-scientist. Publicity was more important than methodology for these hothouse doctrines that bloomed overnight and wilted fast. Collyer's claim for a share in the discovery of inhalation anesthesia depended on just such pseudo-scientific talents.

On June 15, 1836, Collyer disembarked in New York City, where he immediately set up as a popular lecturer.[10] At the university he had learned something about microscopes, and having brought one with him, he offered to reveal "The Wonders of the Microscopic World" to all who had the price of admission.[11]

Friends soon urged him to take advantage of his acquaintance with the late Dr. Spurzheim, whose tour a few years earlier had made phrenology fashionable with Americans.[12] It would not take much study to memorize the phrenological charts that located the thirty-four faculties and propensities on the skull; after that, it was more a matter of eloquence than of knowledge. Encouraged by "the success that had attended several private examinations" (like palm readings, of the cranium), Collyer left his microscopic wonders for the more lucrative phrenological lecture circuit.

He said that he was not in the field "for any pecuniary benefit," and in fact he often lectured without a fee—but that was because there was more money to be made in private consultations. This sharp practice earned him the contempt of the world-famous Scots phrenologist George Combe, whose own itinerary happened to cross Collyer's in 1839. There were three phrenological lecturers billed for Hartford on the same night: Combe was charging $3 a ticket for his series of twelve lectures;

a Mr. Young promised to cover the subject more economically in only two lectures, enlivened by magic lantern slides; but Collyer stole away both audiences by advertising that he would unfold the whole science in a single night, free ("and might be consulted at his hotel as to character, &c.").[13]

Collyer soon realized that the essence of his calling was advertising. It helped to be able to refer to his "personal friend" Spurzheim, and he never failed to take advantage of the most scraping acquaintance, writing letters to celebrities like Charles Dickens just so he could print their replies.[14] A typical pseudo-scientist, he had his own magazine in which to do so. He also wrote his own *Manual of Phrenology,* which he sold after his lectures and also distributed, with its charts personally annotated for the client during private consultations, using up four editions in as many years.[15]

During the late 1830s Collyer was one of dozens of such wandering showmen-scientists, fingering skulls in Lancaster, Harrodsburg, Baltimore, Louisville, Columbia, Savannah, all the way to New Orleans,[16] where his father, also an emigrant, was running a distillery.[17] This lecturing from town to town was born of revivalism and circuit riding, though now the subjects were secular—not merely phrenology but all the latest scientific doctrines—geology, electricity, chemistry. Charles Lyell's audiences rivaled both Combe's and Dickens's when he toured the U.S. during the same period.

Footloose as he was, Collyer found time for "graduate work," as we call it, to supplement his training in London. He took a "quickie" degree at the Berkshire Medical College in Pittsfield, Massachusetts.[18] But that was mere ornament; like most pseudo-scientists, he had his true laboratory on the stage where he performed. Collyer made his first scientific discovery during his phrenological travels in the South. Each plantation owner was asked to point out the most musical of his slaves, and after examining some three hundred natural minstrels, Collyer announced that he was moving the organ for Tune up an inch from where Gall and Spurzheim had located it on the temple, squeezing Humor and Ideality but leaving its old spot vacant for an organ Collyer invented to fill the gap, Proper Names. (Tune, by the way, was to be found large not only in Negroes, but also "in Handel, Mozart, Van Weber, Gluck, Rossini, Malibran, and in all singing birds.")[19]

Just before graduation from medical school Collyer was introduced to the new craze that was beginning to steal phrenology's thunder—mesmerism, or animal magnetism.[20] Soon he was giving lectures on the subject, using his own little brother, who joined him from New Orleans, as a somnambulist.[21]

Mesmerism too could be profitably divided into lecture and private consultation. Instead of character readings the animal magnetist offered medical diagnosis: when he put little Frederick into the clairvoyant state, the newly credentialed Dr. Collyer had his own X-ray. He also treated headache and various nervous disorders by direct magnetic applications.

Public appearances consisted in exhibiting the further range of clairvoyant perception. One night, for instance, Collyer's performance was capped by this convincing experiment:

> A well known citizen of Boston, Mr. R.T.S. wished to be put in correspondence with one of my subjects....He took the subject mentally to his house in _____ street, South End, and asked him a number of questions respecting the disposition of the furniture, the rooms, &c. &c. to all of which he obtained correct answers, and so communicated to the audience. He then took the subject to his bedroom. "Who do you see now?" asked the gentleman.
>
> "A young lady dressed in her night-clothes—she wears a ruffled cap, and a white gown—upon the table is a lamp and a white ewer."
>
> "Admirable!" said the gentleman, taking out his watch, "that lady is my wife, and it is just the time that she generally goes to bed"; then turning to the subject, he said, "do you see anything more?"
>
> "Yes!" replied the subject, "I see a young man dressed in black, he is very good-looking, and wears a pair of black whiskers and an imperial upon his chin!"
>
> "Mercy on us!" exclaimed the old gentleman, turning pale, and dropping the hand of the subject, "who can be there with my wife! Really, Doctor, I must go home and see."[22]

In full flower as a pseudo-scientific celebrity, Collyer missed no opportunity to enliven his act. Audiences would tire of imaginary tours of private homes, no matter how amusing a few of them might turn out. It was necessary to provide something to watch on the stage itself. It was now that he laid the basis for his claim to a share in the discovery of anesthesia. Collyer added to his routine a dramatic demonstration of his power to control the perceptions of his subjects: their very teeth could be yanked from their jaws without their knowing it.[23]

Had that been all there was to it, Collyer would not have had much to say for himself in the anesthesia debate. All the mesmerists had this trick in their repertoire, and the teeth extracted in front of wincing audiences in 1842 would have made a sizable pile.[24] But Collyer went further. He also used "stimulating and narcotic vapors" to achieve the same painless results. Collyer's drugs were merely alcohol and opium, the old standbys; but that was not the issue as he saw it later.[25] Perhaps he was right. The question is, was he methodically experimenting with different kinds of painkillers, and thus drawing public attention for the first time to the possibility of a science of anesthetics? He claimed that both Wells and Morton had attended his lectures in the early 1840s and stolen their experiments with laughing gas and ether from him.[26] (Wells actually admitted getting the idea of using nitrous oxide from an itinerant lecturer on popular science—not Collyer however, but Samuel Colt, who made a living demonstrating laughing gas before inventing his famous revolver.)[27]

Supposing that some such project was in Collyer's head, the writer for the *Lancet* wondered, why did he himself not take the next step and proceed systematically with his idea? "As it was, after throwing out a fine suggestion, he virtually deserted it himself, as if he did not himself see the whole of its extensive application and importance."[28]

It was true. Collyer's use of mesmerism as a painkiller involved neither a discovery nor a recognition; he simply did not have the scientific habit of mind that sees phenomena in their systematic relations. It was characteristic of his harum-scarum manner of thought that the idea for his "stimulating and narcotic vapors" came, not from Professor Turner's chemistry lectures at University College, where Collyer himself had been put to sleep by a whiff of ether,[29] but from his father's distillery, where in 1839 a Negro slave who had been "sniffing" under the canvas cover of a vat of rum passed out and fell ten feet, dislocating his hip. Collyer reduced the dislocation, which was severe, without causing "Bob" any pain, and *that* was his first experiment in anesthesia—bizarre enough, but really no different from the experience of many surgeons who got their patients drunk before operating.[30]

Collyer never put two and two together. The point of performing painless dentistry during his lectures, sometimes by mesmerism, sometimes by drugs, was not to advance the idea of anesthesia at all, but to offer a pseudo-scientific hypothesis about the physiology of trance. He called this "the magnetic or congestive state of the brain," and explained that it could be produced not only by mesmerism but also "by mental excitement, accompanied with musuclar action; the inhaling of narcotic and stimulating vapors;...or by the will of the individual himself."[31]

So much for Collyer as a scientist. Yet as a pseudo-scientist—that is, as a publicist of unsubstantiated scientific fantasies—he probably did, unknowingly, contribute something to the discovery of anesthesia. Perhaps his claim is best argued in the words of anesthesia's most vehement opponent, the famous surgeon François Magendie, who tried to prevent the French Academy of Sciences from honoring any of the discoverers: "I consider that the new method conflicts both with sound reason and with moral responsibility. Behind the whole matter lies this, that certain European doctors have been led astray by an American advertiser, and are now trying to enlist the Academy of Sciences in the puffery."[32] Magendie had William Morton in mind, who had taken out a patent and was advertising his "Letheon" apparatus at home and abroad; but it was Collyer who was the expert in puffery, and who, as the *Lancet* put it, "beckoned and called, however oddly, others to follow."[33]

What do we learn from this tawdry story? First of all, let us recognize that this is not the founding of a science but merely a technology, and that none of its initiators were serious scientists, only indifferent practitioners of dentistry and medicine, crafts barely out of the hands of barbers and apothecaries. The practical consequences have been enormous but not really scientific, just as the discovery itself owed less to chemistry than to hearsay, ballyhoo, and luck.

Nonetheless we are obviously reluctant to call anesthesia an achievement of pseudo-science—not so much, I think, because of our distaste for its vulgarities, as because of a need to buttress faith in our own technological society: if it works, it's science; if it's pseudo-science, it can't possibly work.

But the truth is that science and pseudo-science were—are—closer than we like to think. The history of anesthesia is not the only example of a technological breakthrough propelled by pseudo-science. Much of what we now think of as orthodoxy, especially in social sciences like psychology, was actually taking shape in this welter of *isms* and *ologies.* A majority of the early authorities on insanity—the asylum superintendents who founded the American Psychiatric Association—were phrenologists. This does not mean that phrenology simply evolved into psychiatry; but phrenological concepts of brain function certainly influenced men like Isaac Ray and Amariah Brigham, who accordingly assumed that mental aberration always had physiological concomitants; insanity was a disease of the body, like any other, and therefore treatable. This was a radical view in the nineteenth century.[34]

Moreover, the norms of behavior were assumed to fit neatly within the system of propensities found on phrenological charts, and not only by asylum superintendents but also by prison wardens, reformers of fallen women, and philanthropists of every description. Such an authoritative codification of faculty-psychology had a profound effect on popular notions of human nature.[35] To take a single striking example, the phrenological distinction between Amativeness and Propagativeness was used by the early advocates of birth control to justify contraception.[36]

The influence of pseudo-science tended to be social or medical rather than purely scientific, though even here there were important contributions. After all, the phrenologists were right in their guess about the localization of brain function, and Gall's anatomical technique is now recognized as epoch-making, though the misguided theory of bumps prevented his followers from going any farther physiologically.[37]

Compared to their orthodox rivals, the pseudo-sciences were often more advanced or enlightened. Nineteenth-century medical orthodoxy (called "allopathy") never proved itself better able to heal the sick than hydropathy, homoeopathy, Thomsonianism, and so on, although the A.M.A. finally succeeded in squeezing them out. On the contrary, the homoeopathists were the first to condemn the huge allopathic doses of calomel and opium, and the bleeding and blistering which killed so many patients.[38] Their own prescriptions, diluted to "potencies" that would not cover a pinpoint, may have served only as placebos, but the homoeopathists were ahead of everyone else in recognizing the need for an experimentally derived pharmacopoeia, even if it was full of "microscopic sugar-plums," as Oliver Wendell Holmes put it.[39] Similarly, the hydropathists were the first to demonstrate the importance of diet, rest, and exercise in the prevention and cure of disease; their health spas were the best the nineteenth century had to offer.

The fact is, although science must finally be systematic to be true, its acquisitions, and especially its applications, do not always come in an orderly way. Science must make room for novelty, and relinquish a system when it can no longer bear the weight of its anomalies and exceptions. This is the loophole that gave the pseudo-scientists their place in the scientific enterprise. Their enthusiasms drew attention to phenomena that could not be explained according to orthodox theories.

Even the best scientists knew next to nothing about the problems of human consciousness that many of the pseudo-scientists were interested in. The old religious psychology had broken down, and an extremely mechanistic view of experience and behavior was taking its place, seen, for example, in the development of statistics, the nosology of mental disease, and the anatomical work of the early neurosurgeons. Finally, as the behaviorists drew their net tight around whatever in mental life could be measured, William James would reach back to Jonathan Edwards's *Freedom of the Will* for a fresh start on spiritual questions.

Meanwhile the pseudo-scientists muddled through, applying their vocabulary of fluids and mediums and congestions to processes of mind that are spiritual. It was part of the general tendency of nineteenth-century science. While Faraday was hacking away at the "empty" Newtonian universe of forces acting on bodies completely without material agency, the animal magnetists thought they had discovered the ultimate medium of human will, a universal energy that passed, like electricity or light, between mind and mind, explaining all the mysterious phenomena of mesmerism and clairvoyance, and opening up the possibility of communication with the spiritual realm inhabited by the disembodied.

Again Collyer was in the vanguard.

One night Collyer found himself magnetizing a difficult subject, who would not obey his will. Someone in the audience suggested that he try magnetizing the phrenological organ of Benevolence, whereupon the subject immediately became pliant and cooperative. This was the birth of phrenomagnetism, a pseudo-scientific amalgam that not only harmonized two sets of doctrines, thereby proving their validity, but also gave rise to new speculations about the sources of mesmeric power—perhaps "the vital principle" itself.[40]

Animal magnetism was a form of electricity—that seemed obvious; if Galvani could produce reflexes in a frog's leg with his crude apparatus, why not the magnetist, passing his positively charged fingers over the negatively receptive cranium of the somnambulist? Now that there was a means of artificially exciting the organs of the mind one by one, their locations could also be conclusively settled—just as neurosurgeon Wilder Penfield was able to determine the functions of the cortex when, two generations later, he stimulated it with his electrodes.

Then, in a development that perfectly illustrates everything that was wrong with pseudo-science, the phrenomagnetists suddenly realized that they had not only authenticated all the organs charted by Gall and Spurzheim, but had found a technique for discovering a whole series of new ones. Dread of Death, Desire for Money, Love of Stimulants, Boasting, Sarcasm, Love of Pets, Desire for Seeing Ancient Places, Perfection, Gratitude, etc., etc.—soon the skull was so crowded with new faculties that their locations would no longer fit on the cranial maps published in the handbooks.[41]

There was a race to see who could stake out the available space first, and Collyer soon had several rivals for the distinction of having discovered phrenomagnetism. In order to be famous like Gall or Mesmer, it was necessary to have one's own pseudo-science. The discovery of a few new organs was not enough: anyone could add a gargoyle or two to the edifice; the glory belonged to the architect.[42]

In the contest that ensued Collyer fought for his priority with the same relish he later displayed in the anesthetic controversy. He accused one of his rivals (LaRoy Sunderland, ex-preacher and author of the phrenological list I have just quoted) not only of stealing his idea but of making up new organs just as he fancied: "This LRS has new organs for love of cold water, love of strong drink, organs of suavity, organs of molasses and water, gin-slings, hot whiskey punches, organs for eating Bologna sausages, organs for sucking molasses, mush and milk, organs for kicking foot-ball, for knocking down watchmen, organs for kissing women, organs for jealousy, organs for swindling the public out of their money, organs for claiming certain discoveries in Mesmerism, that the individual never thought of, &c. &c."[43]

The satire is effective until one remembers Collyer's own discoveries of Tune and Proper Names. At least he never claimed to have located them phrenomagnetically. In fact, perhaps as a result of his interchange with Sunderland, Collyer now began to criticize phrenology as "a glaring absurdity, an insult to the intelligence of an enlightened public." He even recanted phrenomagnetism (while still claiming priority in it!) because he found he could get the same results, so long as his subjects did not know the phrenological charts, by magnetizing their elbows.[44]

One reason that Collyer was so willing to renounce phre-

A: The operator, directing the image of his thoughts to point C.
B: The recipient receiving the reflected image on his brain from point C.
C: The angle AC being equal to the angle CB.

Fig. 2.2. Collyer's "bowl of molasses" experiment. From Collyer's *Psychography* (Philadelphia, 1843).

nomagnetism is that he had now discovered still another pseudo-science, this one entirely his own, which he christened "psychography." It was, he hoped, his ticket to fame. He had found the fundamental scientific explanation for all the phenomena of telepathy and clairvoyance. Collyer argued that the trance travels of somnambulists were really a form of mind reading, effected by photographic principles: "I was obliged to *embody* the image[s]...in my own mind, before they could be recognized by the recipients; whose brain during the congestive state was so sentient that the impression was conveyed to the mind similar to the photographic process of Daguerre."[45] Collyer now added the "bowl of molasses experiment" to his act. Someone from the audience would sit opposite his somnambulist, gazing into a bowl of molasses ("any other dark fluid will answer"), and the mental images of the one were reflected into the mesmerized consciousness of the other. In the illustrations for his new pamphlet the lines of psychographic force were dotted in with comic-book literalness.[46]

Both phrenomagnetism and psychography were attempts to explore the physiological basis of psychic life. It was hard for the pseudo-scientists to accept Benjamin Franklin's opinion, given as a member of the famous French committee investigating Mesmer, that the magnetic phenomena could be explained by "the excited imagination of the patient, and by the involuntary instinct of imitation."[47] But both Franklin and the mesmerists missed the real point—that the phenomena were all the more extraordinary when considered as the effects of mere suggestion. At bottom the mesmerists agreed with the orthodox scientists of the Bailly Committee, that only what could be measured was worth studying. Mesmerism and phrenology were doomed as sciences of mind because they neglected the interesting questions they had their fingers on, questions of faith and will, desire and attention, consciousness and unconsciousness.

Whether or not Collyer's motives were what we would call "scientific" in exposing the absurdities of phrenology and phrenomagnetism, the upshot was that orthodox pseudo-scientists began to treat him as a renegade. Sunderland retaliated in *The Magnet*: "We have now before us, letters and affidavits of respectable persons, in which he is charged with conduct the most infamous. Indeed, we have just received a letter from a respectable female whom he had been in the habit of magnetizing, in Boston, in which she charges him with *deception, falsehood, profanity,* and an attempt to defraud her; and, also, with extreme *cruelty* towards her while in the magnetic state."[48]

Orson Fowler himself, the dean of phrenology in America, accused Collyer of being "utterly destitute of moral principle." When Collyer countered with a libel suit, Fowler advertised for witnesses to testify to his "having committed immoralities or crimes, great or small, or…dirty deeds, or his having committed seduction, or adultery, or having even gone off without paying his debts."[49]

Here we begin to see the underside of pseudo-science. Whether or not Collyer was the villain Fowler and Sunderland said he was, such rumors circulated freely about most of the itinerant mesmerists. It was bound to happen in a calling that combined traveling salesman and mad scientist. In his *Mesmeric Magazine* Collyer had boasted of curing a girl of infatuation, at her mother's request and without the patient's knowledge;[50] could he not just as easily transfer her affections to himself? This possibility was the theme of many stories and novels based on the mesmeric phenomena, including the darker corners of Hawthorne's *House of the Seven Gables* and *The Blithedale Romance.* George Lippard's sensationalist *Quaker City* depicted an entire harem of sexy somnambulists drawn from "the best homes" all over the world by an irresistible magnetist.[51]

In short, the public image of the pseudo-scientist was Janus-faced: Collyer might be seen as he no doubt saw himself, a dedicated scientist, never hesitating to question even his own earlier enthusiasms, or as his rivals saw him, a dissolute fraud and opportunist. Reports about him were so antithetical as to lead a modern historian of phrenology to posit *two* Robert H. Collyers, the one a respectable visiting scientist from England, the other an impostor following his trail and trading on his reputation.[52] The conjecture is not so far-fetched: Collyer's enemy Sunderland, for instance, complained that someone "stole the entire name, advertisement, hand-bills, and testimonials" of his professional identity, "for a course of lectures on Pathetism."[53] Some of these people changed their names every time they changed pseudo-sciences—perhaps, as Fowler hinted, to escape paying their old hotel bills. But finally there is no hard evidence for the twin Collyer theory; it is more reasonable to assume that he had as many public faces as audiences wanted to see.

Like media personalities today, the pseudo-scientists were fantasy creations of the popular imagination. Mesmerism in particular was a catalyst for all sorts of cultural mythologizing. The best place to see this is in the works of the popular writers, especially Poe and Hawthorne.

Poe actually knew Collyer; they met at one of revival preacher William Miller's mass meetings in the spring of 1843, when the Millerites were expecting the Last Judgment at any moment.[54] Poe and Collyer, both students of the power of the imagination, were naturally intrigued by this new metamorphosis of the evangelical impulse, twisting its way toward later science-and-religion sects like Christian Science and Scientology. Obviously there was something like mass hypnosis at work; when the end of the world failed to materialize, one of the disillusioned leaders announced that the whole movement was nothing but mesmerism.[55]

Poe probably knew as much pseudo-science as Collyer, while Collyer was equally adept at keeping an audience spellbound. They must have had much to say to one another. Collyer's *Psychography* was not yet out (he was seeing it through the press at the time), but he might have given Poe Chauncey Townshend's *Facts in Mesmerism,* which had an appendix reporting his own experiments.[56] Collyer had presented a copy to Poe's friend John Neal soon after its publication.[57] Somehow Poe obtained this book, because he used it extensively in writing a series of mesmeric hoax-tales not long after his meeting with Collyer.[58]

The most successful of these—as hoax if not as literature—was "The Facts in the Case of M. Valdemar," an account of suspended animation achieved by mesmerism. This gruesome fancy was widely reprinted in the mid-1840s, when readers were eager to swallow whatever wonders a pseudo-scientist might dangle in front of them. Many took Poe's fabrication hook, line, and sinker, the mesmerists most greedily of all. An English expert, Thomas South, was thoroughly gulled by the

> announcement lately made by Mr. Poe...of a dying man magnetised by him in *articule mortis,* and though inevitable death did certainly supervene, yet there in his chamber and in testimony of a crowd of witnesses, for seven months consecutively lay the undemagnetised corpse, and when questioned by the magnetiser Poe, in a sepulchral voice gave utterance that he was dead, dead, and should not be disturbed; and then, when at the intervention of others, Poe made the demagnetising passes, the outward body, the whole perfect form instantly dissolved into one shapeless mass of intolerable corruption. This is well and publicly attested, yet few even of the faithful will believe, though one spoke from the dead. But be it true or false to this generation, "Ye shall see greater things than these."[59]

Poe of course was gratified by such reactions. Even more delectable was the response of his friend and informant Collyer, who wrote a fan letter to Poe's *Broadway Journal:*

> DEAR SIR—Your account of M. Valdemar's Case had been universally copied in this city, and has created a great sensation. It requires from me no apology, in stating, that I have not the least doubt of the *possibility* of such a phenomenon; for, I did actually restore to active animation a person who died from excessive drinking of ardent spirits. He was placed in his coffin ready for interment.
>
> I will give you the detailed account on your reply to this, which I require for publication, in order to put at rest the growing impression that your account is merely a *splendid creation* of your own brain, not having any truth in fact. My dear sir, I have battled the storm of public derision too long on the subject of Mesmerism, to be now found in the rear ranks—though I have not publicly lectured for more than two years, I have steadily made it a subject of deep investigation.
>
> I sent the account to my friend Dr. Elliotson of London; also to the "Zoist,"—to which journal I have regularly contributed.
>
> Your early reply will oblige, which I will publish, with your consent, in connection with the case I have referred to. Believe me yours, most respectfully.[60]

Poe toyed with his victim: "We have no doubt that Mr. Collyer is perfectly correct in all that he says—and all that he desires us to say—but the truth is, there was a very small modicum of truth in the case of M. Valdemar—which, in consequence, may be called a hard case—*very* hard for M. Valdemar, for Mr. Collyer, and ourselves. If the story was not true, however, it should have been—and perhaps 'The Zoist' may discover that it *is* true after all."[61] To which there was little for Collyer to reply.

Poe was so hard on Collyer because he asked for it. Given his career, and the tone of his letter, one might also suspect the doctor of having invented his revivification just to cash in on Poe's. The truth was, Collyer actually had had the adventure he reported, though the facts were not quite what his letter implied. In the spring of 1841 Collyer had "revived" a sailor who had drunk himself into a stupor ("No perceptible respiration, no pulse, surface cold and clammy")—but his technique had not been mesmerism at all, rather "a *hot bath*, and constant friction of the whole body, which was continued for over three hours."[62] Collyer fails to mention the hot bath and chafing in his letter to Poe; that would have spoiled *his* story.

One obvious response to pseudo-science is simply to make fun of it like this, which is our modern stance. But it was possible to take it much more seriously and still condemn it. This was the reaction of Hawthorne, who had less faith in all science than Poe, and who saw pseudo-science as demonic.

There is some evidence that Hawthorne may have seen Collyer perform—he mentions him in one of his sketches,[63] and the portrait of an evil mesmerist in *The Blithedale Romance* bears some resemblance; but Hawthorne's condemnation was not directed at any single individual so much as at the whole pseudo-scientific fad. He particularly deplored any science of the psyche that seemed to meddle with spiritual nature, for this was blasphemous. When his fiancée announced her intent to be mesmerized (for her migraines), Hawthorne wrote her anxiously: "I am unwilling that a power should be exercised on thee, of which we know neither the origin nor consequence, and the phenomena of which seem rather calculated to bewilder us, than to teach us any truths about the present or future state of being....I have no faith whatever that people are raised to the seventh heaven, or to any heaven at all, or that they gain any insight into the mysteries of life beyond death, by means of this strange science....Keep the imagination sane—that is one of the truest conditions of communion with heaven."[64]

These sentiments found their way into many of his stories. "The Birthmark," for example, shows us Poe's ghoulish mesmerist several centuries earlier, as an alchemist pursuing the same life-and-death researches. Using his esoteric sciences to remove a tiny birthmark from the cheek of his wife, Aylmer finds his technology too powerful—or rather, what comes to the same thing, the birthmark turns out to be no mere blemish but the very stigma of mortality. In eradicating it he uproots life itself. Hawthorne's work parades a dozen such pseudo-scientists before the reader to enforce this fervent moral: every materialistic endeavor to lay bare the secrets of human life and spirit is nothing but *hubris*, the ancient sin of pride and blasphemy.

In secular terms that his villains might more readily understand, Hawthorne's critique accused them of promoting a crass psychology of weights and measures, cause and effect, in which the most complicated and subtle problems of ethics, love, and faith are reduced to electrochemical instrumentalities. It was not that Hawthorne thought their formulas and entities delusions—though in most cases he probably did—but rather that he foresaw a terrible contraction and deadening of human spirit in these new sciences of mind.

At this level of his indictment, our modern distinction between true science and pseudo-science may not seem very relevant. Even though the fuzzy doctrines of pseudo-science have been largely debunked by our more painstaking investigators, we have too much accepted their aims while rejecting their methodologies. I am not thinking merely of obvious examples like chemotherapy for "hyperactive" children, genetic engineering, or artificial intelligence research, but of the twentieth-century attitude that assumes scientific wisdom consists in knowing which technology to apply in a given instance.

Indeed, from this point of view the Victorian pseudo-scientists often knew better than we do. The refusal of homoeopathists and hydropathists to dose their patients with the nineteenth-century miracle drugs might well be imitated by modern practitioners. This does not mean that all scientific discoveries are panaceas from Pandora's box, for clearly no one believes that. But Hawthorne's warning ought not be ignored.

The modern tendency to conflate science and technology as a single unified discipline, to rush every scientific truth into application before we have thoroughly understood it, is precisely *our* pseudo-science, complete with all the characteristics that we deplore in Collyer's career—the reduction of psychic phenomena to materialistic explanations, the reckless experimenting with human subjects, the substitution of publicity for candor, the eagerness for marketable results, the assumption that whatever new problems technology may create it can also solve, that there is always some new discovery in the offing that will explain what is unknown and set everything to rights.

Our test of a science seems to be whether or not we can derive a profitable technology from it, the same criterion applied in Collyer's day to theories we now think of as pseudo-scientific. Some, like psychography, proved worthless and ended on the junkheap; others grew respectable through success. Consider the history of daguerreotypy, or the metamorphosis of Dr. Coult, the pseudo-scientific lecturer on nitrous oxide, into Samuel Colt, the revolver king. Or the fact that Alexander Graham Bell's father was the inventor of something called "visible speech, the science of universal alphabetics." Or the fact that in the 1840s Congress debated (half-seriously) whether mesmerism ought not be subsidized along with Morse's proposed telegraph, as an analogous form of magnetism.[65]

Collyer's own later life makes the point dramatically. The anesthesia controversy of 1847 was the last major pseudo-scientific effort of his career. He seems then to have realized that he had missed the one chance to make a name for himself that way; thereafter he turned to pursuits more practical and socially useful. During the next decade he practiced medicine on the Isle of Jersey, went West with the Gold Rush, was in charge of a cholera hospital in Mexico City. He focused his fertile imagination on sober, patentable inventions—a new method for crushing quartz, a new amalgamating process, an improved breech-loading cannon (all associated with his California adventures); after finally settling down in England in the mid-1850s, he continued to experiment with new processes and devices: for making paper, for cleaning wheat, for a chemical ink pencil, for telegraph cables, and so on.[66] A born technologist, he was equally at home in mind or matter, so long as there was a profit to be made there.

Collyer never turned his back on the pseudo-science of the psyche while concentrating on more mundane engineerings. Having been one of the first to claim the power to talk with the dead, Collyer now amused himself by sending in occasional contributions to *The Spiritualist Magazine,* getting out all his old press clippings in order to convert his theories of somnambulism to the new mediumship. When the world-famous "slate-writing" medium Henry Slade was sentenced to three months' hard labor for fraud, Collyer published an article defending him. His own research convinced him that "all the varied phenomena" of psychic experience could be explained "on a material hypothesis"—that is, that science and religion were reconcilable. Even more, the decades he devoted to "the practical sciences of electricity, chemistry, engineering, mining, &c. ...tended to confirm my ideas that all things were merely different states of materiality."[67]

Here was Hawthorne's mad scientist to a *t*, grinding everything spiritual down to its secular atoms. When he announced his discovery of psychography in 1843, Collyer betrayed an enormous ambition: "I know that my age will not give me the credit I demand, but I know that posterity will carry out what I have begun, and when scarcely a tombstone of this generation has been left behind, when all party strife and private animosity shall have been buried and forgotten, then will these experiments take their proper rank in the temple of knowledge; nor is the expectation vain, when I declare, that they will form the cupola of human attainment."[68] If we consider his contribution in his own narrow terms—the discoveries of Tune and Proper Names, of phrenomagnetism, psychography, or even of anesthesia—his claims are false and his ambitions thwarted; but seen more broadly, as part of the overwhelming technological revolution that has usurped both science and pseudo-science in our day, it must be admitted that Collyer was right: the attitude he represented has come into its own, with achievements beyond his somnambulist's wildest clairvoyance, and with both ecological and spiritual costs not even the gloomy Hawthorne could imagine.

Notes

1. H.A. Simon and A. Newell, "Heuristic Problem Solving: The Next Advance in Operations Research," *Operations Research* 6 (Jan.-Feb. 1958): 8; quoted in Joseph Weizenbaum, "The Computer in Your Future," *New York Review of Books*, Oct. 27, 1983. Dust jacket of Geoff Simons, *Are Computers Alive? Evolution and New Life Forms* (Brighton, Eng.: Harvester, 1983) quoted in H.C. Longuet-Higgins, "On the Altar of AI," *Times Literary Supplement*, Oct. 28, 1983.

2. Carol Kahn, *Beyond the Helix: DNA and the Quest for Longevity* (New York: Times Books, 1985), p. 260.

3. The history of the ether controversy is told in many standard sources. Collyer's part is presented by the anonymous *Lancet* writer in "The History of Anaesthetic Discovery: II," *Lancet*, June 11, 1870, 840-44.

4. Ibid., p. 843.

5. R.H. Collyer, *Manual of Phrenology*, 4th ed. (Dayton, Ohio: B. F. Ells, 1842 [copyright 1838]), p. 34.

6. Robert H. Collyer, *Exalted States of the Nervous System*, 3rd ed. (London: Henry Renshaw, 1873), p. 6; *Mesmeric Magazine* [Boston] 1 (July 1842): 26; *Lancet*, p. 841.

7. *Mesmeric Magazine*, p. 16; Robert H. Collyer, *Lights and Shadows of American Life* (Boston: Redding & Co., 1843), p. 15.

8. *Lancet*, p. 842.

9. Anon., *The History and Philosophy of Animal Magnetism, by A Practical Magnetizer* (Boston: J.N. Bradley & Co., 1843), p. 7.

10. Collyer, *Lights and Shadows*, p. 15.

11. Ibid.

12. Ibid.

13. Charles Gibbon, *The Life of George Combe*, 2 vols. (London: Macmillan, 1878), 2:74.

14. *Mesmeric Magazine*, p. 28.

15. Collyer's use of his *Manual of Phrenology* in these ways is assumed from the practice of others in the field.

16. Collyer, *Manual of Phrenology*, pp. 33-39.

17. Collyer, *Exalted States*, p. 5.

18. Robert H. Collyer, *Psychography* (Philadelphia: Zieber & Co., 1843), p. 5; *Exalted States*, p. 49.

19. Collyer, *Manual of Phrenology*, pp. 99-100.

20. Collyer, *Psychography*, p. 5; *Exalted States*, pp. 48-49.

21. Collyer, *Psychography*, p. 32.

22. Collyer, *Lights and Shadows*, p. 35.

23. *Mesmeric Magazine*, p. 13.

24. LaRoy Sunderland, *Ideology*, 2 vols. (Boston: J.P. Mendun, 1885), 1:31-35, lists nineteen such cases he himself attended.

25. Collyer, *Psychography*, p. 26; *Exalted States*, p. 126, and passim.

26. Collyer, *Exalted States*, p. 21.

27. Bernard Jaffe, *Men of Science in America* (New York: Simon and Schuster, 1944), pp. 163-64; Collyer, *Exalted States*, p. 124.

28. *Lancet*, p. 842.

29. Collyer, *Exalted States*, p. 6.

30. Ibid., pp. 5-6, 127.

31. Collyer, *Psychography,* p. 26.

32. René Fülöp-Miller, *Triumph over Pain,* trans. Eden and Cedar Paul (New York: Literary Guild, 1938), p. 211.

33. *Lancet,* p. 843.

34. See J.K. Hall, ed., *One Hundred Years of American Psychiatry* (New York: Columbia Univ. Press, 1944), pp. 54, 67.

35. See John D. Davies, *Phrenology: Fad and Science* (New Haven: Yale Univ. Press, 1955), passim.

36. John Humphrey Noyes, *Bible Communism* (Brooklyn: Office of the [Oneida] Circular, 1853), p. 47.

37. Gordon Rattray Taylor, *The Science of Life* (New York: McGraw-Hill, 1963), pp. 197-98.

38. See Martin Kaufman, *Homoeopathy in America* (Baltimore: Johns Hopkins Univ. Press, 1971), passim.

39. Oliver Wendell Holmes, *Homeopathy and Its Kindred Delusions* (Boston: William D. Ticknor, 1842), p. 54.

40. Collyer, *Psychography,* pp. 5-6; *Exalted States,* p. 49.

41. LaRoy Sunderland, "Mental Organs," *Magnet* 1 (Oct. 1842): 107-9.

42. See, for example, *Magnet* 1 (June 1842): 13; Collyer, *Psychography,* pp. 12-13.

43. Collyer, *Lights and Shadows,* pp. 16-17.

44. Collyer, *Psychography,* pp. 15-16; *American Phrenological Journal* n.s., 5 (Feb. 1843) 94-95.

45. Collyer, *Psychography,* p. 30.

46. Collyer, *Psychography,* p. 31.

47. Frank Podmore, *From Mesmer to Christian Science* (New Hyde Park, N.Y.: University Books, 1963 [c. 1909]), p. 59.

48. *Magnet* 1 (July 1842): 34.

49. *American Phrenological Journal* n.s., 5 (Feb. 1843): 94-95; (July 1843): 331-32.

50. *Mesmeric Magazine,* pp. 31-32.

51. George Lippard, *The Quaker City* (New York: Odyssey, 1970 [c. 1845]), pp. 526-27.

52. Davies, *Phrenology,* pp. 132-33.

53. LaRoy Sunderland in *Spirit World* 3 (Sept. 1851): 117.

54. Collyer, *Exalted States,* pp. 66, 110.

55. Clara Endicott Sears, *Days of Delusion* (Boston: Houghton Mifflin, 1924), p. 243.

56. Chauncy Hare Townshend, *Facts in Mesmerism,* 1st Amer. ed. (Boston, 1841).

57. The copy Collyer gave to Neal is in the possession of Dr. Jacques M. Quen, New York City. It is inscribed "September 7, 1841."

58. See Sidney E. Lind, "Poe and Mesmerism," *PMLA* 62 (1947): 1077-94. Lind thinks Poe used the edition of 1844, but Collyer's 1841 edition is equally possible.

59. Thuos Mathos [Thomas South], *Early Magnetism in Its Higher Relations to Humanity, as Veiled in the Poets and the Prophets* (London: H. Balliere, 1846), p. 116.

60. *The Broadway Journal* 2 (Dec. 27, 1845): 390-91.

61. Ibid.

62. Collyer, *Exalted States*, p. 55.

63. "The Hall of Fantasy," *Pioneer* 1 (1843): 55.

64. Oct. 18, 1841. Huntington Library.

65. Hal Sears, *The Sex Radicals* (Lawrence: Regents Press of Kansas, 1977), p. 14.

66. Collyer, *Exalted States*, pp. 14, 28, 128.

67. Robert H. Collyer, *Automatic Writing: The Slade Prosecution* (London: H. Vickers, 1876); Robert H. Collyer, "My Brother's Ghost," *Spiritual Magazine*, May 1, 1861, p. 235.

68. Collyer, *Psychography*, p. 25.

JOHN L. GREENWAY

3. "Nervous Disease" and Electric Medicine

Browsing through popular and even learned periodicals from the late nineteenth century, a modern researcher is apt to be both amused and amazed by advertisements asserting that a device prefixed by "electric" will cure most of the ailments known to man. In the *Illustrated London News* for April 10, 1886, for instance,the Medical Battery Co., Ltd., describes its "ELECTROPATHIC (Battery) BELT" (figure 3.1), just 21 shillings. The company claims unreservedly that the device has taken care of "over a quarter of a million patients," who have been "successfully treated for rheumatism, lumbago, sciatica, gout, kidney complaints, paralysis, indigestion, constipation, female complaints, general and local debility, functional disorders, etc." The advertisement asks, "Can you afford to die?" reminding readers that "all disorders of the Nervous System, Impaired Vitality, and Defective Organic Action can be speedily, effectually and permanently cured by wearing the ELECTROPATHIC (Battery) BELT, which is guaranteed to restore vital energy."

Ads for similar devices (such as electric cigarettes) purporting to cure "nervous ailments" festooned the pages of other periodicals and late Victorian walls.[1] The modern reader, even while smiling, might seriously ask, "How was such credulity possible?" While one can always retreat to the eternal "caveat emptor," the key to understanding the popularity of this array of curative electric belts, rings, brushes, garters, towels, tooth-

ELECTROPATHIC (BATTERY) BELT

PRICE 21s., POST-FREE. WILL LAST FOR YEARS.

OVER A QUARTER OF A MILLION PATIENTS HAVE BEEN SUCCESSFULLY TREATED FOR RHEUMATISM, LUMBAGO, SCIATICA, GOUT, KIDNEY COMPLAINTS, EPILEPSY, PARALYSIS, INDIGESTION, CONSTIPATION, FEMALE COMPLAINTS, GENERAL AND LOCAL DEBILITY, FUNCTIONAL DISORDERS, &c.

The following are selected from thousands of reports received. The originals may be seen at the Company's Rooms.

GOUT. "Completely cured me."—Major PAKENHAM, Armagh.

HYSTERIA. "The Belt has done wonders."—Mrs. M. ORIEL, Dowlais.

LUMBAGO. "It has been an untold comfort to me."—Miss HUDSON, Twyford.

RHEUMATIC FEVER. "I can speak positively of its advantages."—Dr. C. LEMPRIERE, D.C.L., Senior Fellow St. John's College, Oxford.

SCIATICA. "Worth fifty pounds."—Mr. R. J. WATSON, Harwich.

KIDNEY DISORDERS. "I am like a new man."—Mr. W. P. POUGHER, Plymouth.

BRONCHITIS. "A wonderful change."—Rev. E. AUBREY, Ystrad, Pontypridd.

NEURALGIA. "A most complete success."—M. A. LANGDALE, Esq., Leacroft.

RHEUMATISM. "Completely cured me."—W. TURNER, Esq., Ashby-de-la-Zouch.

NERVOUS HEADACHE. "Derived much benefit."—Mr. W. HOLT, New Stafford.

INDIGESTION. "I wish I had purchased one before."—Mr. C. HITCHCOCK, Bicester.

NERVOUS DEBILITY. "My health has improved every day."—Mr. W. BLISSETT, Wallingford.

CAN YOU AFFORD TO DIE?

Can you afford to drag on a miserable existence? Can you afford to pay doctor's bills? when all disorders of the Nervous System, Impaired Vitality, and Defective Organic Action can be speedily, effectually, and permanently cured by wearing the ELECTROPATHIC (Battery) BELT, which is guaranteed to restore impaired vital energy, to invigorate the debilitated constitution, stimulate the organic action, promote the circulation, assist digestion, and promptly renew that vital energy the loss of which is the first symptom of decay. Every man and woman suffering from Rheumatism, Lumbago, Sciatica, Indigestion, Constipation, or any Disorder of the Nervous System, should at once stop physicking, and send a P.O.O. or Cheque for 21s., for an ELECTROPATHIC BELT (post-free), and obtain immediate relief.

LIVER COMPLAINT. "I have no pain now."—Mr. T. SMITH, Hey, Lees.

EPILEPSY. "Wonderfully improved."—Mrs. GODWIN, Andoversford.

SHORTNESS OF BREATH. "Greatly relieved."—Mrs. C. FRAYER, 72, Elm Park-gardens, S.W.

ASTHMA. "Quite left me."—Mrs. J. LOW, Stirling, N.B.

CONSTIPATION. "A wonderful effect."—Mr. H. T. STOKES, Demerara.

WEAKNESS. "Still improving."—Mrs. MENHENICK, Colwyn Bay.

DYSPEPSIA. "I feel altogether stronger and better."—Miss WELLS, Scarboro'.

PILES. "Better in every way."—Mr. R. STRINGER, East Bradenham.

BAD CIRCULATION. "Feel like a different person."—JOHN ALGAR, Esq., Campsey Ashe, Wickham Market.

PALPITATION. "Quite free."—Mr. G. GATE, St. Helier, Jersey.

PARALYSIS. "Very great benefit."—Mrs. SHARP, Maidstone.

WRITER'S CRAMP. "A complete cure."—Miss E. HASTINGS, Eastbourne."

SPINAL WEAKNESS. "Rapid improvement."—Mr. W. WATSON, Newspynie, N.B.

MR. C. B. HARNESS, the Eminent Consulting Medical Electrician, has been specially retained by the Company, and may be consulted daily (without charge) on all matters relating to health, and the application of Curative Electricity. Residents at a distance, and those unable to avail themselves of a personal consultation, are invited to write for a PRIVATE ADVICE FORM, which will be forwarded POST-FREE on application to the MEDICAL BATTERY COMPANY, LTD., 52, OXFORD-STREET, LONDON, W.

On receipt of Post-Office Order or Cheque, value 21s., crossed "London and County Bank," the MEDICAL BATTERY COMPANY, LIMITED, 52, OXFORD-STREET, LONDON, W., undertake to forward the ELECTROPATHIC (Battery) BELT, as described above, for either Lady or Gentleman, free by post to any part of the United Kingdom.

"ELECTROPATHY; or, HARNESS' GUIDE TO HEALTH," will be sent, post-free, on application to the

Medical Battery Co., Ltd., 52, OXFORD-STREET, LONDON, W.

Fig. 3.1. The Electropathic (Battery) Belt, as advertised in the *Illustrated London News*, April 10, 1880.

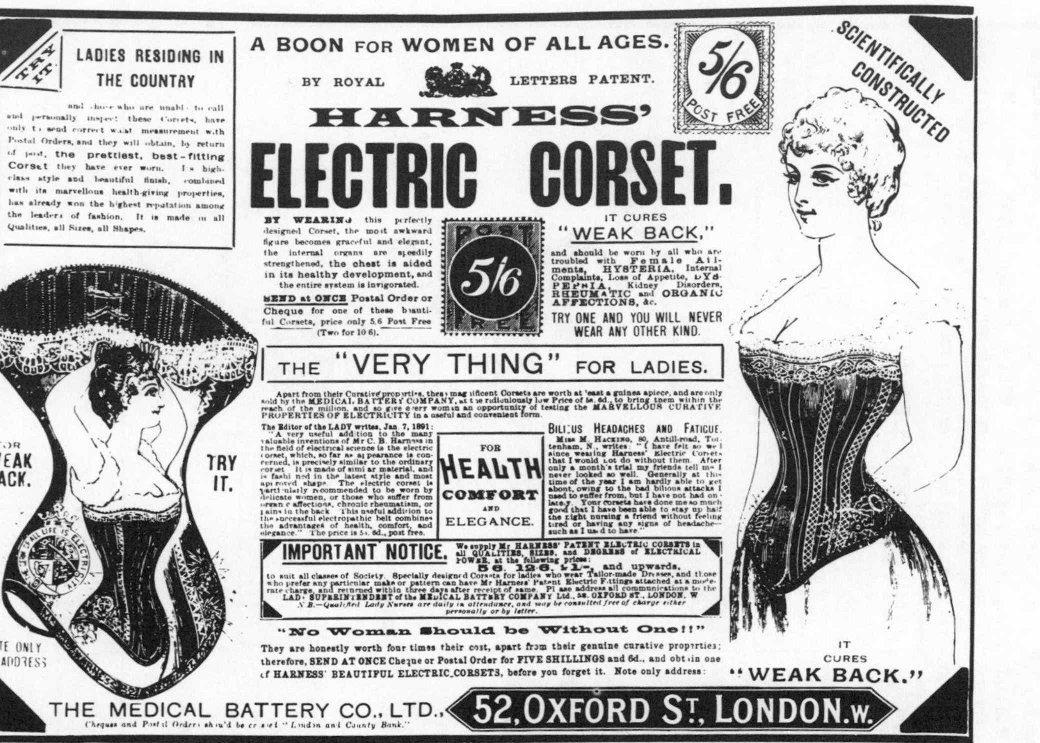

Fig. 3.2. Harness' Electric Corset, advertised in *The Queen*, March 12, 1892.

brushes, and corsets lies in understanding the premises governing contemporary inquiry concerning the nature of electricity and its relationship to the nervous system.

While the electrical aspect of popular medicine should not be isolated from patent medicines and other nostrums, we can from that aggregation of gadgets suggest that the gulf between it and what was considered legitimate research was not as vast as one might suppose. Indeed, given the assumptions regulating researchers' questions, Harness' Electric Corset (figure 3.2) seemed hardly less plausible as a cure for "nervous exhaustion" than those advocated in medical journals and texts. As bizarre as such illustrations seem today, at the time they embodied metaphors of a new but legitimate field for biological research.

"Biology" as a normative term did not come into play until 1802, so the newness of electricity as a field for scientific research, plus the lack of norms within the field, invited the exotic speculations of Mesmer and mystical advocates of animal magnetism. By the mid-nineteenth century physiological criteria rephrased the relationship between electricity and organic life, but prior to that time the therapeutic effects of the unseen world of electricity seemed equally unintelligible to scientists and quacks alike. Furthermore, until the acceptance of the germ theory of disease, there was little physicians could do to intervene in the course of a disease in any manner other than trial and error. Assertions of electricity's therapeutic efficacy outside the community of normal science played upon just this element of the unknown.

The scientific establishment of the Enlightenment, though hostile or indifferent to the exotic showmanship of Mesmer,[2] was by no means uninterested in the relationship of artificial electricity to the weather and man. In France, Mauduyt's therapeutic premises of fluids clearing blockages in the nerves differed from Mesmer's only in the lack of exotic trappings. Mauduyt performed several experiments with electricity where he immersed the patient in "electric baths," or drew sparks to increase the flow of nervous fluid, or attempted to free neural blockages through shocks from a Leyden jar, a drastic measure Mesmer did not try.[3]

Still, the absence of anything but conjecture as to why these experiments stemming from sanctioned research should sometimes show startlingly beneficial results prompted pseudo-scientific ingenuity to answer the question in dramatic terms, satisfying the imagination in a way conventional medicine and science could not. At these fringes of legitimate inquiry into electricity and biology we encounter a modern version of shamanism. In 1779 a Dr. James Graham, intrigued by Franklin's experiments, established the Temple of Health in London. For a fee of one hundred pounds one could avail oneself of his "medico-electrical apparatus" and his three great medicines: "Electrical Æther, Nervous Ætherial Balsam, and Imperial Pills," while breathing "electrical, dephlogisticated and vivifying atmosphere." For another fee, one could lie in his Celestial Bed to insure "propagation of Beings, rational and far stronger and more beautiful than the present puny, feeble and nonsensical race of probationary mortals." Graham told the curious that this genesis was accomplished through 1,500 pounds of electromagnets, while he communicated the "celestial fire, ...the fluid which animates and vivifies all," to the fructifying bedchamber. While Graham was notorious as the "emperor of quacks," he coopted his scientific opposition by asserting his pious intentions and scientific credentials, warning the public all the while against the "electrizing quacks" on every corner.[4]

Graham may have been the first of the electrical quack doctors, but popular faith in the efficacy of his Temple stemmed from the scientific suspicion that this manmade fluid had healing properties similar to those of atmospheric electricity, the latter being the subject of a quite legitimate research program undertaken by Mauduyt as part of the general Enlightenment interest in the relationship between weather and health. The popular interest in such phenomena is shown, for instance, in the *New-York Weekly Journal* for May 9, 1748: "For the Entertainment of the Curious. To Be Shown, The most surprising Effects of Phenominas on the Electricity of Attracting, Repelling, & Flemmies Force, particular to the New Way of Electrifing several Persons at the same Time, so that Fire shall Dart from all Parts of their Bodies....And it's tho't to be of Service to many Ailments."

Although part of the early interest in electrotherapy went the way of entertainment and quackery, it must be borne in mind that "quackery" often becomes obvious only in retrospect. In the 1790s Dr. Elisha Perkins had, according to his letters, a firm belief that his "metallic tractors" were based upon Galvani's theories, and would cure "pains in the head, face, teeth, breast, stomach, back, rheumatism, and all joint pains," as well as "paralysis, lameness, and deformities of all types..." since "far the greatest part of our pains is caused by a surcharge of the electric fluid in the parts affected." The tractors were described as looking like a pair of horseshoe nails. For an advised twenty minutes a day, one passed them downwards or outwards over the afflicted area; never upwards. Although the Connecticut Medical Association expelled Perkins in May 1797, many cures were said to have been effected, and "Perkinism" spread to Denmark and Germany. Even George Washington bought a pair.[5]

Generally, the medical use of electricity in the early nineteenth century was usurped by the mesmerists, the magnetizers, and the philosophic biology of the *Naturphilosophen,* and as such fell into official disfavor. By mid-century, however, electrotherapeutics became part of normal science through being rephrased in terms of a radically new but acceptable research program: physiology. Although electrotherapeutics developed as a legitimate research program in this context, on its frontier it was still complemented by the popular imagination.

Electrophysics as practiced by Coulomb and Ampère had been accepted as a legitimate direction of research in the new field, probably because its theories of fluids were less flamboyant than the biological speculations of the mesmerists. Faraday's discussions of electromagnetism and induced currents in the 1830s revived the medical establishment's interest in electricity. Furthermore, the stern rejection by Claude Bernard and other physiologists of the previous generation's speculative, philosophically grounded biological theories helped to clear the field of the taint of animal magnetism and speculation in favor of a new, reductionist biology based upon experiment.[6]

The physiologists focused their experimental energies upon the fashionably radical research program of vivisection.[7] Though socially controversial in the extreme, vivisection allowed the physiologist for the first time to intervene directly in the metabolic processes of life forms and to attempt to control them. Electrotherapy did not attract the heated controversy of vivisection, but Du Bois–Reymond's experiments upon the electrical activity of living tissue in 1843 established the field as legitimate science, away from romantic speculation upon the electrical essence of life. Returning to the question of harnessing this electrical activity for therapeutic use, Duchenne's papers in France (1849) and Remak's *Galvanotherapie* in Germany (1858) reestablished the respectability of electricity in diagnosis and therapy of neural disorders.

To the physiologically trained generation of researchers, any biological effect had of necessity a physical cause. In discussing neural disorders, for instance, it was no longer sufficient to state that Madame was suffering from "vapeurs." "Nervousness is a physical state not a mental state," asserted George M. Beard, "and its phenomena do not come from emotional excess or excitability...but from nervous debility and irritability."[8] This generation of Du Bois–Reymond, Helmholtz, and Ludwig assumed lesions of the brain or nervous system to be the only possible cause of mental illness, and that such physical causes should be counteracted by physical means. In this context, not only did electric medicine become respectable, but Wilhelm Erb managed to imply that electrotherapeutics was the newest of the new by stating that its relationship to physiology was similar to that of physiology to biology. Calling his field "electrophysiology," he asserted that this research "has led, in many respects, to a depth and exactness of knowledge, such as are scarcely excelled in any other branch of physiology."[9] Later in the century Erb's *Handbuch der Electrotherapie* and von Ziemssen's *Elektricität in der Medicin* became basic texts for the programs of a new generation of researchers. Julius Althaus, in the third edition of his *A Treatise on Medical Electricity* (1873), more modestly admitted that electrotherapy lay on the fringes of scientific respectability and, as such, he declared that the newness of galvanism as a research program combined with the vastness of the field to make discoveries of principles (as opposed to empirical guesswork) difficult and uncertain. Althaus warned against a kind of quack within the scientific community: those experimenters, ignorant of physiology, whose empiricism had brought the field into disrepute. The field could be freed from the taint of speculation, Althaus contended, only by scientific study of electricity's physiological effects.[10]

Metaphor and analogy gave a certain narrative quality to these medical texts, and the popular imagination was to seize upon these metaphors and graphically dramatize them. The most frequently used metaphor expressing the relationship of electricity to human physiology was that of the battery. As A.D. Rockwell wrote in his text on electrotherapeutics of 1903, "Chemic action of any sort whatsoever is attended by the evolution of electricity," so in the nerves "energy is undoubtedly stored, possibly in the same sense, although not in the same demonstrable way that chemical action is stored in the ordinary storage batteries."[11]

The battery metaphor seemed persuasive to the medical imagination of the time. Beard's use of the metaphor is typical: "Men, like batteries, need a reserve force, and men, like batteries, need to be measured by the amount of the reserve, and not by what they are compelled to expend in ordinary daily life." Lesions of the nerves come from "unusual drains," continued Beard (a friend of Edison's) and cause "overload."[12]

Beard's great achievement lay in combining medical theory with social theory in a manner that appealed to both the scientific and the popular imagination. Beard gathered a number of real and imagined "symptoms" of "nervousness" (at one time, some three dozen) into a collage and popularized the lot as "neurasthenia." Nervous exhaustion became the fashionable disease of the *fin de siècle.* For this generation, Beard provided a scientifically plausible (that is, physiological) explanation for the exhausted businessman, the wasted, superfluous youth languishing in late-century novels, and the erratic, hyperexcitable, swooning women who appeared so frequently in these novels. Redefining the criteria for naturalistic characterization, the dramatist August Strindberg declared in 1887 that "we are all neuropaths."[13]

Popular advertising, published in an age with next to no

formal regulation, capitalized upon the popularity of neurasthenia; eye-catching graphics and rhapsodic testimonials promised what the physician could not: cures. The technique of reproducing pictures had just replaced stylized type arrangements,[14] and the graphics of these advertisements for cures of "nervous disease" became part of a complex interplay of science, pseudo-science, and non-science late in the century. Indeed, it was often difficult to tell the difference.

Whether Beard used the language of the advertisements or vice versa is unclear, but in his *Practical Treatise on Nervous Exhaustion (Neurasthenia)* of 1880, he described neurasthenia as "general debility, spinal weakness, and nervous prostration." In a noteworthy parallel, Dr. Dye's Voltaic Belt could cure those with "Nervous Debility, Lost Vitality, Lack of Nerve Force and Vigor, Wasting Weaknesses." Beard attributed the physiological causes of neurasthenia to the unique stresses in contemporary social environment: "steam power, the periodical press, the telegraph and the mental activity of women."[15]

Initially, physicians regarded neurasthenia as a disease of men, with women's neural exhaustion expressing itself as hysteria, "found usually in those whose emotional natures greatly predominate" and "is connected in many instances with some sexual or uterine derangement."[16] By the end of the century physicians began to question this distinction, but in the 1870s and 1880s neurasthenia was fashionable for weary males, hysteria for anxious females.

Women, being as a rule of smaller stature than men, were assumed to have less "nerve force" than men. Naturally, they would be more prone to nervous overload as they attempted mental activity. Medical objections to the "new woman" of the eighties and nineties were, given the assumptions regulating the research done, quite sound. Feminists wishing to argue their case on scientific grounds had some difficulty, particularly in matters pertaining to race. Comparisons of cranial capacities, for instance, showed women's skulls to be not only smaller than those of Caucasian men, but comparable to those of Bushmen.[17]

Many feminists had also been abolitionists, and even scientists in favor of women's suffrage were put in the uncomfortable position of either losing their case or accepting qualitative racial differences in discussions of mental and neural resources. Ludwig Büchner, discussing "The Brain of Women" in 1893, says that if a "dirty, idiotic negro" male can vote, it would be absurd to deny Caucasian women with similar cranial capacities the same privilege.[18] As the demands upon the nervous system coming from the environment were the same for men and women, women would, given their smaller physique, be proportionally more depleted, physicians warned.

Given the kinds of questions considered legitimate by researchers in the nineteenth century, it was on the whole a difficult time for feminists to use science to buttress their campaign. The American Medical Association debated the suitability of women for the medical profession for some time in its *Journal,* the editor in 1891 expressing grave doubts about the feminine constitution to withstand the rigors of the profession. As a compromise, however, he suggested that a woman might succeed by treating patients of similar mental resources—that is, other women or non-Aryan peoples.[19] We will see below how the commercial world responded to this constitutional deficiency in women. Mental activity by women was, then, regarded as unusual, debilitating, and, some argued, unnatural. Given the criteria used to formulate the questions researched, the arguments seemed tenable.

As mentioned above, physiologists generally assumed the cause of any disease to be somatic. Unfortunately, neither Beard nor anybody else could detect any neural lesions or any other physiological manifestations, but Beard and those interested in the new disease (actually, only the label was new) retreated to a faith that scientific progress would ultimately explain this lack of evidence. Rather than question the premises underlying his research, Beard blamed the coarseness of contemporary instrumentation and anticipated the exquisite devices to come, feeling assured that his theories would "in time be substantially confirmed by microscopical and chemical examinations of those patients who die in a neurasthenic condition."[20]

Beard's description of nervous exhaustion met with considerable—albeit not universal—acceptance.[21] His book had a second edition within a year, was soon translated into German, and "neurasthenia" began to earn multiple-column entries in medical encyclopedias. While part of Beard's success must be attributed to his explaining contemporary attitudes in appropriate physiological language, his significance for cultural history lies in his fusing a somatic description of neurasthenia with the social Darwinism of Herbert Spencer. Writing in *Atlantic Monthly* in 1879 on the "Physical Future of the American People," Beard described Darwinism as the "highest generalization that the human mind has yet reached," and placed his scientific facts in the context of current social theory. Noting as an accepted fact that differences in nerve force are hereditary ("nervous diathesis"), he explains these differences by contending that the farther the species progresses in its evolution and the more complex becomes its life, the greater becomes the strain upon the neural reserves of even the strong. Hence, it stands to reason that neurasthenia would afflict the wealthy, the refined, and the sensitive.[22]

Conjectures concerning the relationship between atmospheric electricity, the climate, and human health had prompted legitimate research for over a century. Beard plausibly argued that America's fluctuating climate produced singular changes in atmospheric electricity, which have a deleterious effect upon the neural balance of the refined. Beard was confident that the neurasthenia that plagued his time was but a contemporary sympton of the evolution fo a superior race.

As Rosenberg notes in his study on Beard, his view became popular not through its novelty, which would have signaled a genuine scientific revolution, but through its familiarity.[23] Specifically, Beard's etiology of "nervous disease" fused two accepted research programs in different disciplines, putting the morphological emphases of contemporary scientific research into the narrative structure of Spencerian Darwinism. However obsolete his scientific premises sound today, Beard did begin the modern interest in social origins of mental illness. By the end of the century specialists such as Wilhelm Erb became somewhat skeptical of the myriad of vague "symptoms" covered by the term "neurasthenia," but had to concede it to be "the fashionable neurosis of the present time."[24] Hysteria, the female counterpart of neurasthenia, seemed to be equally popular, and by the time Freud began to redefine the physiological premises of neural disorders, neurasthenia and hysteria were the two most accepted targets for research in the field of mental illness.[25]

Might it be possible to recharge the neural battery through harnessing electricity? Therapies for neural disorders have often taken a somewhat bizarre turn, but they contribute to our understanding of nineteenth-century medicine and of how it was complemented by the popular imagination. Appealing to the latter, Dr. Scott's Electric Hair-Brush (figure 3.3) appears to be at the frontier of research. "(Made of Pure Bristles, NOT WIRES), Warranted to cure Nervous Headache in 5 minutes" and to "immediately soothe the weary brain," this device appeared less preposterous to the consumer than it does now. It was simply part of the dramatic novelty of another technological breakthrough: in this case, applied electricity. With Miss Liberty holding one of the new electric lights on the cover, the German Electric Belt Agency appealed to faith in progress in its sober little pamphlet called "The Electric Age" (ca. 1889). Soon, the brochure argued, everything would be done by electricity, and the "subtle fluid" of its belt would be without doubt the "coming method of treating all forms of disease." The reader might well infer that the company's belt was the latest advance in electrical medicine, its therapeutic apex.[26]

Even the scientific establishment, although it eventually rejected Mesmer and his magnetic fluids as a "public menace," could not deny that cures were effected. Similarly, legitimate scientists could not gainsay the claims of the belt makers, for their research was proceeding along the same lines, if in more discreet language. Du Bois-Reymond had shown all muscles and nerves to be seats of neural currents; Duchenne, who apparently invented the term "faradization," suggested localized treatment to repair lesions in his *De l'electrisation localisée* in 1855. The next generation of researchers—Remak, von Ziemssen, Althaus, and Erb—began mapping body electricity physiologically.[27] Applying such maps became the task of electrotherapeutics experts such as Rockwell (Beard's early collabor-

Fig. 3.3. Dr. Scott's Electric Brush, advertised in *The Graphic*, October 13, 1883.

ator) and Erb. In 1871 Beard and Rockwell described "general faradization" thus: one electrode was placed on the feet, the other moved in a systematic manner over points of the chest, back, abdomen, neck, extremities, and head. This resulted in "a stimulating tonic with a powerful sedative influence" and was allegedly an "agent for improving nutrition."[28] Electrotherapy was frequently employed for treating hysteria: Bischoff had used electricity of a sort as early as 1801, while Beard and others found it "indispensable."[29]

The 1880s saw a plethora of advertisements for electric garments of all sorts designed to rehabilitate "spinal weakness," "nervous debility," and everything else, for that matter, through a simple extension of the electrotherapeutics metaphor. If Erb and Rockwell described "faradization" verbally, Harness' Electric Corset did so visually. To be sure, researchers within the scientific community had been aware of "electrizing quacks" since the time of Dr. Graham's Celestial Bed. Althaus, it will be recalled, voiced concern over the use of electricity by those untrained in physiology, but warnings such as his did little to clarify the border between what was seen as legitimate science and pseudo-science.[30] Since at the frontiers of research the border is not always obvious, scientists shared in the ignorance of the charlatans if not in their profits, and the gadget makers had used Althaus's strategy from the beginning. Dr. Graham warned against unscientific frauds in announcing his "Temple of Health," and the German Electric Belt Company gave Bismarck as a reference and intoned the credentials of the inventor, a P.H. Van der Weyde, M.D. ("President of the New York Electrical Society"). In addition, the company warned sternly of "bogus imitations," and offered to pay $500 if a galvanometer did not register a current.

On the scientific front, neurasthenia still resisted detection by physiological means in the 1890s. Many of those involved in the research program kept the faith that the new instrumentation would discover anatomical changes, as did Savill, publishing his lectures on neurasthenia in 1899.[31] Electricity's service in treating "nervous disease" encountered a similar dilemma. Erb, who with Rockwell became one of the leading late-century advocates of electrical therapy, met Beard in 1904. By that time even he had to admit that he had not the faintest idea how electrotherapy worked, and that he still could find no physiological evidence of its efficacy. Though he continued to advocate research in electrotherapeutics, the best he could say of it was that "its office consists in the removal of the nutritive disorder of the nervous system, in strengthening the entire organism, and in combating individual and especially annoying symptoms."[32] By this time he had abandoned the battery metaphor, but popular advertising retained its semipoetic prose and scientific pretensions. The demarcation remained indistinct.

In 1891 Rockwell addressed the American Medical Association, remembering how some thought electrotherapy for neurasthenia to be quackery; he maintained, however, that it could now be accepted as a legitimate science, its future assured. Rockwell's confidence turned out to have been misplaced, however. The integrity of the research program as he understood it had suffered seriously by the turn of the century, and from several sources. First, the basic imagery regulating the understanding of electricity had changed. By 1903 even Rockwell not only had to concede that he, too, did not understand why the treatment worked, but also that researchers had been wrong all along about the nature of electricity. Not only was there no neural fluid, electricity was not a fluid after all. By that time he realized that some previously accepted terms such as "current" and "flow" could now only be used metaphorically, for "electricity is now believed to be identical with the luminiferous ether."[33] After Einstein's paper in 1905, of course, the ether itself as a medium began its eclipse into obsolescence.

Beard, in the fifth edition of his *Practical Treatise on Nervous Exhaustion (Neurasthenia)* (1905), was fully aware of competing research concerning mental illness, but still insisted upon the physiological basis of the disease and its treatment. He still viewed electricity as having the "ability to restore the conductibility of the neuron that has become resistant to the nerve current. The inherent energy of the nerve cells is liberated, new paths of conduction form, resulting in modification of both motor and sensory process."[34]

The assumptions with which one approaches a research project tend to dictate the range of conclusions. When expected results do not occur, the researcher either recognizes the inadequacy of the original premises (most difficult to do, as we have seen thus far) or keeps faith in the original analogies and in the progress of science to validate them. The author of an article on "The Similarity of Electric and Nerve Forces" in the *Journal of the American Medical Association (JAMA)* of August 1885 realized that something was wrong somewhere, and reexamined the whole set of analogies, beginning with the therapeutic use of discharges from the torpedo fish. He recognized that modern research demanded "a knowledge of the brain and of the network of the nervous system" and an appreciation of the "exaltation or depressing of nerve power" as an agency in this. Eloquently describing the progress of science into the "ocean of truth," the author had to admit that "just how electricity acts as a therapeutic agent, no experimenter has satisfactorily explained." Unwilling to abandon the battery metaphor, however, he resorted to a topos in some schools of biological research, romantic in origin, that the expected results must be forthcoming, for "we will maintain our text: 'the unity of Nature.' "[35]

On a less elevated level, the increasing dominance of physiology led to a weakening of training in pharmacology and a general deemphasis of therapeutics in the medical school curricula—a fact of which the merchandisers of belts and nostrums were happily aware. Claude Hopkins, writing of *My Life in Advertising* in 1927, recalled that those writing advertising copy and selling medicines to physicians often knew more about pharmacy and therapeutics than did their customers.[36] Further eroding the already blurred line between the medical and the popular conception of therapy came the marketing practices of reputable companies. Parke-Davis, for instance, sold "Videopathy" treatments along with its legitimate preparations, and Seabury & Johnson played upon new words in the scientific vocabulary in marketing "Radiozone."[37]

Illustrating the unfortunate vacuum in medical training, Erb suggested in 1878 the following cure for neurasthenia, which deserves quotation in detail. The patient must

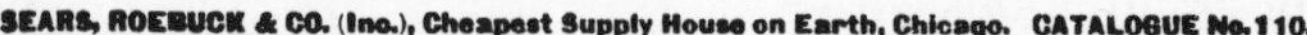

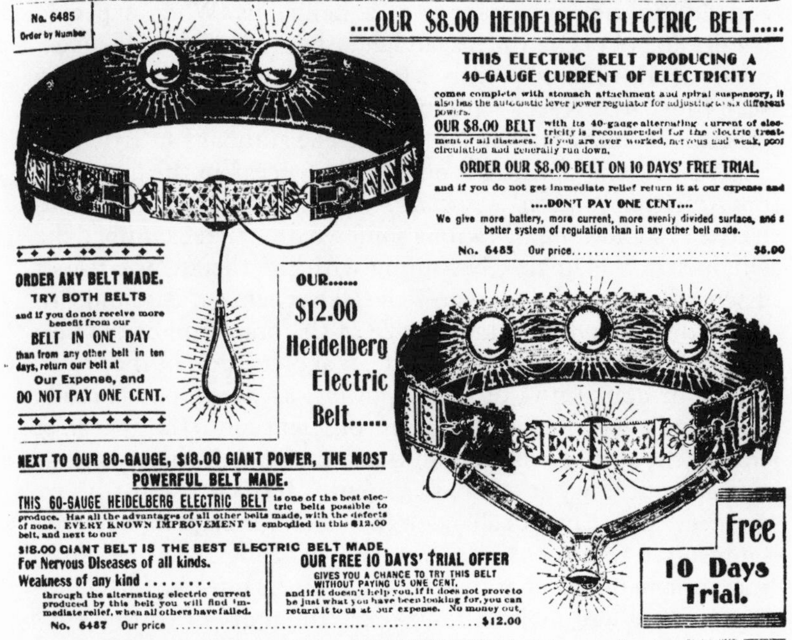

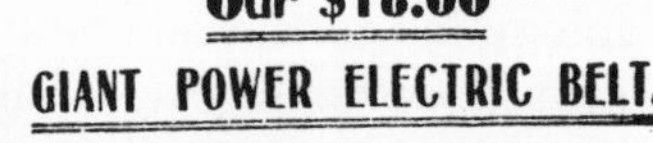

Fig. 3.4. The Heidelberg Electric Belt, from Sears, Roebuck and Company, *Consumer's Guide*, Fall 1900, p. 39.

live a regular and healthy life in every respect, and must continue this plan with the greatest perserverance. He must work little, and only at fixed hours, with frequent interruptions; must go to bed early and sleep as much as he can; must have an abundance of strong, easibly digestible food, at not too great intervals; spirituous drinks are allowable in moderation; much moving about in open air...is absolutely necessary; patients who are very easily exhausted must sit a great deal out of doors in good air; the sexual act must be restricted as much as possible, but... sexual excitement without gratification must be avoided as much as possible.[38]

Erb continues by suggesting therapy in Switzerland or the Tyrol; scant wonder Beard found neurasthenia popular among the wealthy.

The gulf between popular treatments for "nervous diseases" and those suggested by physicians was not as great as one might suppose, in that both operated upon a combination of faith (either in the efficacy of the device itself or in the progress of instrumentation) and ignorance. According to Beard, the symptoms of neurasthenia resemble those of syphilis, and have similar cures. It is difficult to read without a shudder the "cure" offered by a quack in New York for syphilis, or "self-abuse." "The patient sat naked upon a sort of toilet throne, his bare back resting against a metal plate, his scrotum suspended in a whirling pool."[39] The plate and pool were linked by wire to a power source; therapy began when the circuit was completed. While this therapy doubtless cured lads of some of the vices in question, normal therapy worked from much the same (albeit less graphic) premises. Erb suggested, for "flaccidity of the testicles" due to sexual excess, "the passage of a moderately strong faradic or galvanic current through the testicles for a few minutes,"[40] while the *JAMA* of March 19, 1892, reported that M. Kronfeld of the General Hospital of Vienna treated syphilis with an electric bath. Dommer, in the meantime, suggested treating "sexual neurasthenia" by passing a faradic current between one electrode in the urethra and the other in the rectum.[41]

So the popularity of electrical devices promising fast, fast, fast relief from "spinal weakness" cannot be solely ascribed to charlatanism and gullibility. The advertisements shared the premises and language of legitimate research programs. They often visualized their metaphors through the new technique of reproducing pictures. Such an ad for Harness' Electric Corset (females, particularly the "new woman," would need neural refreshment more than men) showed a well-rounded beauty leaning out of the apparatus with a bemused smile, while "magnetic rays" darted from the electrified stays (figure 3.2). For "diseases of men" the German Electric Suspensory Belt, mentioned previously, had four batteries pulsing electricity. More elaborate yet, the radiant illustration of the Heidelberg Electric Belt in the Sears *Consumer Guide* for 1900 seizes the eye with its gaudy array of apparatus (figure 3.4). The pouches were detachable, so the belt could be worn by both sexes.

One should not isolate the discussion of popular electric therapy from patent medicines and nostrums of the time. Part of the competitive appeal of medical electricity, however, lay in its scientific, invisible, and drugless nature. Morphine addiction was common to veterans of the Civil War, and some of the putative cures for alcoholism were themselves forty proof. After Samuel Hopkins Adams, writing in *Collier's Magazine* in 1905, exposed the alcohol, morphine, opium, and cocaine contents of patent medicines, new tonics appeared in Sears catalogues purporting to cure alcoholism and drug addiction.[42] The Sanden Electric Company, however, declared that "electricity, properly applied, will do more for you than all the drugs ever compounded."[43] Rockwell, too, contended that one of the virtues of electrotherapeutics lay in the ability to experiment without drugs.[44]

If we look at the popular cures from the point of view of the advertiser rather than the scientist, another aspect of the relationship between normal science and popular culture emerges. Claude Hopkins confesses about his early career that he probably should not have published the medical ads, but notes that the nostrums did more good than harm, in that "people bought results, not medicine." These results, Hopkins surmises, came "largely through mental impressions": in other words, suggestion.[45]

Ironically, Hopkins's marketing instinct solved the problem

which had confronted the scientists who had once rejected Mesmer, Graham, and Perkins as frauds—the sometimes startling remissions of maladies hitherto inaccessible to conventional treatment. Hopkins recalls the success of his ploy the commercial guarantee, particularly the one affixed to "Dr. Shoop's Rheumatic Cure." "It worked like magic," he asserted. Hopkins was right in several ways. Essentially, the guarantee increased the suggestive power of the purchase by telling the buyer that the element of risk or danger had been removed. In effect, the cure lay in the act of purchase rather than in the product itself. The advertisements for the garments, the testimonials from authorities, the scientific terminology, and the visual depictions of scientific metaphors all lent plausibility to the products and increased their suggestive power. The German Electric Belt Company, for instance, details in its pamphlet the credentials of the two inventors, and, while never saying precisely how the invention works, gives the reader a vague feeling of having been scientifically edified.

The manufacturers also sensed that the impact of visual impressions to suggest security to the consumer went beyond language and graphics. In his investigations for *Collier's*, Samuel Hopkins Adams noted of a certain C.J. Thatcher of Chicago that "he wore a magnetic cap, a magnetic waistcoat, magnetic insoles, and...his legs...swathed like a mummy's in magnetic wrappings."[46] So plausible were the electrical cures that when A.D. Crabtre exposed in *The Funny Side of Physic* (1872) all the bleeders, patent medicines, and other forms of "humbug," he made no mention of electrical garters, oils, tablets, and toothbrushes.

By the end of the century "nervous diseases" and their electrical treatments were beginning to lose their power over the medical imagination. Skepticism crept into the medical literature, at least in part because such diseases doggedly refused to exhibit any physiological manifestations. Electrotherapy also resisted explanation, and lost favor partly because, as even Erb had to admit, it failed more often than not. Ironically, the new instrumentation for which so many had hoped showed that, while electrotherapy could make abnormal cells less pathological, this was done at the expense of normal cells, causing "electrical neurosis."[47]

More importantly, the falling into disfavor of neurasthenia and electrotherapeutics as research programs reflected a change in the assumptions regarding the mind and mental illness. The insight on the part of the advertisers as to the element of suggestion was not far removed from an emerging research program within the scientific community which was not physiologically based, and which would contend with and eventually replace the electrotherapeutic assumptions of Beard and others. In 1884 Engelskjön noted that in certain cases hot and cold water had the same therapeutic effect as electricity, and in the *Reference Handbook of the Medical Sciences* (1903) Bailey draws from "hints" that traumatic neuroses (neurasthenia and hysteria) come from "mental impressions" (the same term used by Hopkins) rather than from physical injuries.[48]

We see here the beginnings of a change in the medical imagination stemming from the experiments on suggestion by Charcot and Bernheim in the 1870s. Bernheim noticed that the patient's belief in the efficacy of the cure was often of more importance than the technique of the cure itself.[49] In 1843 James Braid rescued therapeutic suggestion from disgrace by renaming it, first, "neuryphnology," and, finally, "hypnotism." In 1891 a Frankfurt Congress, convened to discuss "Elektrotherapeutische Streitfragen," was sharply divided upon just this possibility that suggestion produced the results attributed to electricity.[50] Freud, though interested in Beard's work, especially his later emphasis upon the sexual etiology of neurasthenia, shifted the assumptions regulating the term away from physiology and radically restricted its use.[51]

Among non-scientific texts one sees a similar shifting of assumptions and imagery. *Harper's Bazaar* 42 (1908) showed the change in scientific and popular tastes by carrying Alice Fallows's article on "Mind Cure for Women's Ills," in which the author tells her readers (on p. 266) that for "functional nervous diseases" (neurasthenia had been described as such) "mind-trance by suggestion" is the best cure. Interestingly, the set of gynecological assumptions concerning women's neural re-

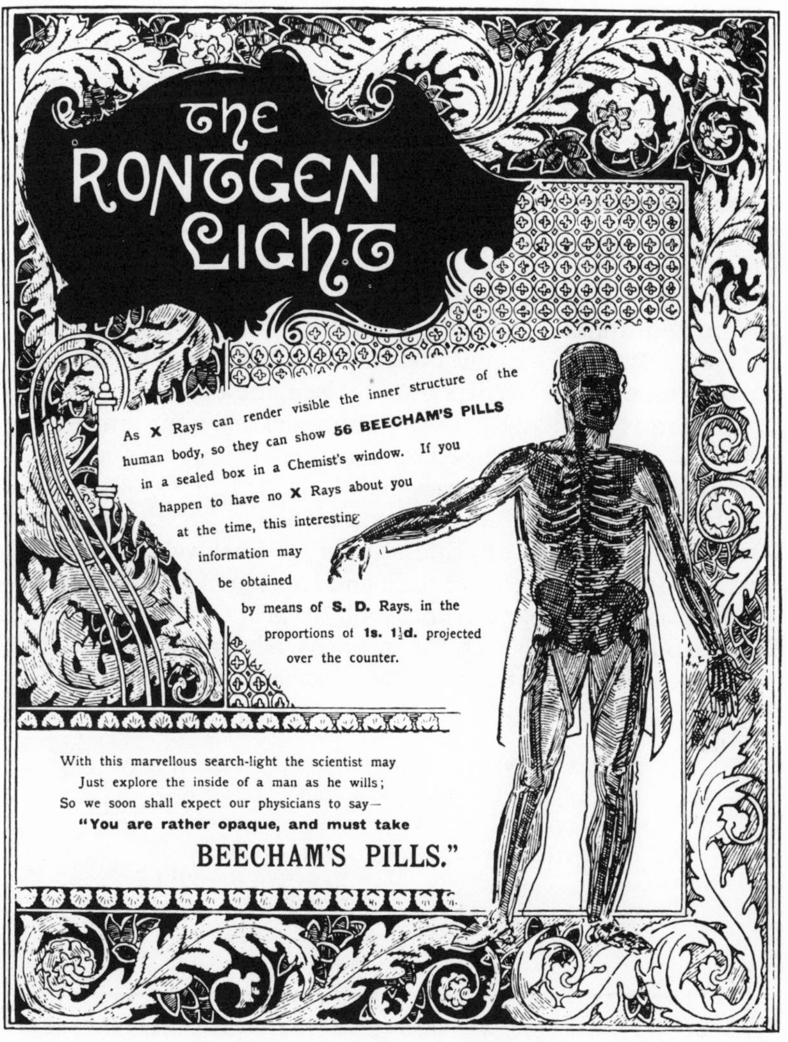

Fig. 3.5. Beecham's Pills advertisement, from the *Illustrated London News*, May 9, 1896.

serves were changing as well: an article in the *JAMA* in 1894 questioned the blanket use of "female weakness" as a concept that only obscured ignorance and sometimes led to unnecessary surgery.[52]

The enigmatic nature of the unseen world of energy continued to provide a frontier to the imagination in which the lines between science and pseudo-science were often blurred. The Sears *Consumer Guide,* for instance, provides an excellent mirror to changing popular taste. By 1909 the Heidelberg Belts that pulsed from the pages of the 1900 fall *Guide* were gone, although patent medicines and elixirs such as Beef and Iron Wine continued. Electricity continued to be of some use in therapy, although without the earlier underlying physiological assumptions. The discovery of the dramatic characteristics of other forms of energy, however, prompted reactions similar to those attending electricity. The *New York Medical Week* of January 10, 1925, carried a page of advertisement extolling the "ethereal virtue" of "Elixir of Radium." Roentgen's discovery of X-rays in 1895 lent a breathless quality to Rockwell's introduction to the 1903 revision of the eighth edition of his and Beard's *Practical Treatise on the Medical and Surgical Uses of Electricity,* but as one might suspect, the inventive advertiser in the *Illustrated London News* (figure 3.5) went science one better in 1895:

> With this marvellous search-light the scientist may
> Just explore the inside of a man as he wills;
> So we soon shall expect our physicians to say—
> **"You are rather opaque, and must take**
> **BEECHAM'S PILLS**."

Notes

Research for this chapter was supported by the program in Humanities, Science and Technology of the National Endowment for the Humanities.

1. See the collections of Victorian advertisements in Gerald Carson, *One for a Man, Two for a Horse* (New York: Doubleday, 1961); L. De Vries and Ilonka van Amstel, *The Wonderful World of Advertising,*

1865-1900 (Chicago: Follett, 1972); Adelaide Hechtlinger, *The Great Patent Medicine Era, or, Without Benefit of Doctor* (New York: Grosset & Dunlap, 1970). For an illustration of the omnipresence of advertisements, see the illustrations in Diana and Geoffrey Hundley, *Advertising in Victorian England, 1837-1901* (London: Wayland Publishers, 1972), chap. 1, "The Media."

2. On Mesmer, see Robert Darnton, *Mesmerism and the End of the Enlightenment in France* (Cambridge: Harvard Univ. Press, 1968); Rudolph Tischner and Karl Bittle, *Mesmer und sein Problem: Magnetismus, Suggestion, Hypnose* (Stuttgart: Hippokrates, 1941); René Kaech, "Om mesmerismens ursprung och föregångere," *Ciba Journal* 1 (1947): 274; and Maria M. Tatar, *Spellbound: Studies on Mesmerism and Literature* (Princeton: Princeton Univ. Press, 1978), chap. 1, "From Mesmer to Freud," pp. 3-44.

3. See Geoffrey Sutton, "Electric Medicine and Mesmerism," *Isis* 72 (1981): 384-86.

4. On Graham, see Charles J.S. Thompson, *The Quacks of Old London* (London: Brentano, 1928), pp. 333-35; Grete de Francesco, *The Power of the Charlatan,* trans. Miriam Beard (New Haven: Yale Univ. Press, 1939); Geerto Snyder, *Wunderglaube and Wahn: Aus der bunten Welt der Scharlatane* (Munich: Bruckmann, 1965), pp. 145-46. For an eyewitness account of Graham's "magnetic magic," see Joseph Ennemoser, *Geschichte der Magie* (Leipzig, 1844), p. 924, and his *Anleitung der mesmerischen Praxis* (Stuttgart: Cotta, 1852). For Graham's description of his apparatus, see his "A Sketch, or, Short Description of Dr. Graham's Medical Apparatus &c" (London, 1780).

5. See Thompson, *Quacks of Old London,* 338-42, and Jacques M. Quen, "Elisha Perkins, Physician, Nostrum-vendor, or Charlatan?" *Bull. Hist. Med.* 37 (1963): 159-66.

6. Everett Mendelsohn, "The Biological Sciences in the Nineteenth Century: Some Problems and Sources," *History of Science* 3 (1964): 39-54. See also Werner Leibbrand, *Romantische Medizin* (Heidelberg and Leipzig: H. Goverts, 1937), chap. 5, " 'Thierischer Magnetismus' und romantische Totalität," pp. 119-43.

7. For a sense of vivisectionists' militancy and heroic self-depiction, see the preface to Elie de Cyon, *Methodik der physiologischen Experimente und Vivisectionen* (Giessen: J. Ricker, 1876): "Soll die Medizin ernst eine streng wissenschaftliche Basis in allen ihren Zweigen erhalten, so muss sie dieselbe in erster Linie von der Physiologie erwarten" (p. 8). For the controversy, see Victor D. French, *Antivivisection and Medical Science in Victorian Society* (Princeton: Princeton Univ. Press, 1975).

8. George M. Beard, *American Nervousness, Its Causes and Consequences (Supplement to Nervous Exhaustion)*, 1881, in *Medicine and Society in America*, ed. Chas. Rosenberg (New York: Arno Press, 1972), p. 17. See also S. Weir Mitchell, *Diseases of the Nervous System, Especially in Women* (Philadelphia: Henry C. Lea, 1881), p. 219. Generally, see Francis G. Gosling, *American Nervousness: A Study in Medicine and Social Values in the Gilded Age, 1870-1900* (Norman: Oklahoma Medical College, 1976), and George Frederick Drinka, *The Birth of Neurosis: Myth, Malady, and the Victorians* (New York: Simon and Schuster, 1984).

9. Wilhelm Erb, *Handbook of Electro-Therapeutics*, trans. L. Putzel, Wood's Library of Standard Medical Authors (New York: Wm. Wood, 1883), p. 33.

10. J. Althaus, *A Treatise on Medical Electricity, Theoretical and Practical, and its Use in Paralysis, Neuralgia, and Other Diseases*, 3d ed. (London: Longmans, Green, 1873), pp. xi-xii.

11. Alphonso David Rockwell, *The Medical and Surgical Uses of Electricity, Including the X-Ray, Finsen Light, Vibratory Therapeutics, and High-Frequency Currents* (New York: E.B. Treat & Co., 1903), p. 21; *JAMA* 20 (1893): 73.

12. George M. Beard, *American Nervousness*, pp. 11, 98. For more on the battery metaphor, see John S. and Robin M. Haller, *The Physician and Sexuality in Victorian America* (New York: Norton, 1977), pp. 9-24.

13. "Själamord (apropos *Rosmersholm*)," *Samlade Skrifter*, ed. Landquist, 22 (Stockholm: Bonniers, 1920): 189.

14. "Spreading the Word," *Printers' Ink* 184 (July 28, 1938): 84.

15. Beard, *American Nervousness*, p. 96. For assessments of Beard, see Charles E. Rosenberg, "The Place of George M. Beard in Nineteenth-Century Psychiatry," *Bull. Hist. Med.* 36 (1962): 245-59. Philip P. Wiener, "G.M. Beard and Freud on American Nervousness," *Journal of the History of Ideas* 17 (1956), has the best list of Beard's numerous if duplicatory publications; and generally, see Haller and Haller, *Physician and Sexuality*, chap. 1, "The Nervous Century."

16. Allan McLaine Hamilton, *Nervous Diseases: Their Description and Treatment* (Philadelphia: Henry C. Lea, 1878), p. 378.

17. Seminal to craniometry was Emil Huschke's *Schädel, Hirn and Seele des Menschen und der Thiere nach Alter, Geschlecht and Race...* (Jena: Mauke, 1854). For overviews of this research program, see Stephen Jay Gould, *The Mismeasure of Man* (New York: Norton, 1981), chaps. 1-3; Haller and Haller, *Physician and Sexuality*, pp. 48-61; J. Haller's paper on "Neurasthenic Women: The Medical Profession and

the 'New Woman' of the Nineteenth Century," *New York Journal of Medicine* 70 (1970) 2489-97.

18. Ludwig Büchner, "The Brain of Women," *New Review* 9 (1893): 176.

19. "On the Province of Women in Medicine," *JAMA* 19 (June 20, 1891): 893.

20. George M. Beard, "Neurasthenia or Nervous Exhaustion," *Boston Medical and Surgical Journal* 80 (1869): 217.

21. In a review of Beard's *Practical Treatise on Nervous Exhaustion,* E.L. Spitzka commented upon Beard's prolific writings as a "diarrhoea of words and a constipation of ideas." *St. Louis Clinical Record* 7 (1880-81): 92-94.

22. George M. Beard, "The Physical Future of the American People," *Atlantic Monthly* 43 (1879): 727. The *Saturday Review,* though not given to the more sensational advertisements, ran one during 1879, the height of neurasthenia's popularity, which declared that "brain work is undoubtedly far more exhausting than bodily labour," and extolled "Grant's Morella Cherry Brandy" as a restorative.

23. Charles E. Rosenberg, "The Place of George M. Beard in Nineteenth-Century Psychiatry," *Bull. Hist. Med.* 36 (1962): 245.

24. Erb, *Handbook,* p. 290.

25. Henri F. Ellenberger, *The Discovery of the Unconscious* (New York: Basic Books, 1970), p. 244.

26. "The Electric Era: The German Electric Belts & Appliances" (Brooklyn: The German Electric Belt Co. [n.d.], 1899[?]), copy in the National Library of Medicine, Bethesda, Md. Copies of the Pulvermacher Galvanic Co. of New York's "Electricity, Nature's Chief Restorer...Cure of Nervous and Chronic Diseases without Medication (New York, 1878) and the Volta Belt Co.'s "Electricity, The Best Curative Agent..." (n.d.) may be found in the Cincinnati Historical Society archives.

27. A concise survey of the theories may be found in Irving Samuel Cutter, "History of Physical Therapy and its Relation to Medicine," *Principles and Practice of Physical Therapy,* ed. Harry E. Mock et al. (Hagerstown, Md.: W.F. Prior, 1932), pp. 57-58.

28. George M. Beard and Alphonso David Rockwell, *A Practical Treatise on the Medical and Surgical Uses of Electricity, Including Localized and General Electrization* (New York: William Wood, 1871). See Edward Stainbrook, "The Use of Electricity in Psychiatric Treatment during the Nineteenth Century," *Bull. Hist. Med.* 22 (1948): 166-67.

29. Stainbrook, "Use of Electricity," p. 172. George M. Beard, "The

Treatment of Insanity by Electricity," *Journal of Mental Science* 19 (1873-74): 355.

30. See the papers in Thomas Hardy Leahey and Grace Evans Leahey, *Psychology's Occult Doubles: Psychology and the Problem of Pseudoscience* (Chicago: Nelson-Hall, 1983) for discussions of the difficulty in distinguishing between the two terms in any manner save in retrospect.

31. Thomas D. Savill, *Clinical Lectures on Neurasthenia* (New York: Wm. Wood, 1899), p. 22.

32. Erb, *Handbook* p. 103. He adds, "And who will affirm that there are not other at present unknown effects of electricity upon the living organism, upon which the most important therapeutic results depend?" (p. 104). See the results of Engelskjön below for the unintended irony of this statement.

33. Rockwell, *Medical and Surgical Uses,* p. 20.

34. George M. Beard, *A Practical Treatise on Nervous Exhaustion (Neurasthenia),* ed. A.D. Rockwell (New York: E.B. Treat, 1905; Kraus Reprint Co., 1971), p. 284.

35. John J. Caldwell, "The Similarity of Electric and Nerve Forces," *JAMA* 5 (1885): 227. On the romantic basis of this biological theme, see L.S. Jacyna, "Perceived General Physiology: The Comparative Dimension to British Neuroscience in the 1830s and 1840s," *Studies in History of Biology* 7 (1984): 61-68.

36. Claude Hopkins, *My Life in Advertising,* (Chicago: Advertising Publications, 1966), pp. 73-77.

37. David L. Dykstra, "The Medical Profession and Patent and Proprietary Medicines during the Nineteenth Century," *Bull. Hist. Med.* 29 (1955): 88, 90-99.

38. H. von Ziemssen, "Diseases of the Spinal Cord," in *Cyclopaedia of the Practice of Medicine* trans. Geoghean et al. (New York: William. Wood, 1878), 7:380-81.

39. For the description, see Champe Seabury Andrews, *A Century's Criminal Alliance between Quacks and Some Newspapers* (New York: Stettiner Bros, 1905), pp. 7-8, cited in James Harvey Young, "Device Quackery in America," *Bull. Hist. Med.* 39 (1965): 158.

40. Erb, *Handbook,* p. 350.

41. F. Dommer, "Urethrale Faradisations-Elektroden," *Deutsche Praxis* 10 (1898): 23.

42. Lydia Pinkham's Vegetable Compound, for instance, was 14 percent alcohol, while "croup tonics" would induce your tot to sleep tight by means of morphine, laudanum, or cocaine. His *Collier's* arti-

cles were reprinted in Samuel Hopkins Adams, *The Great American Fraud* (Chicago: AMA Press, 1912). See also Edward Bok, "The 'Patent-Medicine' Curse," *Ladies' Home Journal* 21 (May 1904): 18, and E. S. Turner, *The Shocking History of Advertising!* (New York: Dutton, 1953), pp. 203-6.

43. Arthur J. Cramp, *Nostrums and Quackery* (Chicago: AMA Press, 1936) 2:721. The German Electric Belt Co. said that its products would cure opium and morphine addiction, since these were but "an electric disturbance in the system."

44. Rockwell, *Medical and Surgical Uses,* p. 22.

45. Hopkins, *My Life in Advertising,* p. 77.

46. Adams, *Great American Fraud,* p. 95.

47. C. Engelskjön, "Die ungleichartige therapeutische Wirkungsweise der zwei elektrische Stromsarten und die elektrodiagnostische Geschichtsfeldsuntersuchung," *Archiv für Psychiatrie und Nervenkrankheiten* 15 (1884): 138.

48. Ibid., p. 139; Pearce Bailey, "Nervous System," in *Reference Handbook of the Medical Sciences* 6 (New York: William Wood, 1903): 240.

49. Bernheim's experiment cited in Robert Hillman, "A Scientific Study of Mystery: The Role of Medical and Popular Press in the Nancy-Salpêtrière Controversy on Hypnotism," *Bull. Hist. Med.* 39 (1965): 170.

50. *Elektrotherapeutische Streitfragen* in *Verhandlungen der Electrotherapeuten-Versammlung...,* ed. Ludwig Edinger et al. (Wiesbaden: Bergmann, 1892).

51. Henry Alden Bunker, "From Beard to Freud: A Brief History of the Concept of Neurasthenia," *Medical Review of Reviews* 36 (1930): 113-14.

52. C.E. Ruth, "Female Weakness," *JAMA* 19 (Sept. 8, 1894): 389-90.

MARSHALL SCOTT LEGAN

4. Hydropathy, or the Water-Cure

The principles of hydrotherapy have occupied a time-honored position in man's arsenal against disease and infirmity. Hydropathic remedies have enjoyed a continuum in the annals of medical practice from antiquity to the present. But never has so much emphasis been placed on the value of hydrotherapeutics as in the period 1820-60, when its practitioners developed their own unique "system," known as Hydropathy or the Water-Cure. To persuade the uninitiated of the soundness and legitimacy of their new "discovery," the hydropaths produced an elaborate structure of methodology and a vast panoply of "scientific" literature. Negatively, hydropathy, like Thomsonianism, homoeopathy, and other single-theory cures came to reject many of the valid practices in the pantheon of regular medicine. However, as a system devoted to the improvement of health, the water-cure deserves analysis as one of the least harmful, at least in its regimen, of the pseudo-sciences.

The originator of the hydropathic or water-cure system which enjoyed such vogue in the "age of the common man" was the Silesian peasant Vincent Priessnitz. Born October 4, 1799, in the vicinity of Gräfenberg, Silesia, Priessnitz, while aiding his father with farm chores, observed the efficacious effects of cold water compacts in sprains, bruises, and tumors on horses' hoofs. In addition, an old man who employed cold water in diseases of cattle shared his knowledge with the inquisitive youth. But it was not until 1816 when Priessnitz was injured while baling hay that he became an unconditional convert to the therapeutic merits of cold water for human ailments. Kicked in the face by the horse and run over by the wagon, Priessnitz suffered two broken ribs and a severely bruised left arm. An attending physician from nearby Freiwaldau declared that the injured boy could never be cured in such a manner as to be again fit for work.[1] Unwilling to accept the prognostication, Priessnitz determined to treat himself. Leaning his belly against a chair, he forced the fractured ribs into their natural position. Applying wet cloths as bandages on his ribs and face, he drank plenty of cold water, ate sparingly, and observed perfect repose. Within ten days, Priessnitz was able to go out, and at the end of a year, he had resumed working in the fields.[2]

The success of his self-cure stimulated Priessnitz's imagination, and he began to broaden his investigations into the general curative effects of cold water and into which laws of hydrotherapeutics were most applicable in relieving human maladies. Ultimately, he devised a hydropathic system which employed at least three modes of treatment: (1) general application of water to the external body by either a bath or douche;[3] (2) local application of water to particular parts of the body through the method of ablution, and (3) internal use of water by drinking, lavements, and injections.[4] As his therapeutic reputation spread locally, especially his success in relieving gout and rheumatism, Priessnitz established a hydropathic institute in Gräfenberg in 1826. Meeting with limited success initially, he found his notoriety did not begin to spread until 1830 when the Austrian government granted him authority to receive patients and treat them under his own "system."[5] A close viewer of the hydropathic scene, R.T. Claridge, reported the number of individuals treated by Priessnitz at his establishment. Starting with only 45 patients in 1829, the numbers had increased to 469 by 1836, and in 1840 1,576 took the cure. Between 1829 and 1841, Claridge calculated, over 7,298 patients followed the regimen of the Silesian hydropath.[6]

Even more remarkable than the numbers was the geographic diversity of the clientele attracted to Gräfenberg, which included patients from "St. Petersburg, Moscow, and Paris, London and Philadelphia, Astrakhan and Constantinople, Vienna,

Berlin, and Warsaw; and all Germany, Hungary, and Italy furnish their several contingents."[7] Indeed, the inmates had a decidedly "upper crust" tinge; for example, in 1841 there resided for treatment an archduchess, ten princes and princesses, at least a hundred counts and barons, military men of all grades, several medical men, professors, lawyers, and other notables.[8]

Because of the growing popularity of the hydropathic cure, initiates on both sides of the Atlantic began to search the records of antiquity for evidence in support of the legitimacy of the water-cure regimen. Citations of proof ranged from the mundane to the sublime, and no shred of support was thought too small to ignore. Euripides' statement "The sea removes each taint of evil from the human race" was cited to describe how the dramatist, traveling with Plato in Egypt, fell ill and was cured by bathing in the sea.[9] In *De Medicina* Aulus Cornelius Celsus, the Roman encyclopedist, advised the following hydrotherapeutic regimen if a patient, bitten by a rabid dog, developed a fear of water: "In these cases there is very little hope for the sufferer. But still there is just one remedy, to throw the patient unawares into a water tank which he has not seen beforehand. If he cannot swim, let him sink and drink, then lift him out. If he can swim, push him under at intervals so that he drinks his fill of water even against his will. For so his thirst and dread of water are removed at the same time." Celsus did warn, however, that "a spasm of sinews, provoked by cold water, may carry off a weakened body." As a palliative to the frigid shock, Celsus believed the patient should be taken straight from the water tank and "plunged into a bath of hot oil."[10] In 1846 the editor of *DeBow's Review*, published in New Orleans, printed an eleven-page article entitled "On the Revival of the Roman Thermae or Ancient Public Baths."[11] Dr. Sam Kneeland, Jr., of Boston described how the moderns had not improved much upon the therapeutics of antiquity in the use of water as he invoked the names of Hippocrates (460 B.C.); Asdepiades, who was surnamed the "cold bather" from his zeal; Musa, who cured Augustus Caesar; Celsus, Galen, Avicenna, Paracelsus, and other notables in the history of medicine.[12] Replying to a sneer in *The Lancet*, a supporter claimed that the water-cure was "as old as the flood, the first grand treatment by that remedy having taken place in the time of the venerable Noah."[13] Even a poetess, Mrs. A.C. Judson, was inspired to contribute several pieces to the *Water-Cure Journal*:

Cold Water Song

All hail to pure cold water,
That bright rich gem from heaven;
And praise to the Creator,
for such a blessing given!
And since it comes in fulness,
We'll prize it yet the more;
For life, and health, and gladness,
It spreads the wide earth oer.[14]

Wash and Be Healed

Go wash in pure water, 'twill gladden thy soul,
And make the diseased clayey tenement whole;
'Twill nerve thee for life's deepest trials and bring
A zest with each joy around thee may spring.[15]

As the evolving panacea had its adherents, it also had its critics, and considerable print and paper were devoted to the fallacies, evils, and potential harms inherent in the hydropathic regimen. The British *Lancet* condemned the itinerant physicians of hydropathy and began to report unsuccessful cures and even deaths in the fallacious attempts to cure every malady with water.[16] One detractor wrote: "The hydropathists have discarded this excessive precaution and boldly used their remedy as a tonic, whenever a tonic is required. They have administered it to the old, the weak, the bilious, the gouty, the scrofulous, the dyseptic, and the paralytic. Neither mucous membranes nor mesenteric glands, infantile weakness, nor senile decrepitude have stood in their way."[17] American periodicals especially delighted in repeating the experience of Jean-Jacques Rousseau with the cure back in 1736. Adopting the cold-water system with little discretion, Rousseau recalled that "it nearly relieved me, not only of my ills, but of my life."[18] Suffering from a languid condition and being sick of a milk diet, Rousseau began to arise every morning and go to the fountain with a goblet to drink, as he walked about, as much as two full bottles of water, while entirely leaving off wine at meals. He graphically described the results:

> The water which I drank was a little hard and difficult to pass, as mountain springs generally are. In short, I succeeded so well, that in less than two months I entirely destroyed the powers of my stomach, which had been very good up to the time. Being no longer able to digest anything, I thought it useless any longer to hope for recovery. At this time an accident happened to me, singular in itself, and in its consequences which will only cease with my life.
>
> One morning when I was no worse than usual, whilst raising up a little table which had fallen, I perceived a sudden and almost inconceivable revolution throughout my whole body. I know not how to compare it better than to a kind of tempest, which arising in my blood, gained in an instant all my limbs. My arteries commenced beating with such force, that I not only felt their beating, but I even heard it, especially the beating of the carotid. In addition there was a great noise in my ears, and this noise was triple, or rather quadruple—to wit a deep hollow—buzzing, a clear murmur like that of running water, a very shrill blowing sound, and the beating which I have mentioned, the blows of which I could easily count, without feeling my pulse or touching my body with my hands. This inward noise was so great, that it destroyed the fineness of hearing which I had had formerly, and rendered me, not entirely deaf, but hard of hearing, as I have continued to be ever since that time.
>
> One may judge of my surprise and consternation. I gave myself up for dead, and took to my bed.... At the end of some weeks finding that I was neither better nor worse, I left my bed, and resumed my ordinary habits of life, with the beating of the arteries and the buzzing in the ears, which from that time—that is to say for 30 years—has not ceased for one minute.[19]

In another critical vein, the *Boston Medical and Surgical Journal* described how obdurate prisoners were subdued by cold showering. An investigation by prison officials concluded that cold water showering, as practiced at the Auburn (N.Y.) State Prison, when continued long enough and in the mode to make an efficient punishment, was "injurious to health."[20] Even a scoffing poet replied in biting verse:

Oh! do not say that doctor's stuff
Could cure my woesome ills;
Or think that ever health is found
In potions or in pills.
No noisome draught could bring relief
No drug my fever quell;
Healthy, rosy maid, like Truth, is found
In the bottom of a well.[21]

And a rhymster in *The Knickerbocker* opined in satirical verse:

It's water, water everywhere,
And quarts to drink, if you can bear:
'Tis well that we are made of clay
For common dust would wash away![22]

Another piece pictured an invalid doused with buckets of water until at last he "turned pale and kicked the bucket."[23]

In spite of its critics, the water-cure system developed by Priessnitz soon spread with major impact into England. The English people had not been unaware of the benefits of cold water in the treatment of disease. In the early 1700s works had appeared in England with such titles as *Psychrolousia, or the History of Cold Bath, both Ancient and Modern,* J.S. Hahn's *The Healing Virtues of Cold Water,* but especially a work by the British novelist and surgeon Tobias George Smollett, entitled *An Essay on the External Use of Water* (1752).[24] Smollett reported: "The efficacy of the *Cold Bath,* tho' unimpregnated with mineral principles, is so well known in *hypochondriac* Disorders, in diseases of the lox fibre, and partial weakness, when the Viscera are not unsound, that there is scarce a Physician, Surgeon, or Apothecary, who has not opportunities of seeing it everyday."[25] With the hydropathic craze infecting England, a London hydropathic institute was organized in 1842, and water-cure centers were hastily established in other localities. A published monograph described English spas, and Malvern, England's leading hydropathic institution, became a center of English society.[26] Older health spas like Bath and Brighton were refurbished and adopted the Priessnitzian regimen. Rules for the bath were minutely prescribed for the decorum-conscious.[27] Even Alfred Tennyson, soon to become the poet laureate of England, testified at a hydropathic establishment in 1844: "Much poison has come out of me, which no physic ever would have brought to light."[28]

As in England, the general tenets of hydrotherapy had been described in America long before the time of Priessnitz. In 1723 an American edition of John Smith's *The Curiosities of Common Water* was released, followed in 1725 by *The Curiosities of Common Water: or the Advantages Thereof in Preventing Cholera.*[29] Americans, quite early, had discovered the delights of mineral and natural springs. Travelers had long extolled the merits of particular locations, two of the more popular being Saratoga Springs, New York, and Hot Springs, Virginia.[30] However, other local promoters published reports of miraculous cures as they undertook to gain similar reputations for their own regional health spas. Readers of the American periodical press were able to follow both sides of the hydropathic debate in Europe throughout the thirties. It was not until the beginning of the 1840s that the brand of therapy advanced by Priessnitz began to spread to the United States.

In the 1820s the American nation had entered the period known as the "age of the common man," when little credence was given to professional credentials. Consequently, the mood of the nation was ripe for the spread of the pseudo-sciences, in part because of reaction against the excessive practices of regular medicos who often depended on the radical use of phlebotomy, vomiting, blistering, sweating, purging, and intemperate medication. It is little wonder that Americans, observing the debilitating effects that eclectic physicians had on patients, would seek cures that promised less shock to the body and seemed, at least initially, just as effective in their curative powers. Americans had always taken water with their meals—a habit which Europeans tolerated only in the interest of international goodwill.[31] Under these conditions the water-cure would blossom full-blown as the handmaiden of health in the egalitarian American society.

The spread of hydropathy became another example of the readiness of the American public to accept anything new. The "system" devised by Priessnitz had scarcely reached the United

States before several water-cure journals began to be published, two medical schools of hydropathy opened, and in a few years a hundred or more practitioners, male and female, were dispensing therapy with positive hygienic results. No doubt, the establishment of bath houses was a direct contribution of hydropathy to improved hygienic conditions throughout the United States.[32] No section of the nation enjoyed a monopoly on the "system," and hydropathic institutes were erected in all sections. The Northeast, however, by virtue of its more diverse society, often looking for leisure as well as relief, both real and perceived, proved most amenable to the panacea. It would be this section that would nurture the system's leaders, publish its monographs and periodicals, refine the methodology of the new practice, and carry its "message" into all sections of the nation.

The "Big Four" in American hydropathy became Dr. Joel Shew, Dr. Russell Thacher Trall, Mrs. Mary Sargeant Gove Nichols, and Dr. Thomas Low Nichols. In 1843 Shew abandoned the "regular" practice of medicine and adopted the tenets of hydropathy exclusively by opening the first hydropathic establishment in America in New York City.[33] As sole proprietor or partner in several other water-cure enterprises, Shew became a leading supporter as well as editor of the *Water-Cure Journal* between 1845 and 1848. Numerous articles and published monographs with such titles as *Hydropathy, or the Water Cure, Cholera Treated by Water, Children: Their Hydropathic Management,* and *The Hydropathic Family Physician* appeared under his authorship. When Shew died in November 1855, a post-mortem examination revealed an enlarged liver and internal lesions, which may have been due to his exposure to chemicals like mercury, iodine, and bromine in his earlier career as a photographer.[34] In essence, one could conclude that there were certain ailments that were beyond the pale of water-cure therapy. Dr. Trall followed closely after Shew in establishing a hydropathic institute in New York City in 1844. Initially doing as much as any single person to advance hydropathy's cause, Trall, with his diverse interests in hygiene, food reform, sensible living habits, phrenology, temperance, and vegetarianism, would later help to integrate the principles of hydrotherapy into the hygienic cult.[35]

The husband-wife team of Dr. Thomas Low Nichols and

particularly Mary Sargeant Gove Nichols proved to be among the most described hydropaths, if articles appearing in the periodical press are an indication. Mrs. Nichols, born in 1810, had become dedicated to helping women relieve themselves of the physical and mental suffering caused largely by their ignorance of health matters. Embarking on a lecture career to eliminate such abuses, she was attracted to the water-cure system in the 1830s after successfully applying the European techniques she had read about to healing herself and her daughter. Affiliating with the Brattleboro (Vermont) Water-Cure, she lectured on health matters, but after several misadventures eventually located in New York City. In 1847 she met Nichols, who had abandoned Dartmouth College as a medical student for journalism. Nichols, however, continued his interest in medicine, and ultimately completed his M.D. degree at New York University. Soon thereafter Nichols transferred his medical allegiance to the water-cure regimen, and in 1851 the couple established the American Hydropathic Institute, essentially a coeducational medical school for aspiring hydropaths. The Nicholses, however, soon became alienated from the other leaders of the water-cure movement because of their "heretical" views concerning diet and dress reform, health education, women's rights, and the relations between the sexes. Abandoning the East, they moved to Cincinnati, and largely dissipated their efforts by affiliating with too many cultic crusades.[36]

The professional's and layman's Bible of the hydropathic panacea became the *Water-Cure Journal and Herald of Reform,* which under various titles survived from 1845 until the eve of the twentieth century. Initially edited by Dr. Joel Shew, the periodical enjoyed remarkable success, claiming a circulation of fifty thousand shortly after 1850.[37] Its prospectus in 1845 claimed that the journal would be devoted to "explaining in a way the new system...to provide information on Bathing, Cleanliness, Clothing, Ventilation, Food, Drinks, and in general the prevention of disease."[38] When the new periodical experienced financial difficulties in its early existence, it was taken over in April 1848 by the publishers of the successful *American Phrenological Journal,* Lorenzo N. Fowler, Orson S. Fowler, and

Samuel Wells. Essentially, the hydropathic journal lasted, in its original form, from 1845 until 1862, when it became the *Hygienic Teacher and Water-Cure Journal,* and under other titles such as the *Herald of Health* and *Journal of Hygiene and Herald of Health* until 1897.[39] Hydropaths were also able to find edification in the *Water-Cure Monthly* (1859-60), published in Yellow Springs, Ohio, the *Water-Cure World: A Journal of Health and Herald of Reform* (1860-61) published in Brattleboro, Vermont, *Nichols' Journal of Health, Water-Cure and Human Progress,* and assorted local publications.[40]

As the definitive authority on the new pseudo-science, the *Water-Cure Journal* became the principal butt of the critics' scorn. Even before Fowler and Wells, who published the *American Phrenological Journal,* fell heir to the *Water-Cure Journal* in 1848, they were criticized for including hydropathic articles in their publication. In an article "Phrenological Hydropathy" O.S. Fowler's disposition to favor the cold water practice was criticized by the *Boston Medical and Surgical Journal,* which concluded that hydropathic articles were "quite out of place in a purely phrenological publication where the reader has in past time been regaled with those noble and lofty views which are the characteristics of Mr. Fowler's philosophy. It is not possible to mix hydropathy with phrenology; the oil will rise to the top; and therefore it is not out of place to say that Mr. Fowler's Journal always excites the most pleasure when it breathes his own elevated sentiments, unmixed with the false scheme of adventurers, who would make the unthinking world believe that moonshine is tangible.[41] Condemning the one-idea system, the same medical journal argued that "all the while water is still water" and Wells and Fowler were taking advantage of those innocents who would place their faith in such a remedy.[42] In 1850 the eclectic medical journal, commenting on the revised format of the *Water-Cure Journal,* stated: "Were the subjects that are discussed in its columns any where near as correct and truly scientific as its mechanical execution is beautiful, it might rank with the first journals devoted to medical science." The editor was inspired to confess that "were we sick, and without any previous knowledge of the first principles of the healing art, we might possibly choose those doctors who give no medicine."[43]

Indeed, it was the proposed mild regimen of the hydropaths that proved most attractive to the public's desires. Although refinements in cures might differ from locale to locale and practitioner to practitioner, they generally followed the pattern of Dr. Shew in his New York establishment. Water, an extremely versatile and potent substance which could be used in treating all kinds of disease, functioned best when administered gradually through the skin. The wet sheet became the approved technique, although other hydropaths might employ alternative methods for administering such treatment. Generally, a sheet of cotton or linen dipped in cold water was spread on several thick woolen blankets. The patient would then be wound in the sheet and blankets by an attendant who would secure the wrap with large pins and tape. Over the encased patient was thrown a feather bed, and the patient would remain in his cocoon for twenty-five minutes to several hours, depending upon the seriousness of his condition and his ability to work up a good perspiration. As soon as he was sweating freely, the victim was unswathed and cold water poured over him, or he was plunged into a cold bath, finally being briskly rubbed dry.[44]

For patients with weak constitutions, the shock of the wet sheet treatment was determined to be too radical. An alternative was the wet dress, a gown with extra wide sleeves which was dipped in cold water before being put on, although the excellent results obtained by the wet sheet could not be guaranteed. The wet dress became the model of the so-called bloomer costume, designed in one of the hydropathic institutions, which would add zest to the dress reform movement. Introduced to the fashion world by Elizabeth Smith, daughter of abolitionist Gerrit Smith, the bloomer, while neither immodest nor ungainly, consisted of a loose fitting dress or coat reaching below the knees and a garment similar to Turkish trousers gathered at the ankles into walking boots or neatly fitted above house slippers. Because of frequent bathing, wearers usually cut their hair short for easy drying, and felt themselves emancipated from the prevailing dress codes of trailing skirts, petticoats, corsets, and corkscrew curls. The hydropathic costume suffered when it became the badge of women prominent in the suffrage movement. The bloomer dress came to be accepted as a manifestation of female radicalism, and its *aficionados* were suspected of "free love" notions and of a desire to be rid of all feminine graces and restrictions.[45]

Another therapeutic variation was the water girdle, made of toweling three yards long and soaked every three hours in cold water. Prescribed for varying periods in the day, in extreme cases the girdle might be kept on continuously for twenty-four hours. Treatment by these methods was made even more effectual by the baths. Baths of every kind were utilized, foot, head, finger, elbow, and arm, but the most popular was the sitz bath which employed cold water just deep enough to cover the abdomen. Only the part of the patient actually immersed was bare; otherwise, he was clothed. With his head, arms, trunk, and legs at strange angles, the patient remained in the sitz for twenty to thirty minutes, or as long as his acrobatic talents permitted. The most powerful dousing stimulant employed was the shower bath, but even the milder douche was used with greatest caution, for water falling on the head from an extended height or for an extended period was deemed extremely dangerous.[46]

Another essential ingredient of the hydropathic cure was water drinking for internal cleansing. Most patients were directed to drink copious amounts of water, the quantity varying from five to forty tumblers in twenty-four hours.[47] The *Water-Cure Journal* extolled water drinking and advised that twelve to twenty-four tumblers should be the minimum and maximum doses. Through the regimen of water drinking, the elements of the body were clarified—the blood purified. The process when sufficiently repeated for a significant time would "evacuate anything acid, acrid, irritating, effete; and without the forced, unnatural, and exhausting efforts of the organism which drugs induce."[48] More unpleasant to the patient consequently not discussed as openly as water drinking were lavements and injections of cold water. Enemas were prescribed for constipation and in certain cases of diarrhea, with two pints, enough to produce distension of the colon, the recommended dose. In treatment of diseases, however, the warning was given that such techniques must be administered under professional direction. Cold injections into the urethra and vagina were of "indispensable necessity in all chronic or acute mucous or muco-purulent discharges of those passages." To obtain maximum benefit in the ills of leucorrhoea and uterine catarrh, a small tube was inserted into the passage while the patient took a hip bath. The instrument used was described as four inches long, of various calibers from half an inch to two inches in diameter, and made of a sheet of zinc wire-work. Allowing water to come into contact with the walls of the afflicted passage, the water-cure physician claimed "its introduction is not painful; and its salutary results inconceivable by those who have not used it."[49]

Dietetic regimen was also an important ingredient of the Priessnitzian cure, for he believed that the intake of hot food was injurious to all men. His remedy was to eat cold food, use water for drink, and regulate the patient's diet. Every stimulant was taboo, from brandy and claret to mustard and pepper. Luxuries imported from foreign ports, such as coffee, tea, and every kind of spice, were deemed harmful. No warm beverage whatever was permitted throughout the day, and most of the food served in the hydropathic establishments was considerably cooled, although those inmates slightly affected were allowed to consume warm meats. The caloric value of the dietetic regimen may not have been as nourishing as promised, though most patients bore their reduction in weight willingly. It may be correctly assumed that there were cases of obesity where a loss of weight was indeed beneficial. A patient in a cold water asylum in Massachusetts joyously proclaimed after five months' treatment that he had weighed 127 pounds when he entered the asylum but had been relieved of 33 pounds of bad flesh and now felt that he had been made over.[50] One wonders how much of the Priessnitzian diet he could have endured. Another patient, however, wrote his wife that the table d'hôte of Chester Springs, Pennsylvania, had resulted in his gaining eight pounds.[51]

A final significant element in the hydropathic therapy was exercise, which was generally prescribed at the time of water drinking. Patients were expected to take large amounts of exercise periodically through the day, but especially after the cold baths, which would stimulate the proper therapeutic reactions. The most popular form was walking in the open air, for many hydropathic institutions were located in rural settings where a person ambulating along rustic forest paths could easily commune with nature. In case of inclement weather or lameness, gymnastics, dancing, and sawing or chopping wood were utilized. In an age when fainting and frailty were considered desirable for young females of the better classes, the use of dumbbells, skipping rope, and other forms of exercise must have helped the ladies.[52] The Round-Hill Water-Cure Retreat in Northampton, Massachusetts, in its advertisements, emphasized its extensive gymnasium, bowling alleys, billiard room, shady walks, the beautiful valley with the Connecticut River winding through its center, and the rich and varied scenery designed to offer everyone sources of amusement and health. The proprietors claimed that their "great variety of amusements and accomodations [*sic*] [were] not inferior to any hotel in the country."[53] At the Wild Wood Springs in Franklin County, Mississippi, planters who had been shackled by rheumatism for twenty-five years could be seen dancing in the ballroom, while the Waterford Water-Cure Establishment in Maine claimed that no place in New England affords "superior natural advantages" in the most beautiful and varied mountain and lake scenery. Six to ten dollars a week purchased treatment, room, and board at the Jamestown Water-Cure beside "the lucid lake of Chautauqua," offering "an abundance of water of dewey [*sic*] softness and crystal transparency, to cleanse, renovate, and rejuvenate the disease-worn and dilapidated system."[54]

The growing army of hydropathic practitioners and the proliferation of hydropathic establishments soon found Americans of all backgrounds actively seeking the water-cure. Water for drinking, bathing, compresses, and every other purpose imaginable became the great panacea, and persons high and low, north, south, and west, extolled its benefits. Even William Shakespeare was quoted in support of hydropathy as Dr. E.A. Kittridge, writing in the *Harbinger*, reported the London bard saying, "Throw physic to the dogs; I'll none of it."[55] Harriet

Beecher Stowe, soon to become much better known, remained almost a year in the water-cure at Brattleboro, Vermont, and her husband, who during her absence had relapsed into hypochondria, decided that he too needed a cure, remaining in Brattleboro for fifteen months. Another literary figure, Charlotte Forten, claimed that Dr. Seth Rogers, who had treated her during one of her breakdowns at the Worcester, Massachusetts, water-cure, had done her "a world of good—spiritually as well as physically."[56] William Gilmore Simms, distinguished editor, novelist, and historian, wrote about the cure in the *Magnolia; or Southern Apalachian.* His letter to James Henry Hammond, dated Charleston, June 17, 1842, stated: "One fact, I have been more than a month following his [Priessnitz's] rules and never half so well in my life—but twice have I had the headache in the time, and before that I had it almost every other day."[57] In defense of the water-cure Simms included an article on hydropathy in his literary journal, observing that "we are really of the opinion that the remedial virtues of cold water are very great, and superior, in some cases to those of any other specific....For our literary and professional readers—for those who like ourselves, are compelled by frequent physical suffering, incident to the habits of the student, which the allopathist and Homeopathist have alike ministered in vain,—it may be well to see what is promised by hydropathy."[58]

In nearly all water-cure establishments miraculous cures were claimed and testimonials appeared frequently in the popular press. The experience of three members of the William S. Hamilton family may be taken as indicative of the system's success. Spending time in a Biloxi, Mississippi, institution run by Dr. Alexander Byrenheit in 1851, Kitty Hamilton wrote of the institution's proprietor: "I have never had to deal with a Physician possessed of the same delicacy and consideration for female modesty. He is a perfect gentleman."[59] The good doctor diagnosed her illness as a combination of two acids in the blood, but "Miss Kitty's" constitution was so strong that the acids had not attacked her stomach nor her lungs, which would have caused consumption. Fortunately, the malady had settled in her bladder, a condition which water could remedy. Her sister, Penelope, declared in a letter: "It is a happy change indeed from poisonous drugs to pure cold water. Would to heaven, I had come here when I was first taken sick; instead of being butchered by Pill givers. How many hours of pain and anguish I might have been spared."[60] John Knight, a successful Mississippi merchant who suffered from a throat infection and dyspepsia, wrote his wife from a water-cure in Pennsylvania that his health was good, and that he was eating stale brown bread, rice, and either boiled mutton or roast beef. He spurned coffee or any vegetable but rice, and although he had had several "sudden, severe, but short attacks of indisposition," his doctors had told him the attacks were "critical" and highly favorable. Indeed, he claimed that his whole system was now under the full force and effect of the water treatment. He wrote that the treatment left none of the terrible after-effects of mercury and other medicines.[61]

While the *Water-Cure Journal* is the most useful source of testimonials for hydropathy as well as other sectarian cures, no tabloid was immune from extolling cures wrought by water. The Vicksburg, Mississippi, *Weekly Sentinel* joyously reprinted a letter from the New Orleans *Delta* describing how cold water could cure the most dreaded malady in the South, yellow fever.[62] The Vidalia, Louisiana, *Concordia Intelligencer* extracted the following from a New Jersey paper in support of hydropathy: "The watercure treatment of the various diseases to which civilized humanity is subject, is assuming an importance of which those who take [but] slight notice of passing events, can have but one conception. Less than a quarter of a century ago, it was entirely unknown; and now water-cure Establishments exist in every part of Europe and the U.S. throughout which countries, it is crowned by a success unparalleled in the history of the healing art....The intelligence of the civilized world seems enlisted in its favor."[63]

The paper's editor may well have had mercenary motives, for in the same issue as this glowing review there appeared under "Hydropathy Advertisement" the notice of a Dr. Gray, who had moved his water-cure location to "Wild Wood Springs," twenty-three miles east of Natchez. Gray claimed success in such acute diseases as fevers, inflammation, measles, smallpox, scarlet fever, whooping cough, as well as the following chronic diseases: debility, obesity, nervousness, neuralgia, epilepsy, insanity, gout, rheumatism, dysentery, diarrhea, headache, dyspepsia, disease of the spine, liver, and spleen, all skin diseases, all female diseases, scrofula and consumption in the first stages, hemorrhages, dropsy, white swelling and hip joint disease, and all other minor diseases "too tedious to name."[64] Notwithstanding the amazing panoply of cures the doctor could handle, he still required each patient to furnish on his own two coarse linen and two cotton sheets, two thick blankets, two heavy cotton comforts, three yards of coarse linen and three of cotton, and four coarse linen towels. He also informed the readers that "all diseases are Chronic, after they have continued 40 days."[65]

In spite of the widespread popularity of water-cure therapy, pessimistic reports concerning the validity of the single cure system continued to appear in print, especially in American medical journals, which took great delight in pointing out the weaknesses or hazards of the system.[66] Oliver Wendell Holmes, professor of anatomy at the Harvard Medical School, traced the evolution of a water-cure practitioner, Dr. Bigel, through the cult of allopathy to homoeopathy to hydropathy. John Townsend Trowbridge, who spent some time in a water-cure institute, complained of little benefit from the douching, soaking, or skin friction to which he was subjected. While praising the restful conditions provided by the institution, he bitterly denounced the society of people inhabiting the water-cure whose invalidism was their chief interest in life and topic of conversation.[67] At Brattleboro, Vermont, the prominent abolitionist Thomas Wentworth Higginson, decrying the inclement weather, wrote that "we thought it best to take all the moisture together and so we had a party of Hydropaths. Some came in tubs, other paddled in punts, and the most desperate invalids came in douches through the ceiling. We had large pails of water for supper."[68] The American writer John W. DeForest, traveling in Europe and "pursued by the fretting enmity of a monotonous invalidism," decided to consign himself to *the* water-cure at Gräfenberg. After describing his first wet sheet treatment he reported that the attendant, Franz engineered me into a side room, and halted me alongside of an oblong cistern, brimming with black water, supplied by a brooklet, which fell into it with a perpetual chilly gurgal. In a moment his practiced fingers had peeled me like an orange, only far quicker than any orange was ever yet stripped of its envelope. As I shuffled off the last tag of their humid coil, the steam coiled up from my body as from an acceptable sacrifice, or an ear of hot boiled corn. Priessnitz pointed to the cistern like an angel of destiny signing to my tomb, and I bolted into it in a hurry as wise people always bolt out of the frying pan into the fire, when there is no help for it. In a minute my whole surface was so perfectly iced that it felt hard, smooth, and glossy, like a skin of marble.[69]

Complaining of the treatment, the climate, the institution's regimen, and the food as "an insult to the palate and an injury to the stomach," DeForest abandoned the water-cure.[70] Like DeForest, many inmates in American water-cures soon concluded that there were aspects of the water-cure therapy as rigorous as heroic medicine.

By the mid-1850s the water-cure mania had reached its crest. The *Boston Medical and Surgical Journal* printed an article in 1850 on its downfall and reported that water was proving unsuccessful in the most thorough hydropathic institutes.[71] However, this does not indicate that hydropathy disappeared, for the vogue of the water-cure system lasted until the Civil War. Indeed, in an era peculiar for its pseudo-sciences, each enjoyed a brief career which eventually yielded to more rational and consistent views. Advancing medical science was already proving receptive to selecting the best of the pseudo-scientific practices to incorporate into eclectic materia medica.

The fate of hydropathy was not its collapse or disappearance, but rather its sublimation into the general hygienic cult. Its claim to exclusiveness as a single cure system would be lost as it merged into other health reforms. Dr. Russell Thacher Trall and his followers, using hygiene as the motivation, superimposed the cult of Grahamism upon it.[72] Dietetic regimen, exercise, and hydrotherapeutic principles continue to be extolled as proper ingredients in maintaining holistic health even today. Not a physical fitness center, health and beauty spa, or athletic training room fails to provide its patrons with some form of hydrotherapeutic agent, be it a whirlpool bath, a swimming pool, or a steam room. Medical science currently debates the validity of a trend in European obstetrics which prescribes natural childbirth delivery underwater.[73] The availability of bottled mineral water, spring water, or jugs of distilled water which line the grocer's shelves, often at outlandish prices, gives continuing testimony to the public's faith in the efficacy of water (and distrust of public water supplies). Indeed, the humbugic aspects of the water-cure may still be found, as in a contemporary advertisement to "Add Up to 3 Inches to Your Bustline" with the Hydrotherapy Contour Cup.[74] The conclusion to be drawn is that certain aspects of the pseudo-science of water-cure have found an honored place in the mind-set of the American public, and will remain. Some of the perceptions are medically and scientifically valid, but those that are not will continue to flourish because of the deep taproots of American egalitarianism best embodied in the phrase "Physician, heal thyself."

Notes

1. R.T. Claridge, "Hydropathy; or the Cold Water Cure as Practised by Vincent Priessnitz, at Gräefenberg, Silesia, Austria," *Edinburg Medical and Surgical Journal* 58 (1842): 161.

2. Ibid.; "The Founder of the Cold-Water Cure," *Boston Medical and Surgical Journal* 27 (Nov. 30, 1842): 282-86; "History of Vincent Priessnitz by Capt. Claridge," *Water-Cure Journal,* n.s. 1 (Jan. 15, Feb. 1, 1846): 49-52, 65-68; John Forbes, "The Water-Cure, or Hydropathy," *Western Journal of Medicine and Surgery,* n.s. 7 (1847): 38-47; and Harry B. Weiss and Howard R. Kemble, *The Great American Water-Cure Craze: A History of Hydropathy in the United States* (Trenton, N.J.: Past Times Press, 1967), pp. 3-17.

3. A douche was a stream of cold water falling from varying heights on the afflicted portion of the patient's body.

4. Claridge, "Hydropathy," p. 169; "Treatment of Disease by Cold Water," *Boston Medical and Surgical Journal* 23 (Sept. 16, 1840): 99-100.

5. Louis Fleury, "Hydrosudapathia, or a Therapeutic System Founded on the Combined Action of Cold Water and Exciting Cutaneous

Perspiration," *Western Journal of Medical and Physical Sciences* 12 (May, June, and July 1838): 134-35.

6. Claridge, "Hydropathy," p. 164.

7. "Hydropathy in Germany: Gräefenberg and Priessnitz," *Lancet* 2 (1842-43): 275.

8. "Founder of the Cold-Water Cure," p. 283; "Hydropathy in Germany," p. 276; "Editor's Remarks," *Medical Examiner,* n.s. 1 (April 30, 1842): 280. The editor of the *Medical Examiner* was little surprised at the presence of European nobility at Gräfenberg and at Priessnitz's "considerable reputation as a quack." But after reporting that the water-cure proprietor had earned about £50,000, he was forced to concede: "We should not be surprised to hear of it in time in our own country."

9. *New Orleans Daily Crescent,* March 11, 1851.

10. Berton Roueché, *The Medical Detectives* (New York: Times Books, 1980), pp. 51-52.

11. *DeBow's Commercial Review* 2 (Oct. 1846): 228-39.

12. Sam Kneeland, Jr., "Hydropathy, or the Use of Cold Water for the Prevention and Cure of Disease," *American Journal of Medical Sciences,* n.s. 14 (1847): 76-77.

13. "Hydropathy," *Lancet,* 1842-43, 2:814.

14. *Water-Cure Journal,* n.s. 2 (Sept. 1, 1846): 111.

15. *Water-Cure Journal,* n.s. 3 (April 15, 1847): 125.

16. Robert Dick, "The Treatment and the Mal-treatment of Disease by Water, Hot and Cold," *Lancet,* 1842-43, 1:241-44; "The Attempts to Cure Everything with Water," *Lancet,* 1842-43. 2:415; R.S. Hutchinson, "Trial of Cold Water as a Remedy for Supposed Disease: Death: Post-Mortem Appearances" *Lancet,* 1843-44, 1:511-12; "Hydropathy Practiced Fatally amongst the North American Indians," *Lancet,* 1847, 1:14; C.B. Garrett, "Hydropathy and Its Evils: Report of a Case," *Lancet,* 1849, 1:62; "Hydropathic Quackery: Alleged Death from the Imprudent Application of Cold Water: Inquest and Verdict," *Lancet,* 1849, 2:243-44.

17. "The Reviewer's Estimate of 'Hydropathy, or the Cold-Water Cure,' " *Lancet,* 1846, 2:513.

18. "The Water Quackery in the Year 1736," *New York Journal of Medicine and the Collateral Sciences* 7 (July 1846): 108-9; "Hydropathy: The Water Quackery in the Year 1736 as Described by the Celebrated Rousseau," *Medical News* 4 (Aug. 1846): 72-73.

19. "Water Quackery, 1736," pp. 108-9; "Hydropathy as Described by Rousseau in 1736," pp. 72-73.

20. "Cold Water Punishment in Prisons," *Boston Medical and Surgical Journal* 21 (Dec. 4, 1844): 366.

21. "The Water Cure: A Hydropathic Ballad," *Medical News* 1 (Sept. 1843): 101.

22. Frank Luther Mott, *A History of American Magazines, 1850-1865* (Cambridge: Harvard Univ. Press, 1938), p. 87.

23. Frank Luther Mott, *A History of American Magazines, 1741-1850* (New York: Appleton, 1930), p. 441.

24. Madge E. Pickard and R. Carlyle Buley, *The Midwest Pioneer: His Ills, Cures & Doctors* (New York: Henry Schuman, 1946), p. 218; G.S. Rousseau, *Tobias Smollett: Essays of Two Decades* (Edinburgh: T. & T. Clark, 1982), p. 3; Cecil K. Drinker, "Doctor Smollett," *Annals of Medical History* 7 (March 1925): 31-47.

25. Claude E. Jones, ed., "An Essay on the External Use of Water, by Tobias Smollett," *Bulletin of the Institute of the History of Medicine* 3 (1935): 55. G.S. Rousseau describes Tobias Smollett's participation in a controversy in English balneology which largely centered around the sulphur content of the waters of English spas and their efficacy in the treatment of disease (pp. 144-57).

26. "Hydropathy: Itinerant Physicians," *Lancet*, 1841-42, 2:429-30; review of Dr. A.B. Granville's *The Spas of England, and Principal Sea-Bathing Places, Blackwood's Edinburgh Magazine* 49 (June 1841): 725-33; review of Richard J. Lane's *Life at the Water-Cure; or, a Month at Malvern: A Diary, Blackwood's Edinburgh Magazine* 64 (Nov. 1848): 515-42; "The Monarch of Bath," *Blackwood's Edinburgh Magazine* 48 (Dec. 1840): 773-92.

27. Joseph Wechsberg, *The Lost World of the Spas* (New York: Harper & Row, 1979), pp. 10-45.

28. Christopher Ricks, *Tennyson* (New York: Macmillan, 1972), pp. 180-81; John W. Dodds, *The Age of Paradox: A Biography of England, 1841-1851* (London: Gollancz, 1953), p. 369; *Alfred Lord Tennyson: A Memoir by His Son*, 2 vols. (London: Macmillan, 1897), 1:221.

29. Weiss and Kemble, *Water-Cure Craze*, p. 18; Pickard and Buley, *Midwest Pioneer*, p. 219.

30. Wechsberg, *Lost World of the Spas*, pp. 180-205. A history of balneology, particularly mineral springs and spas, parallels the story of hydropathy; the following references should provide some understanding of their importance in America: Carl Bridenbaugh, "Baths and Watering Places of Colonial America," *William and Mary Quarterly*, 3rd ser., 3 (April 1946): 151-81; William Edward Fitch, *Mineral Waters of the United States and American Spas* (Philadelphia: Lea and Febiger,

1927); S. Hoffius, "Healing Waters," *Southern Exposure* 6 (1978): 54-58; Billy M. Jones, *Health-Seekers in the Southwest, 1817-1900* (Norman: Univ. of Oklahoma Press, 1967); Ruth Irene Jones, "Antebellum Watering Places of the Mississippi Gulf Coast," *Journal of Mississippi History* 18 (Oct. 1956): 268-301; H.A. Meeks, "Stagnant, Smelly and Successful: Vermont's Mineral Springs," *Vermont History* 47 (1979): 5-20; Henry E. Sigerist, "American Spas in Historical Perspective," *Bulletin of the History of Medicine* 11 (Feb. 1942): 133-47; Henry E. Sigerist, "The Early Medical History of Saratoga Springs," *Bulletin of the History of Medicine* 13 (May 1943): 540-84; Henry E. Sigerist, "Rise and Fall of the American Spa," *Ciba Symposia* 8 (1946): 327-36; C.B. Thorne, "The Watering Spas of Middle Tennessee," *Tennessee Historical Quarterly* 29 (1970-71): 321-59; and R. Woodlief, "North Carolina's Mineral Springs," *North Carolina Medical Journal* 25 (1964): 159-64.

31. Richard Harrison Shryock, *Medicine and Society in America, 1660-1860* (New York: New York Univ. Press, 1960), p. 89; James Harvey Young, "American Medical Quackery in the Age of the Common Man," *Mississippi Valley Historical Review* 47 (March 1961): 579-93.

32. Dr. Thomas L. Nichols, *Forty Years of American Life,* 2 vols. (London: John Maxwell, 1864), 2:21; James C. Whorton, *Crusaders for Fitness: The History of American Health Reformers* (Princeton: Princeton Univ. Press, 1982), p. 137; Harold Donaldson Eberlein, "When Society First Took Baths," *Pennsylvania Magazine of History* 67 (1943): 30-48.

33. "Joel Shew," *Appleton's Cyclopaedia of American Biography*, 6 vols. (New York: Appleton, 1888), 5:508-9; Russell Trall, "Death of Dr. Shew," *Water-Cure Journal* 20 (Nov. 1855): 104-5; Weiss and Kemble, *Water-Cure Craze,* pp. 69-70; James C. Whorton, "Joel Shew," *Dictionary of American Medical Biography,* ed. Martin Kaufman, Stuart Galishoff, and Todd L. Savitt, 2 vols. (Westport, Conn.: Greenwood Press, 1984), 2:677-78.

34. Weiss and Kemble, *Water-Cure Craze,* p. 70.

35. "Russell Thacher Trall," *Appleton's Cyclopaedia of American Biography* 6:154; Weiss and Kemble, *Water-Cure Craze,* pp. 80-89; Whorton, *Crusaders for Fitness,* pp. 138-40; Ronald Numbers, "Health Reform on the Delaware," *New Jersey History* 92 (1974): 5-12; James C. Whorton, "Russell Thacher Trall," *Dictionary of American Medical Biography* 2:751.

36. Bertha Monica Sterns, "Mary Sargeant Neal Gove Nichols and Thomas Low Nichols," *Dictionary of American Biography* (1934) 13:495-97; William Walker, "The Health Reform Movement in the

United States," Ph.D. diss., The Johns Hopkins University, 1955, pp. 156-60; Weiss and Kemble, *Water-Cure Craze,* pp. 33-35, 72-80; Philip Gleason, "From Free-Love to Catholicism: Dr. and Mrs. Thomas L. Nichols at Yellow Springs," *Ohio Historical Quarterly* 70 (Oct. 1961): 283-307; Nichols, *Forty Years of American Life;* Bertha Monica Sterns, "Two Forgotten New England Reformers," *New England Quarterly* 6 (Nov. 1933): 59-84; Virginia G. Drachman, "Mary Sargeant (Neal) Gove Nichols," *Dictionary of American Medical Biography* 2:552-53; John B. Blake, "Mary Gove Nichols, Prophetess of Health," *Proceedings of the American Philosophical Society* 3 (1962-63): 219-34.

37. Mott, *History of American Magazines, 1741-1850,* p. 441; Weiss and Kemble, *Water-Cure Craze,* pp. 25-28.

38. *Water-Cure Journal,* n.s. 1 (Jan. 15, 1845): 64.

39. John D. Davies, *Phrenology: Fad and Science: A 19th-Century American Crusade* (New Haven: Yale Univ. Press, 1955), p. 112; Weiss and Kemble, *Water-Cure Craze,* p. 26; Whorton, *Crusaders for Fitness,* p. 140.

40. Mott, *History of American Magazines, 1850-1865,* p. 87; Weiss and Kemble, *Water-Cure Craze,* pp. 28-29. For other publications see the following articles in the *Boston Medical and Surgical Journal:* "Water-Cure Journal," 31 (Nov. 20, 1844): 324-25; "Cold Water Cure," 34 (Feb. 4, 1846): 21-22; "Journal of Hydropathy," 34 (March 4, 1846): 105; "Water Cure Reporter," 37 (Nov. 24, 1847): 345; "Water-Cure Almanac," 39 (Sept. 7, 1848): 145-46; and "Water-Cure Era," 39 (Dec. 20, 1848): 426.

41. "Phrenological Hydropathy," *Boston Medical and Surgical Journal* 34 (July 15, 1846): 485-86; Davies, *Phrenology,* p. 112.

42. "The Water-Cure Journal," *Boston Medical and Surgical Journal* 39 (Aug. 9, 1848): 45-46.

43. Ibid., 43 (Dec. 25, 1850): 428.

44. Pickard and Buley, *Midwest Pioneer,* pp. 218-20; "Biographical notice of a *Manual of Hydrosudopathy, or the Treatment of Diseases by Cold Water, Sweating, Exercise and Regimen; According to the method employed by V. Priessnitz at Gräfenberg,*" *Medical Examiner* 3 (Aug. 15, 1840): 521-23; "A Letter on the Cold-Water Treatment of Priessnitz at Gräefenberg," *Medical Examiner,* n.s. 1 (June 4, 1842): 360-61; Licentiate Blich, "Trial of the Cold Water System," *Medical Examiner,* n.s. 1 (Aug. 27, 1842): 551-55; "Cold Water Cure," *Boston Medical and Surgical Journal* 27 (Sept. 28, 1842): 134-35; "Hydropathy, or the Water-Cure: Its Principles, Modes of Treatment, etc." *New York Journal of Medicine* 4 (1845): 401-5; "New York Correspondence: Hydropathy,"

Boston Medical and Surgical Journal 35 (Nov. 18, 1846): 325-27; "The Water-Cure," *Boston Medical and Surgical Journal* 35 (Jan. 13, 1847): 490-96.

45. Alice Felt Tyler, *Freedom's Ferment: Phases of American Social History to 1860* (Minneapolis: Univ. of Minnesota Press, 1944), p. 441; D.C. Bloomer, *Life and Writings of Amelia Bloomer* (Boston: Arena Publishing Co., 1895), pp. 65-81.

46. Pickard and Buley, *Midwest Pioneer,* p. 220; *The Letters of William Gilmore Simms,* ed. Mary C. Oliphant et al., 5 vols. (Columbia: Univ. of South Carolina Press, 1952-55), 2:503; 4:570-71; Kneeland, "Hydrotherapy," pp. 81-96; Fleury, "Hydrosudapathia," pp. 136-37; and *New York Journal of Medicine,* 3rd ser., 7 (July 1859): 114-15.

47. Forbes, "Water-Cure," pp. 42-43; "Biographical Notice of a *Manual of Hydrosudopathy,*" p. 522.

48. "The Drinking of Water," *Water-Cure Journal,* n.s. 1 (Jan. 1, 1846): 35-36.

49. "Lavements and Injections," *Water-Cure Journal,* n.s. 1 (Jan. 1,1846): 36-37.

50. "Water-Cure," *Scientific American* 3 (May 6, 1848): 257; "Diet Used at the Table d'Hote of Priessnitz," *Boston Medical and Surgical Journal* 29 (Nov. 15, 1843): 308; "Biographical Notice of a *Manual of Hydrosudopathy,*" pp. 521-23; Forbes, "Water-Cure," pp. 42-43.

51. Weiss and Kemble, *Water-Cure Craze,* p. 201.

52. Forbes, "Water-Cure," pp. 42-43; John Duffy, "Medical Practice in the Ante-Bellum South," *Journal of Southern History* 25 (Feb. 1959): 70; John Duffy, ed., *The Rudolph Matas History of Medicine in Louisiana,* 2 vols. (Baton Rouge: Louisiana State Univ. Press, 1962), 2:39.

53. "Round-Hill Water-Cure Retreat," *American Journal of Homoeopathy* 3 (May 1, 1848): 12; "Water-Cure Establishment," New Orleans *Commercial Bulletin,* May 21, 1853.

54. Vidalia (La.) *Concordia Intelligencer,* Oct. 2, 1852; "Waterford Water-Cure Establishment," *The Harbinger: Devoted to Social and Political Progress* 5 (June 26, 1847): 48; E. Douglas Branch, *The Sentimental Years: 1836-1860* (New York: Appleton-Century, 1934), p. 264. In a lengthy appendix authors Weiss and Kemble, *Water-Cure Craze,* fully document the establishment of hydropathic institutions in the United States, and the pages of the *Water-Cure Journal* are replete with announcements of the openings of new water-cures.

55. "The Water Cure," *Harbinger* 4 (Dec. 12, 1846): 1; Mott, *History of American Magazines, 1741-1850,* p. 441.

56. Edmund Wilson, *Patriotic Gore: Studies in the Literature of the*

American Civil War (New York: Oxford Univ. Press, 1962), pp. 28, 248.

57. *Letters of William Gilmore Simms,* 1:314.

58. William Gilmore Simms, "Hydropathy; or the Cold Water Cure," *Magnolia; or Southern Apalachian,* n.s. 1 (Oct. 1842): 257.

59. Duffy, "Medical Practice," p. 69; Duffy, ed., *Rudolph Matas History,* 2:38-39.

60. Duffy, "Medical Practice," p. 69; Duffy, ed., *Rudolph Matas History,* 2:38.

61. Weiss and Kemble, *Water-Cure Craze,* p. 200.

62. Vicksburg (Miss.) *Weekly Sentinel,* Sept. 1, 1847; Jo Ann Carrigan, "Yellow Fever in New Orleans, 1853: Abstractions and Realities," *Journal of Southern History* 25 (Aug. 1959): 351.

63. Vidalia (La.) *Concordia Intelligencer,* June 19, 1852.

64. Ibid.

65. Ibid. In the October 2, 1852, issue, a friend of the editor gave a glowing description of the Wild Wood Springs for interested readers.

66. "Water Curing," *Boston Medical and Surgical Journal* 29 (Jan. 3, 1844): 444; "The Water Workers," *Boston Medical and Surgical Journal* 34 (Feb. 25, 1846): 663; Blich, "Trial of the Cold Water System," pp. 551-55; "The Rising Humbug—Hydropathy," *Medical News* 1 (April 1843): 54-56; "Victim of Hydropathy—Death of Sir Francis Burdett," *Medical News* 2 (April 1844): 31-32; "Sketches and Illustrations of Medical Delusions—Hydropathy," *Medical News* 6 (Sept. 1848): 87; C.B. Garrett, "Hydropathy and Its Evils," *Medical News and Library* 7 (May 1849): 34-35; and "Death from the Effects of Cold Water Treatment," *Western Journal of Medicine and Surgery,* n.s. 6 (1846): 351.

67. Oliver Wendell Holmes, *Medical Essays: 1842-1882* (Boston: Houghton Mifflin, 1888), p. 91; John Townsend Trowbridge, *My Own Story: With Recollections of Noted Persons* (Boston: Houghton Mifflin, 1904), pp. 199-200.

68. Mary Thacher Higginson, ed., *Letters and Journals of Thomas Wentworth Higginson, 1846-1906* (Boston: Houghton Mifflin, 1921), p. 38.

69. Wilson, *Patriotic Gore,* pp. 674-75; James F. Light, *John William DeForest* (New York: Twayne, 1965), pp. 29-31.

70. Wilson, *Patriotic Gore,* p. 675; Light, *DeForest,* pp. 29-31.

71. "Hydropathy Coming Down," *Boston Medical and Surgical Journal* 42 (July 31, 1850): 533-34.

72. Richard Harrison Shryock, "Sylvester Graham and the Popular Health Movement, 1830-1870," *Mississippi Valley Historical Review* 18 (Sept. 1931): 172-83; Stephen Nissenbaum, *Sex, Diet, and Debility*

in Jacksonian America: Sylvester Graham and Health Reform (Westport, Conn.: Greenwood Press, 1980); Whorton, *Crusaders for Fitness*, pp. 137-40; Ronald L. Numbers, "Do-It-Yourself the Sectarian Way," in Judith Walzer Leavitt and Ronald L. Numbers, eds., *Sickness and Health in America: Readings in the History of Medicine and Public Health* (Madison: Univ. of Wisconsin Press, 1978), p. 93.

73. "Giving Birth Underwater," *Newsweek* (Jan. 16, 1984), p. 70.

74. Undated advertisement in the author's clipping file.

ROBERT W. DELP

5. Andrew Jackson Davis and Spiritualism

Among the popular movements which characterized society in mid-nineteenth century America was spiritualism. The discovery of a new science by which communication with the dead could be achieved did not seem improbable to many optimistic Americans who viewed innovative technical inventions and listened to lecturers extol the limitless horizon of the human mind. Spiritualism benefited, too, from the theories of Emanuel Swedenborg, whose works portraying a progressive spiritual world were frequently perused by curious Americans. Although Shaker communities had experienced epochs of "spiritual visitation," the national interest and the magnitude of the phenomenon which erupted in 1848 were unprecedented.[1] In that year two daughters of John D. Fox of Hydesville, New York, insisted that they had heard rappings which they said originated with the spirit of a peddler who had been slain and interred in the cellar of their cottage. The girls responded to the peculiar noises with raps of their own and were soon "conversing" with the world of spirits. They left their rural home and, joined by a third sister, became objects of great curiosity as they performed before large audiences in Rochester and New York City. In spite of ridicule and attacks by conservative religious forces, they inspired others in many areas who attended seances or became mediums who allegedly destroyed the barrier separating the mortal from the immortal world. Soon automatic writing, table levitation, and the playing of "untouched musical instruments" were common occurrences.[2] Spiritualism began and continued to grow as an unguided and undisciplined movement without creed or philosophy, depending only on the enthusiasm of its devotees.

The philosophical foundation lacking in the frenzy of phenomenal spiritualism was provided largely by Andrew Jackson Davis, whose efforts to give intellectual content to the erratic movement consumed the major portion of his long life. Born in the state of New York in 1826, he grew up an unlettered but precocious young man who was reputed to possess a gift of prophecy and an ability to diagnose clairvoyantly and prescribe for disease. While still in his teens, he was popularly known as the "Poughkeepsie Seer." Unlike many adolescents, he was conscious of the atmosphere of change which altered the complexion of America in the Jacksonian period. He was aware of the millennial enthusiasm of William Miller and knew something of the theories of Emanuel Swedenborg and Charles Fourier. On occasion he had also proved an adept subject for those who experimented with the mysteries of mesmerism. In 1845, prior to the celebrated "Hydesville rappings" in 1848, Davis and two associates, Dr. Silas Lyon, a physician with an interest in hypnotism, and the Reverend William Fishbough, a Universalist clergyman, traveled to New York City where, in a hypnotic state, Davis delivered lectures which he announced would herald the advent of a new "harmonial dispensation." In New York his "lectures" were transcribed and edited by Fishbough. Much attention was given in the press to the activities of the youthful clairvoyant. Among others who heard him were Edgar Allan Poe, Albert Brisbane, and George Bush, a professor at New York University and a devoted Swedenborgian.

When Davis's disquisitions were completed in 1847, they were published in a lengthy volume, *Nature's Divine Revelations: The Principles of Nature, Her Divine Revelations, and a Voice to Mankind.* This initial work and an edition published in England were financed by a well-to-do admirer, Mrs. Catherine DeWolf Dodge. Later Davis made this "spirit sister" his wife, although she was many years older than he.[3] She, too, wrote and spoke in behalf of the "cosmic disclosures" brought to light by her husband.[4] The *Revelations* embodied the Harmonial Philosophy, a grandiose master plan for the reorganization and reform of existing social, economic, and religious systems. Davis maintained that his ideas represented the thought of more refined societies of spirits living in other realms. Later, as the Fox sisters created widespread excitement over their alleged communication with the world of spirits, Davis claimed to have foreseen these events and hailed them as harbingers of his promised new dispensation. Although the term "spiritualism" did not come into use until 1852,[5] the phenomenal elements symbolized at Hydesville and the philosophical schema incorporated in the work of Andrew Jackson Davis were parents of a growing and increasingly controversial movement which was destined to influence American cultural history.

It is impossible to arrive at an accurate estimate of the numbers who in the 1850s were involved in spiritualism. Although there were claims of eleven million believers, a recent scholar suggests that there were more likely only several hundred thousand men and women who were to some extent interested in the new "science." Most were scattered in the old Northwest, New York, Ohio, and Massachusetts.[6] Groups of spiritualists were soon holding frequent meetings in these regions. Most often the gatherings were devoted only to the incessant search for demonstrations or "manifestations," but there were instances where speakers were heard and reasonable discussion was paramount. When, for example, Andrew Jackson Davis moved to Hartford, Connecticut, in the early 1850s, he became part of an investigative circle for which he prepared a constitution declaring it a Harmonial Brotherhood dedicated to Universal Liberty, Fraternity and Unity.[7] He lectured regularly to the membership and took issue with the theology of prominent clergy in that city. His religious unorthodoxy was made clear at the well-publicized Hartford Bible Convention.[8] Local spiritualist groups met in larger associations, and on various occasions Davis was accorded a prominent position. In 1852 at a convention held in Boston's Washington Hall, he was consecrated by John Murray Spear, a Universalist convert to spiritualism, to the "harmonial" work, "by everything that is noble, glorious and much to be desired."[9] Afterwards he spoke to a spiritualist convention at Worcester, Massachusetts, presided over by Adin Ballou, Universalist leader of the Hopedale Community in Massachusetts.

During his 1854 lecture circuit of New York and New England, Davis believed his audiences showed a more appreciative interest in the philosophic aspects of spiritualism than in the more dramatic rappings and other methods of contacting the dead.[10] His optimism, however, was not shared by many persons who watched the erratic course pursued by thousands of the faithful. In April 1854 Senator James Shields of Illinois, although derisive of spiritualism, was persuaded to introduce in the United States Senate a *Memorabilia* containing fifteen thousand signatures petitioning that august body to make a thorough investigation of the current spiritual manifestations.[11] The New York *Herald* expressed its sorrow to see "an otherwise sensible man making a fool of himself" by bestowing consideration upon a topic it declared had been "pronounced by all sane persons as the grossest delusion and humbug."[12] Although members of the Senate quickly relegated the giant petition to the oblivion of the table, the repercussions of this irregular move did not elevate the position of spiritualism in the public mind. Even more startling was the effort of John Spear and other spiritualists near Lynn, Massachusetts, to construct a perpetual-motion machine. After viewing the mechanism, Andrew Jackson Davis lamented, "O, when will superstition die!" When the day arrives for its entombment, he declared, "let us unite in prayer that it may never experience a resurrection—never be exhumed by the undeveloped and the imaginative!"[13]

Spiritualism, however, did gain some respected adherents who tirelessly labored to propagate the new theories of life after death. Judge John Edmonds of the New York State Supreme Court, after the death of his wife, attended seances and became a medium. He was the recipient of alleged spirit messages and wrote in a format that created the impression of scientific investigation.[14] Nathaniel P. Tallmadge, elected to the United States Senate from New York in 1833 and later appointed by President John Tyler to be governor of the Wisconsin Territory, was another important convert to spiritualism. New Yorkers, in 1855, were startled by the spectacle of Edmonds and Tallmadge demonstrating their faith in spiritualism before crowded audiences in the famous Broadway Tabernacle.[15] Yet another well-known figure who converted to spiritualism was Warren Chase, originator of the Wisconsin Phalanx and a member of the Wisconsin legislature, who kept a copy of Davis's *Revelations* on his Senate desk and had additional copies for sale.[16]

Andrew Jackson Davis, in the same year that Edmonds and Tallmadge were appearing in New York, delivered a series of lectures in Boston on the larger implicatons of the spiritualist movement. Here he voiced the fear that spiritualism would be adopted by the church and thus made respectable. "To become respectable," he asserted, "is to become almost entirely opposed to the highest interests of the individual and race."[17] In pressing his indictment of the church as the great enemy of human progress, he predicted that it would ultimately fall. Protestantism, he told his hearers, would be replaced by Roman Catholicism, and a climactic religious struggle would take place between the forces of Catholicism representing "monarchy" and those of the Harmonial Philosophy representing "wisdom and love." At the conclusion of this titanic conflict, he said, a new era would emerge when a full and complete communication would be established between earth and the other spheres. Mankind, he held, would then be elevated and sanctified.[18] Davis's continued and sharp criticism of the church made him the object of ridicule and scorn by representatives of traditional Christianity. There were even those within the ranks of spiritualists who called for moderation. One of these, A.E. Newton, editor of the *New England Spiritualist,* advised his readers that Davis viewed theology and the doctrines of the church quite differently from the way "our education compels us to view them...consequently he uses modes of expression which we should not use." Although Davis often condemned in general and severe terms, Newton remarked, "We think it more fitting to use discrimination and kindly efforts to impart a higher and truer interpretation."[19] Among the most vocal defenders of the Boston lectures was William Lloyd Garrison, who thought they were well expressed and extremely practical. Garrison further asserted that he believed Davis completely true to his highest convictions and utterly removed from arrogant dogmatism and self-conceit. He praised him as "the wonder and admiration of multitudes on both sides of the Atlantic" and contended that had he been egotistical or self-seeking he might have claimed superhuman powers and gathered around him followers who were willing to accept him as an infallible source of knowledge and a veritable messiah.[20]

In 1855 Andrew Jackson Davis, following the death of his wife Catherine, married Mary Robinson Love, a co-worker in the field of reform. The couple resided in New York City, where they enjoyed the patronage of William Green, Jr., a respected citizen for whose family Davis often prescribed remedies for physical maladies afflicting them. Davis was also the recipient of frequent loans of money from his "harmonial brother."[21] From his home in New York Davis continued his efforts in behalf of spiritualism and in 1856 published *The Penetralia* and a semi-autobiographical volume, *The Magic Staff.* In the former work he emphasized the progressive and reformatory nature of the nineteenth century and credited a growing affinity with the spiritual world as the leading cause. In addition, he predicted that spiritualism would prove beneficial in augmenting mechanical invention and improving man's standard of living. Ultimately, he added, man would gain more leisure for the pursuit of spiritual ends.[22]

The publishing efforts of Davis did not deter him from becoming active in promoting greater cooperation among spiritualists. He and his wife served on the executive committee to establish an association of spiritualists in New York. In April of 1857, at a meeting in Dodworth's Academy presided over by Judge John Edmonds, it was decided to form the New York Spiritual Association with a regular lectureship, a library, and a reading room to be open day and evening. The new association defined its purpose as the development and propagation of a scientific, philosophical, and reformatory spiritualism and thus placed itself, by implication, in opposition to the more sensational and radical forces. Davis and Edmonds were appointed to the lecture committee, while Mary Davis served on the finance committee. The New York Association's initial lecture was given by Davis, and he praised the new effort as "a triumphal archway to the successful liberalization of the leading minds of the nineteenth century." He made it clear that he saw the work in New York as an excellent opportunity to influence the growth of spiritualism in other areas.[23] Davis, moreover, continued to join reform conventions in which speakers expounded various theories of the regeneration of society. When it became known that he was to address such a convention in Rutland, Vermont, special trains brought throngs of interested people to hear him. At least three thousand persons were reported to have attended the sessions, at which Davis was the leading feature.[24] New York City was also the scene of Davis's attempt to begin a newspaper, the *Herald of Progress,* which he published from 1860 to 1865. In the pages of the *Herald* he gave wide publicity to schemes for improving the human condition. The Children's Progressive Lyceum and the Moral Police Fraternity were designed to provide educational and recreational activities for children and to deal with the increasing problems of crime and poverty in New York.[25] The Lyceum was successful and by 1871 had spread to seventeen states and was beginning to make inroads in the British Isles.[26] But the increasing population of New York City and the enormity of the problems faced by the Moral Police Fraternity led to its demise. Largely because of financial difficulties the *Herald of Progress* published its last issue early in 1865. An element in its failure may have been the editor's lack of emphasis on spiritualist propaganda and on accounts of communication with those who now dwelt in other spheres.[27]

However, as publisher, lecturer, and philosopher, Andrew Jackson Davis was accorded a respectful hearing in the higher councils of the American Association of Spiritualists, earlier called the National Organization of Spiritualists, which, aside from the short-lived Society for the Diffusion of Spiritual Knowledge, was the only attempt to form a national organization before the 1890s. Whenever possible, he and his wife used their influence to implant seeds of liberalism in this early attempt at unity and to prevent its domination by mediums who cared little for the philosophical moorings of spiritualism. At the Philadelphia meeting in 1865 they helped subdue a move to amend the convention's resolutions in a manner which would have excluded "progressive reformers" and resulted in the admission of only "spiritualists."[28] At another meeting of the national group, held in Cleveland, Ohio, in September 1867, Davis played a significant role in an effort to prevent spiritualism from assuming a narrow or parochial stance. Here an already apparent cleavage between the "philosophic" spiritualists and those emphasizing the phenomenal aspects of their faith had become particularly apparent. Smouldering resentment burst into open warfare when the report of a committee on "spiritual phenomena" was presented to the convention containing a frank criticism of the methods employed in the performances of the celebrated Davenport brothers and other mediums who were attracting considerable attention over the country. So antagonistic was the convention toward the report that it was decided to leave the document unprinted for a period of one year.[29] Seeking to bring peace to the troubled waters of spiritualism and yet redeem, as far as possible, a report with which he heartily concurred, Davis rose to suggest that the convention explain its refusal to accept the controversial statement by declaring that its action was motivated only by a desire to "prevent misunderstanding of the value and reliability of physical tests through mediums on both sides of the Atlantic," rather than a desire to stifle "free and discriminating investigation" of mediumistic demonstrations. The assent of the convention to Davis's motion at least prevented the group from assuming a posture which was alien to the moderate course of Davis and those who shared his views. Davis agreed to serve as a member of the executive committee when the national body met again in Rochester, New York, in August 1868. But his silence was conspicuous when a motion was considered to separate the Children's Progressive Lyceum from the American Association of Spiritualists. It was Mary Davis who took the lead in an unsuccessful attempt to halt a separation.[30]

The victory of Davis's opponents left him further disillusioned with the definition of spiritualism accepted by the majority at general gatherings. Before an audience in 1869 which included the Fox sisters, he asserted that spiritualism was not organizable because, he declared, "it is a notification—because it is an announcement." He predicted that those who attempted to make of it an organized enterprise would find themselves "astride a remarkable velocipede that requires...skill to keep it from tumbling upon and hurting them badly."[31] Pursuing his enemies who sought to equate spiritualism with mediums and seances, Davis published a bitter attack against this interpretation in *The Fountain with Jets of New Meaning.* This volume, which appeared in 1870, provoked the denunciation of those within the ranks of spiritualism who disagreed with him and denied that he was a spiritualist. Davis countered his critics by asserting that he was a spiritualist and when occasion demanded exercised the functions of a medium.[32] His opinions were made public in the moderate spiritualist journals the *Religio-Philosophical Journal* and the *Banner of Light,* which led the way in raising several thousand dollars with which to honor him on the occasion of his fiftieth birthday in 1876. The English spiritualist publication the *Medium* also endorsed this effort and referred to Davis as a "saint in the world's calendar." It urged spiritualists everywhere to "love him and aspire to his high estate."[33]

But the mass of spiritualists disregarded this injunction. Instead of accepting the universal principles of the Harmonial Philosophy, they continued to indulge in and proliferate the manifestations. One of the most controversial spiritualists to attract public attention was one Mrs. Suydam, the "fire-test medium," who before more than a thousand citizens of Chicago was exposed as a fraud. Commenting on this and other similar incidents one journalist exclaimed: "How long, O, how long! must Spiritualism carry its load of idots? When will its votaries learn that the Spirit will not submit to be made the plaything with which to amuse the rabble, or the instrument to put money in the pockets of those who endeavor to speculate upon it?"[34]

Davis presumably had "misguided" spiritualism in mind when, in a speech before the anniversary celebration of New

York spiritualists on March 31, 1878, he became quite personal in his criticism and thus precipitated a bitterly fought conflict within the ranks of spiritualists. He spoke disparagingly of Emma Hardinge Britten, well-known medium and early historian of the movement, and Madame Helen P. Blavatsky, founder of Theosophy, whom he described as an outstanding example of "magical spiritualism."[35] Following his address, Davis observed great confusion and much hostility in his audience, and in an effort to calm the gathering his wife delivered a conciliatory message designed, he later wrote, to "extract the stinger from the bee" her husband had set buzzing. However, Davis was not deterred in his assaults on those who engaged in seances or "dark circles," insisting that their very nature led mediums to "deal with the occult, the mysterious, the sleight of hand, and the deceptive."[36] In October of 1878 at two large assemblies of spiritualists in Hartford, Connecticut, he told his audiences that those who put no restraint on "spiritual circles" were in danger of becoming mental and physical shipwrecks.[37] Davis reached the conclusion that the two interpretations of spiritualism could no longer co-exist, and in December of 1878 organized the First Harmonial Association of New York. As chief lecturer, he sought to make a distinction between the Harmonial Philosophy and certain interpretations of modern spiritualism. The former, he averred, had been inspired by "celestial sources," and sought the elevation of the human state through the advance of science, the inventions of "deep thinkers," the work of artists, musicians, writers, and finally by instructions received through mediums. In contrast, he observed, the latter could be summed up in one word, "manifestations." With heightened confidence he promised to pursue the battle until the ranks of spiritualists were cleansed of the "weakness and wickedness and absurdities which now infest them."[38]

The First Harmonial Association of New York, true to its dedication to the advancement of science, endowed a chair in the United States Medical College of New York, an eclectic school of medicine located in New York City. Davis matriculated at the college and emerged with doctorates in medicine and anthropology. Prior to his graduation, he submitted a thesis entitled "The Reality of Imaginary Disease," in which he contended that "every cutaneous disease, every tumor, every disorganization in the substance or appendages or organs is in effect disturbed and diseased psychical or spiritual force." The ordinary bodily functions, he maintained, "originated in, and depend upon corresponding processes going on in the mysterious universe of invisible motion, life, sensation, and intelligence." In short, Davis concluded, all psychical diseases except those "mechanically and chemically, or accidentally" induced were caused by disturbances in the "physical potencies."[39] These theories, he contended, were impressed upon him long ago by a vision which brought another life breaking upon his horizon, enabling him to see and hear by "spiritual sensation instead of the optic nerve and ordinary processes of nature."[40]

While a student in medical school, Davis met and made friends with Della E. Markham, an electic physician whose services he sought during a period of illness. Soon rumors circulated that the two were engaging in an adulterous relationship.[41] The furor occasioned by the insinuations against him led Davis to leave his duties as lecturer at the New York Harmonial Association and take an extended vacation in order to consider his future personal and professional life. He decided to divorce Mary, now the victim of a terminal illness, informing her that they were not "mated in spirit" and that there were "true conjugal counterparts" waiting somewhere for them.[42] In Boston on his fifty-ninth birthday in 1885 Davis was married to Della Markham. Later his new wife recounted that she had been reared with an atheistic perception of life but, discontented, had longed for "something or someone" who could show her the true way out of "the night of mental errors, and the gloom of ignorance, into the full and blessed light of day."[43] The answer to these longings, she said, had come to her in intimations of the Harmonial Philosophy long before she was acquainted with her future husband.[44]

Davis's old spiritualist enemies used his divorce as a reason to denounce him further and to deny that he was a true spiritualist. Emma Hardinge Britten, in a letter to the New York *Herald*, declared that Davis had never professed to be or allowed himself to be called a spiritualist. On the contrary, she contended, she had heard him repeatedly protest against the attempt to confound the Harmonial Philosophy with spiritualism which, she insisted, he uniformly denounced, ignored, and frequently spoke of in terms of ridicule and insult. Once again Davis denied the accusations and asserted his identity as a spiritualist. Indeed, said he, he was more than a spiritualist—namely a philosopher who had formulated the subtle laws by which spirits made their communications to living organisms.[45] He further informed his critics that if they did not cease their attacks he would be forced to embark upon a work of self-justification which, if accomplished, would make many wish that it had not been undertaken.[46] Stung by the vituperative onslaughts of his detractors, Davis and his bride moved from New York City to Watertown, Massachusetts, where Davis, while writing his last volume, *Beyond the Valley*, opened an office and practiced medicine, specializing in "diseases of the mind and body."[47] He used the clairvoyant method of diagnosing disease and readily offered counsel and advice to his patients. His ready wit and perceptive understanding proved of real therapeutic value. Always benevolently inclined, he treated many in the Boston area who could afford to pay little or nothing for his services. His generosity and genuine altruism brought him the esteem and affection of thousands.[48]

While Davis enjoyed the relative obscurity of his new home, the movement in which he had played a leading role declined in significance. Protestant churches grew more liberal and accepted a more democratic interpretation of divine revelation, while the scientific value of spiritualism was seriously questioned as dishonest mediums continued to be exposed.[49] That the scientific contribution of spiritualism was not ignored, however, was evident as an American Society for Psychical Research was organized in the 1880s with the encouragement of William James and the cooperation of several distinguished scientists. The findings of the society's committee on spiritualistic manifestations were not encouraging. Committee members complained of the difficulty of finding mediums who were willing to submit to tests, and those who participated were often unable to understand or correctly recall details of an occurrence. Another inhibiting factor in the scientific examination of alleged manifestations, said the committee, was the seance itself, where because of darkness, fraud and deception were not easily recognized.[50] The new scientific approach to spiritualism in the United States was symbolized, too, by the Seybert Commission of the University of Pennsylvania. Henry Seybert, an enthusiastic believer in spiritualism, presented the sum of sixty thousand dollars to the University of Pennsylvania on the condition that it appoint a commission to investigate "all systems of morals, religion, or philosophy which assume to represent truth, and particularly modern spiritualism."[51] A committee of professors examined several prominent mediums but in its preliminary report denied that it had discovered a single novel fact. The secretary of the committee wrote that spiritualism must be more convincing than slate writing and rapping. He referred to these physical manifestations as but "the mere ooze and scum cast up by the waves on the idle pebble." "The waters of a heaven-lit sea, if it exist, must lie far out beyond," he concluded. He predicted, however, that soon a class of spiritualists would cast loose from these tactics, which, he indicated, were but little removed from materialism.[52]

The report of the Seybert Commission was roundly condemned by spiritualists. They benefited, however, from the association of spiritualism with modern scientific investigation and from the added publicity they received. Mediums continued to materialize spirits, produce spirit photographs, and answer questions posed by lonely and grief-stricken men and women desiring some word from the "other side." When the National Spiritualist Association was founded in Chicago in 1893, it traced its origins to Davis's writings, but it was not the "class of spiritualists" envisioned by the Seybert Commission or Andrew Jackson Davis. Rather, proliferating spiritualist groups assumed the character of traditional evangelical churches.[53] Seldom was the name of Andrew Jackson Davis mentioned in the literature of organized or unorganized spiritualism during the remainder of the nineteenth century. With the beginning of the twentieth century, however, when the disagreements of the past had been largely forgotten, spiritualists again began to inquire of him. Their journals consequently provided their readers with accounts of Davis's early life and contributions. The notorious behavior of a particular segment of mediums and the general unawareness by youthful spiritualists of their historical roots made necessary a new emphasis on the historical and philosophical background of the movement. "How many of the younger converts to this heaven-born and earth-neglected gospel ever heard of Andrew Jackson Davis?" asked one editor. Yet, he added, nothing had been written in the vast literature of spiritualism, the Harmonial Philosophy, Theosophy, or Christian Science that had not been foreshadowed by Davis. Had spiritualists devoted themselves to the principles represented by phenomena and less to the externals of "seeming manifestations," he avowed, the light Davis held aglow "would never have grown dim."[54]

Not only American but European spiritualists were reawakening to Andrew Jackson Davis's importance. James Robertson, a spiritualist writer of Glasgow, Scotland, published a pamphlet, *The Rise and Progress of Modern Spiritualism,* in which he pointed to the fulfilled prophecies of Davis as evidence of the authenticity of his revelations. He further praised Davis as "one of the great marks by which the nineteenth century would be judged and suggested that no single person in the century has done so much to open wide the doors of spirit life."[55] The aging Davis in Boston read with satisfaction these tributes, which differed in such a pronounced manner from the vilification directed at him only a few years earlier. He expressed his gratitude in a letter to a British spiritualist journal, *Light,* which had recently printed his portrait and with it a biographical summary. It was pleasant, he commented, to find no reference to the long-continued gossip associated with his name. He contended that it had never been his policy to correct false allegations, believing in the truth of Whittier's words, "Ever the right comes upmost, and ever is justice done."[56]

The renewed interest in Davis as philosopher and seer resulted in a demand that a way be found to purchase, publish, and perpetuate his writings. Davis himself expressed on several occasions a desire to have his books and stereotyped plates transferred to friendly persons who would keep the list constantly in print.[57] Although plans for the preservation of Davis's writings were never realized, other marks of honor and respect in which he was held continued to encourage him. He was particularly grateful upon reading an address delivered by E. Wake Cook before the London Spiritualist Alliance on "genius in the Light of Spiritualism," in which the British spiritualist praised Davis for his unique powers and entered into a philosophical discussion of the underlying problem of seership and spiritual inspiration.[58] The same author, on a trip to the United States in 1904, requested an interview with Davis whom he called the "Father of Modern Spiritualism and of those various uplifting movements the golden threads of which are being gathered together as the 'new' or the 'Higher thought.' " Cook drove to Davis's Watertown home, where he discovered that the latter had just returned from an unsuccessful attempt to find him at his Boston hotel. Informed of Cook's absence, he had walked back to his residence—a distance of some six miles. There Cook discovered him "bright, young, and alert as ever, his face radiant with knowledge, love and charity." After his conversation with Davis he wrote enthusiastically, "I feel inclined to sing the 'Nunc Dimittis' now that mine eyes have seen that the man is worthy of his glorious message."[59] E. Wake Cook was destined to play a major role in securing the reputation and position of Davis in modern spiritualism and in explaining philosophically the theories he propounded.

As the first decade of the twentieth century wore on, increasing attention was devoted to Davis in the spiritualist press of Great Britain and the United States. Enlarged portraits and laudatory remarks were carried on his birthdays and when, on his birthday in August 1909, the limitations of age made it necessary for him to retire from his medical practice, he experienced the satisfaction of knowing that sixty-two years after his startling *Revelations* he was again remembered, honored, and revered. On January 13, 1910, Davis died at his home in Watertown. The Boston *Globe* led the way by describing him as "the representative Spiritualist of the world." "His reputation," it reported, "was that of thinker, teacher, and prophet." His followers, millions of spiritualists in various countries, it lavishly claimed, almost worshiped him. In nearly every spiritualist home, stated the newspaper, could be found a copy of his *Divine Revelations,* a book of the "most startling propositions" regarding the spirit world.[60]

In assessing the place of Andrew Jackson Davis in the history of modern American spiritualism, it is important to remember that he was a product of the age in which he lived. He rose to fame in the 1840s and reflected an era which Alice Felt Tyler has christened one of "restless ferment."[61] In that experimental period of change, transition, and boundless hope, Davis reflected the basic American millenarian tradition. Excited by the Millerite enthusiasm of 1843, he delivered his *Revelations* somewhat later, when Fourierism and Swedenborgianism preserved the same dream of a new heaven and a new earth. Davis also shared a not uncommon belief that the New World provided an appropriate setting for the millennium. Writing in 1885, he stated that "when America is contemplated with an interior vision...she is seen to be a supernal promise of the happiest land—the foundation and perfect prophecy of a true Spiritual Republic."[62] The vision Davis brought to light was typical of the restless American democracy. One recent scholar has written that Davis did not urge people to lie back and listen to spirits but to *act.* Spiritualism, for him, was only another branch of knowledge designed to better the quality of human life, much as science and technology were attempting to do. In his opposition to religious sectarianism, the clergy, the unfair accumulation of property, and social distinctions, the harmonial philosopher, the same writer maintains, "wanted perfect human beings and the millennium." "When the spirits gave such advice," he concludes, "they were telling Americans to live up to their own ideals."[63] In his expectation of a millennial era, Davis was in accord with general Christian tradition. Also, like many Christian millenarians, he declared that the stimulus for such a perfected epoch must come from forces exterior to the earth. Societies of departed spirits in other worlds, he maintained, were guiding humanity toward a destiny of boundless hope and achievement. With the advent of the purported spiritual communications at Hydesville, New York, he sensed the beginning of the "good work"[64] and in his own day noted that mankind, under spiritual guidance, had reached a position where "the mental sky is fast becoming clear and serene; and the scene is one of grandeur and sublimity."[65] Similarity between Davis's definition of the "harmonial age" and Christian millennial thought, however, is more superficial than actual. He did not agree, for example, with the Christocentric doctrine implicit in traditional millennial speculation. The person of Christ was irrelevant, said Davis, but the coming day was hastened whenever men acted upon the "Christ-Principle," which he described in terms of "loving forgiveness, womanly gentleness, and a hospitality of soul."[66] These, he believed, would be united in the "harmonial brotherhood," which would encompass men and women in "every age and clime," who followed the eternal principles of "Association, Progression, and Development" and taught the "fixed laws of Science and the immortal principles of Philosophy."[67]

In addition to his lectures and the publication of a newspaper and more than thirty volumes, he created a "lyceum" for children and a "fraternity" to elevate the morals of New York City and, implicitly, other growing metropolitan areas. These innovative groups, he taught, would be influential in advancing a new and better day for all men. The controversial spiritual manifestations were for Davis simply one facet of the broader and more universal truth of the Harmonial Philosophy. Although he participated in early efforts to organize a national spiritualist association, he soon tired of the domination of those whose primary interest lay in dramatic exhibitions. He was more content at "reform conventions" where with spiritualist and non-spiritualist advocates of social change he perceived the advent of a new dispensation.

While other authors of nineteenth-century religious works became leaders of new religious movements, Davis never aspired to occupy such a position. In 1884 he remarked, "For myself I have no ambition to be a chieftain; no desire to be any man's leader; but I do enjoy the delights of teaching the principles of the Harmonial Philosophy."[68] E. Wake Cook echoed the same theme when two years before Davis's death he wrote that the latter "always shrank from the position of leader of a new religion...." He desired, said Cook, "fellow-workers, fellow-investigators, not sheeplike followers." He insisted, though, that by the right of priority and the importance of his work, Davis was the "Father of Modern Spiritualism."[69]

As we have seen, American spiritualists in the first quarter of the twentieth century generally shared the reawakened interest in Andrew Jackson Davis.[70] However, no leader so persistently dedicated to his memory or thought arose on this side of the Atlantic. Older spiritualists in America remembered the years of conflict when Davis had denigrated the majority who were either mediums or chiefly interested in that phase of spiritualistic activity. The poorly educated masses, understandably, could not comprehend the philosophical tomes which Davis produced in profusion. Instead, they chose the excitement of the seance in preference to the lengthy and complex theories that he clothed in an often esoteric vocabulary. In spite of assertions that he was not a spiritualist, Davis forcefully insisted that he *was* a medium who communed with those existing in the realms of departed spirits. He believed, however, that true spiritualism implied a great deal more than contacting or communing with those who had once lived on earth. Instead, it was a means of illuminating the darkness of earth with the light of distant realms even then moving earth toward the dawn of a new and brighter day. His imagery may be obscure to those in a less optimistic century; but Davis's life, characterized by extraordinary personal growth and maturity, epitomized the spirit of his age.

Notes

1. Emma Hardinge Britten, *Modern American Spiritualism* (New York, 1870) remains important because of the author's association with the nineteenth-century movement as a medium and historian. A significant account is George Lawton, *The Drama of Life After Death*

(New York, 1932). A recent and valuable treatment of spiritualism and its subsequent influence on psychic investigation to the present is R. Laurence Moore, *In Search of White Crows: Spiritualism, Parapsychology and American Culture* (New York: Oxford Univ. Press, 1977). Gates Brown, Jr., "Spiritualism in Nineteenth-Century America" (Ph.D. diss., Boston University, 1973), and Ernest Isaacs, "History of Nineteenth Century American Spiritualism as a Religious and Social Movement" (Ph.D. diss., University of Wisconsin, 1975), are thorough studies. The place of spiritualism in the history of American reform is evaluated in Ronald G. Walters, *American Reformers, 1815-1860* (New York, 1978). Howard Kerr and Charles L. Crow, eds., *The Occult in America: New Historical Perspectives* (Urbana, 1983) relates spiritualism to other nineteenth- and twentieth-century religious, social, and scientific developments. Helpful references to Andrew Jackson Davis are contained in Allen Johnson and Dumas Malone, eds., *Dictionary of American Biography*, 20 vols. (New York, 1928-36), 5:105; Amy Pearce Ver Nooy, "Dutchess County Men: Andrew Jackson Davis, the Poughkeepsie Seer," *Year Book of the Dutchess County Historical Society* 32 (1947): 39-62; Jan McCarthy, "Andrew Jackson Davis: The Don Quixote of Spiritualism," *Southern Speech Journal* 30 (Summer 1965): 308-16. The contribution of Davis is assessed in Robert W. Delp, "Andrew Jackson Davis: Prophet of American Spiritualism," *Journal of American History* 54 (June 1967): 43-56; idem, "Andrew Jackson Davis' Revelations: Harbinger of American Spiritualism," *New York Historical Society Quarterly* 60 (July 1971): 211-34; idem, "A Spiritualist in Connecticut: Andrew Jackson Davis, the Hartford Years, 1850-1854," *New England Quarterly* 53 (September 1980): 345-62. Manuscript collections relative to Davis include Andrew Jackson Davis Papers (Yale University Library) and Anti-Slavery Letters Written to William Lloyd Garrison and Others (Boston Public Library).

2. Moore, *White Crows*, p. 15.

3. Andrew Jackson Davis, *The Magic Staff: An Autobiography of Andrew Jackson Davis* (Boston: Bela Marsh, 1857), p. 416.

4. Catherine Davis to William Green, Jr., Dec. 22, 1849, Davis Papers.

5. Isaacs, "History," p. 103.

6. Brown, "Spiritualism," p. 112.

7. *Spirit Messenger* (Springfield, Mass.), June 21, 1851.

8. Delp, "Spiritualist."

9. Rochester *Democrat*, Aug. 12, 1852. Later Davis was critical of Spear's more radical interpretation of spiritualism. See Andrew Jackson Davis to William Green, Jr., Aug. 22, 1855, Davis Papers.

10. Andrew Jackson Davis, *Memoranda of Persons, Places, and Events* (Boston: William White & Co., 1868), p. 182.

11. E.W. Capron, *Modern Spiritualism: Its Facts and Fantasies, Its Consistencies and Contradictions* (Boston, 1855), p. 363. See Isaacs, "History," pp. 195-98.

12. New York *Herald*, April 24, 1854.

13. *Spiritual Telegraph* 5 (1855): 188.

14. Moore, *White Crows*, p. 21.

15. New York *Tribune*, Feb. 19, 1855.

16. Frank Podmore, *Modern Spiritualism: A History and a Criticism* (London: Methuen and Co., 1902), 1:209.

17. *New England Spiritualist* (Boston), May 26, 1855.

18. Ibid., Aug. 10, 1855.

19. Ibid., May 26, 1855.

20. *Liberator* (Boston), Aug. 31, 1855.

21. Davis to William Green, Jr., May 14, 1851, July 8, 1856, Davis Papers.

22. Andrew Jackson Davis, *The Penetralia* (Boston: Bela Marsh, 1872), p. 71.

23. *Spiritual Age* (New York City), May 2, 1857.

24. *New York Times*, June 29, 1858.

25. Delp, "Andrew Jackson Davis."

26. *Medium* (London), June 24, 1870.

27. Andrew Jackson Davis, *Beyond the Valley: A Sequel to "The Magic Staff": An Autobiography of Andrew Jackson Davis* (Boston: Colby & Rich, 1885), p. 81.

28. *Religio-Philosophical Journal* (Chicago), Nov. 4, 1865.

29. *New York Times*, Sept. 13, 1867.

30. *Banner of Light* (Boston), Jan. 2, 1869.

31. Ibid., April 24, 1869.

32. Ibid., April 15, 1871.

33. *Medium*, Aug. 4, 1876.

34. *Religio-Philosophical Journal*, March 23, 1878.

35. Davis, *Beyond the Valley*, p. 132.

36. *Religio-Philosophical Journal*, June 22, 1878.

37. Ibid., Nov. 2, 1878.

38. Ibid., Feb. 1, 1879.

39. Davis, *Beyond the Valley*, p. 201.

40. *Religio-Philosophical Journal*, Sept. 15, 1883.

41. Davis, *Beyond the Valley*, p. 206.

42. *Carrier Dove* (Oakland, Calif.), Oct. 1886, p. 236.

43. Della Davis, *Starnos* (Boston: Colby & Rich, 1891), p. 4.

44. Ibid., p. 6.

45. New York *Herald,* Jan. 17, 1885.

46. *Carrier Dove,* Oct. 1886, p. 255.

47. Ibid., p. 236.

48. *Light: A Journal of Spiritual and Psychical Research* (London) 30 (Feb. 5, 1910): 60.

49. Moore, *White Crows,* p. 65.

50. "Formation of the Society," *Proceedings of the American Society for Psychical Research* 1 (July 1885): 232.

51. *Preliminary Report of the Commission Appointed by the University of Pennsylvania to Investigate Modern Spiritualism* (Philadelphia: Lippincott, 1887), p. 5.

52. Ibid., p. 159.

53. Clifton E. Olmstead, *History of Religion in the United States* (Englewood Cliffs: Prentice-Hall, 1960), p. 517.

54. *Banner of Light,* March 23, 1901.

55. *Light,* Aug. 9, 1902.

56. Ibid., Sept. 27, 1902.

57. *Banner of Light,* March 21, 1903.

58. Ibid., Aug. 15, 1903.

59. Ibid., Nov. 19, 1904.

60. Boston *Globe,* Jan. 13, 1910. Davis was honored not only in the United States and Great Britain but in Germany. He corresponded with an association of spiritualists in Leipzig under the leadership of Professor Johann Zollner. The German group renounced superstition and declared its intention to advance and elevate the German people and to propagate the "fundamental principles of immutable natural laws as produced in the *Great Harmonia* by Andrew Jackson Davis and the cognate branches of pure spiritualism." See *Religio-Philosophical Journal,* Jan. 24, 1880.

61. Alice Felt Tyler, *Freedom's Ferment: Phases of American Social History from the Colonial Period to the Outbreak of the Civil War* (New York, Harper and Brothers [Harper Torchbooks] 1962), p. 1.

62. Davis, *Beyond the Valley,* p. 323.

63. Walters, *American Reformers,* pp. 168-69.

64. Davis, *Memoranda,* p. 100.

65. Davis, *The Philosophy of Spiritual Intercourse* (Boston: William White, 1872), p. 294.

66. Davis, *Penetralia,* p. 69.

67. Davis, *The History and Philosophy of Evil* (Boston: Colby & Rich, 1877), pp. 140-41.

68. *Religio-Philosophical Journal,* Aug. 16, 1884.

69. *The Sunflower* (Lily Dale, N.Y.), Jan. 4, 1908. R. Laurence Moore suggests that although Davis's efforts went against the major thrust of American spiritualism, "insofar as spiritualist leaders were able to develop a set of teachings beyond the mere claim that the dead return, Davis deserved the major share of credit." *White Crows,* p. 10.

70. See, for example, Margaret Vere Farrington, *Andrew Jackson Davis and the Harmonial Philosophy* (Boston: Spiritual Journal, 1912).

ARTHUR WROBEL

6. Phrenology as Political Science

"All institutions must be calculated upon a knowledge of human nature; otherwise they cannot be permanent."
—Johann G. Spurzheim

During his 1838-40 lecture tour of most of the major cities of the east coast, George Combe, the noted Scottish phrenologist and founder of the prestigious Edinburgh Phrenological Society, spoke thirteen times on "The Application of Phrenology to the Present and Prospective Conditions of the United States." Combe's address was an exceptionally able piece; it avoided Frederick Marryat's bemused detachment and Harriet Martineau's officiousness in describing American life and prospects. A candid and even-handed critic of American society, Combe tempered criticism with modest optimism about the future of American democracy. He described American national character, assessed the strength of democratic institutions, and proposed some measures to ensure a stable and lasting system of democracy—all according to the precepts of phrenology.[1]

His address represented the first extended attempt to remove political theory and practice from the realm of philosophic speculation and bring democratic government under the purview of a Baconian "science." Compelled by the thought that America was engaged in a "vast moral experiment,"[2] Combe believed this country's destined brightness (not sufficiently appreciated, he felt, by Tocqueville) could be hastened and insured with phrenology's guidance. So skillfully did Combe combine theory with specific recommendations that little doubt was left, at least among his auditors, regarding phrenology's potential use for political discussion. The *Ladies' Companion* judged Combe's "Application," with the exception of Tocqueville's work, "the most sound and able exposition of America and her institutions which ever proceeded from the pen of any foreign traveller." In city after city where Combe lectured, resolutions were unanimously passed like that of the New York Phrenological Society, which declared phrenology "eminently calculated...to improve the institutions of society and of government, and to elevate the condition of the human race."[3]

Combe's discourse was neither fanciful nor singular. Phrenology's potential for political theory had been recognized as early as 1822 when the *Philadelphia Journal of the Medical and Physical Sciences* observed that phrenology could be an invaluable guide in extirpating "tyrannical customs" and checking imperfect legislation. Several periodicals during the next decade—*Knickerbocker Magazine, Eclectic Journal of Medicine,* and *New England Magazine*—ventured similar sentiments.[4] Other phrenologists also asserted phrenology's relevance for political discourse. During his ill-fated 1832 tour of this country, Johann Gaspar Spurzheim discussed political theory in his lectures on "Liberty" and "On Education." The greatest of American phrenologists, Orson Squire Fowler, whose career spanned forty years of aggressive phrenological entrepreneurship from the 1840s onward, regularly and systematically fused romantic Jacksonian optimism and American millennial expectations with phrenological prescriptions.

That phrenology, a science of the mind, came to have relevance for political discussion and a host of budding social sciences is logical. Interested primarily in cerebral physiology, phrenology's founder, Franz Josef Gall, investigated the brain's anatomy and proposed a theory of cerebral localization which argued that: 1) the brain is the organ of the mind; and 2) the mind is a composite of thirty-seven independent faculties, propensities, and sentiments, each being governed by a corresponding organ located in a determinable area or region of the brain. To each of these faculties he assigned a colorful rubric such as

Conscientiousness, Self-Esteem, Spirituality, or even Destructiveness, their sum total comprising the whole of man's intellectual, moral, and affective character. An examination of the cranium's contour, he believed, could reveal the size and thereby the power or strength of the organs located in that area.[5] In asserting that psychological functions possessed some definitive form of representation in the brain, Gall laid the groundwork for phrenology's future role as a pervasive force in educational practice and social theory.

His immediate disciple, Johann Gaspar Spurzheim, helped erect part of this superstructure. A physician by vocation but a philosopher by avocation, Spurzheim argued that man's faculties were given for salutary ends within a wholly benevolent design. He attributed evil to an imbalance among the faculties (unlike Gall, who believed violence originated in man's constitution) and even argued that specific faculties, sentiments, or propensities could be consciously strengthened or inhibited. Not only did this give phrenology a specific psycho-behavioristic dimension, but it paved the way for unlimited human improvement.

Spurzheim's optimistic revisionism drew George Combe to the movement. More interested in human psychology than in his legal practice, Combe saw in Spurzheim's brand of phrenology a lucid exposition of the mind's structure and operation. But, more importantly, he detected the makings of a natural philosophy. Evils, Combe taught, arise not from any flaw in man's constitution but from man's violations of natural laws—those of external nature or his own—through either ignorance or willful disobedience. Happiness ensues when men and their institutions conform to nature's eternal laws in accordance with universal purpose.

By the time phrenology arrived on these shores in the early 1830s, it had all but ceased being primarily a medical science. Rather, it came to resemble a social science, its bright and cheerful patchwork of scientific, religious, and moralistic doctrine promising a rationalistic means for describing man's place in society and his relation to nature's laws.

The Fowler brothers, Lorenzo Niles and Orson Squire, severely damaged phrenology's hard-won reputation among the leading members of America's medical and academic communities—Benjamin Silliman, Joseph Story, Samuel Gridley Howe, John Bell, John C. Warren, Josiah Quincy, and Horace Mann. Ignoring phrenology's startling medical discoveries about the anatomy of the human brain and its orthodox philosophical underpinnings, the Fowlers quickly seized on phrenology's schematization of the human mind to make practical the analysis of a person's character through a "head-reading." They asserted that the various faculties and their actions on one another could be scientifically gauged and regulated for the purpose of modifying human behavior. To many this turn appeared as just so much quackery; but an equally large number of people were enthralled.[6] To the latter, phrenology was "useful knowledge" valuable for solving problems ranging from career choices and human behavior to restructuring social life—education, religion, the fine arts, treatment of the insane and, of course, government, the subject of this essay.

Its champions gained much in promoting phrenology as a science with political bearing. Considering the newness of the American democratic experiment, interest in political theory flourished in this country, though available treatises on the science of government were woefully inadequate. What American thinkers longed for was a science of politics as exact as Newton's discovery of the laws of the physical universe and Locke's discoveries of the laws of human nature. What they got was another matter. Rather than hard and fast axioms, they had to settle for shifting moralistic maxims; instead of science, conventional wisdoms acquired from the study of political thinkers from the ancients onward. They nevertheless remained expectant; John Adams's writings abound in references to "the divine science of politics"; Thomas Jefferson recommended reading Montesquieu and Locke to gain an understanding of "the science of government"; and George Washington left both land and money for the establishment of a "national university" where young men could " 'acquire knowledge in the principles of politics and good government.' "[7]

Their expectations, however, outdistanced existing realities.

Even the writings of the Scottish academic philosophers—Hutcheson, Hume, Smith, Reid, Kames, and Ferguson—which had trained the spokesmen of the Revolution and the framers of the Constitution, were deficient. Their authors' critical method was historical-comparative synthesis; these writers consulted the literary and philosophical works of earlier ages in order to uncover universal principles of human nature common to men of all nations and ages. Such studies, Hume asserted, allow political philosophers to make predictions about legislation "almost as general and certain...as any which the mathematical sciences will afford us." In this way, he rashly asserted, politics "may be reduced to a science." Hardly. Not only did Hume's so-called science of politics lack a "scientific" methodology, but it was even akin to philosophy. Worse, philosophers themselves had recently fallen into disrepute; George Washington and other leaders viewed them with suspicion as the very authors of the Terror in France and the continent's ensuing calamaties.[8]

While these early leaders feared contamination of unrest from abroad, conservatives during the first half of the nineteenth century viewed the threat of internal unrest with equal alarm. In their darkest moments they suspected the very nature of democratic government as flawed. Liberty too quickly degenerated into rank license, in their estimation, and mobility into social instability and even anarchy. Further, the Revolution left the democratic majority suspicious of all traditional authorities. What was to be the nucleus, they wondered, around which the atoms comprising a society were to revolve in orderly and stately fashion?

To many, phrenology had the best if not the only prospects for being a legitimate science of politics. That its doctrines were compatible with the American experience to date, having tapped the same philosophical sources as the speculative writings of the revolutionary period, made phrenology especially compelling. It postulated a deistic cosmos of natural laws that a benevolent Deity created as the foundation upon which men could build an orderly and permanent society. It also gained a heavy infusion of Scottish philosophy under George Combe. In combining natural theology with Baconian induction and Scottish common sense philosophy, phrenology represented intellectual orthodoxy.[9] Believing they uncovered a causal relation between cranial developments, human behavior, forms of government, and nature's laws, the phrenologists were prepared to determine for Americans whether the national republican compact, as formulated by the founding fathers, was scientifically true and founded on natural law. Further, as a comprehensive psychology, it seemed logically equipped to define, establish, and maintain the social order appropriate to a republican government.

Predictably, phrenology attracted a spectrum of adherents with widely differing political persuasions, from conservatives seeking ways to check the vicissitudes of the unruly masses to visionary democrats wishing to enlarge personal freedoms and reduce the presence of government by identifying those few and universal laws upon which lasting government was said to rest. Its doctrines also appealed to those many reformers who taught that evil stemmed from a faulty social environment and legislative codes that ran counter to nature's precepts. To Americans with millennial expectations, phrenology also promised to guide this country to the Great Republic now that the mysterious laws of mind and nature had been unraveled.

Whatever their political or ideological convictions, nobody questioned the doctrine of natural law. In the writings of Locke, Condorcet, Volney, Hutchinson, and Reid, the authors of the American Constitution found broad philosophical principles for transmuting the theory of natural law into the practice of democracy.[10] In his *Defense of the Constitutions of Government* John Adams proudly stated that "The United States of America have exhibited perhaps, the first example of government erected on the simple principles of nature"; he reasoned elsewhere that there is no other source "for the theory or practice of government" except in "nature and experiment, unless you appeal to revelation." The so-called book of nature, however, was a difficult one to read. Even Spurzheim conceded as much: "It is certainly a difficult task to discover clearly the law established by Nature, and to bring all branches of legislation into harmony with the Creator's will."[11] Phrenology volunteered its expertise, promising to do so according to the principles of scientific induction. In the process, Combe, the Fowler brothers, and other followers of phrenology applauded some of America's most precious national beliefs: that every individual has a right to liberty and equality, that government's activities should be restricted, and that man's and society's potential for development is unlimited.

In their study of natural law the phrenologists found confirmation of the conclusions urged in seventeenth- and eighteenth-century treatises—that man's welfare lay in civilized society, not in an untrammeled romantic statelessness. O.S. Fowler, editor of the *American Phrenological Journal,* sounds Shaftsburyean when he writes that man is "a congregating, associating, social being."[12] Judge Elisha P. Hurlbut of the Supreme Court of New York and the vice president of the New York Phrenological Society, held the same view. Writing under the by-line "By a Phrenologist," Hurlbut contributed a two-part series to the *Democratic Review* entitled "On Rights and Government." He asserted that "the state of civilization is the true natural condition of the human race."[13] Only in the safety and order of civilization is man's nature fully exhibited, his faculties permitted to reach their highest development, and his intellect to grow. Civilization enhances the individual's and mankind's progress.

But the writers part company with this tradition over what form of government could best expedite progress. Gall's conservatism, no doubt, would have inclined him toward the crown as the sole means of maintaining civil order. Spurzheim avoided sanctioning any particular form of government, concluding rather that the best government is that which is best suited to its peoples' intellectual and moral character. In fact, he doubted whether human nature, in any of the civilized nations, was sufficiently developed for true republicanism "where every one sacrifices his private interest to the common welfare." Combe and Fowler, however, repudiated monarchical government. For them postulating a chain of hierarchy in nature that sanctions monarchy with its attendant abuses—the maintenance of a profligate peerage and a toadying established church—ignores the demonstrable truths of human and external nature.[14] Proof that self-government is an inalienable right, an ordinance of nature, lay in the very existence of certain faculties—Intellectuality, Conscientiousness, and Self-Esteem.[15]

While Combe and Fowler based their argument on phrenological premises, their reasoning is indistinguishable from the faculty-psychology contemporary writers used in discourses on American government. For instance, the argument of "The Course of Civilization," featured in the *Democratic Review,* defines democracy as "that condition of society which secures the full and inviolable use of every faculty." This reads no differently from Judge Hurlbut's definition of human rights as the gratification of "every innate power and faculty of the mind."[16] George Combe's essay "The Applicaton of Phrenology" is a specific inquiry into the ways different forms of government influence "the *virtuous activity of all the faculties.*"[17] On these grounds he criticized the paternalistic despotisms in Austria and Prussia. When the press is censored, a national church and hereditary peerage maintained, and citizens excluded from the legislative processes,[18] the organs of Intellectuality, Self-Esteem, and Conscientiousness atrophy. Walt Whitman similarly couched an April 1847 editorial for the *Brooklyn Daily Eagle* in the familiar logic of faculty psychology that probably came to him via his own readings in phrenology. He excoriated the "well-ordered governments" of Russia, Austria, and "the miserable German states" for excluding their citizens from political processes and denying them free inquiry. They fall into listless indifference, he asserted, while those faculties related to self-government weaken through long neglect. According to Samuel Gridley Howe, the great educator, crusader, and physician, the remedy seemed obvious. In *A Discourse on the Social Relations of Man* (1837) he wrote: "The society which effects this [the full development of man's faculties] to the greatest possible number of its members, is in accordance with the principles of phrenology, and is good."[19]

The repression of any primary faculties violated as well other rights that nature's government granted man, specifically life, liberty, and the pursuit of happiness. In discussing this trinity the phrenologists had no difficulty reconciling the popular meaning of these terms with their own idiosyncratic vocabulary and precepts. Man's inalienable right to life was evident enough, but a proper definition of the concept of liberty generated wide interest in phrenological circles as it did energetic debate in the whole nation from 1816 to shortly before the Civil War. By settling on a definition such as the one George Lyon proposed in his "Essay on the Phrenological Causes of the Different Degree of Liberty Enjoyed by Different Nations" in the *Edinburgh Phrenological Journal,* phrenology signaled its potential relevance to a romantic liberalism that involved some of its followers in several extravagant manifestations of mid-century individualism—from collectivist experiments to every shade and hue of romantic reform. Lyon defines liberty as "the exercise at will of the whole propensities, sentiments, and intellectual faculties, in so far as this exercise is not prejudicial to, nor inconsistent with, the legitimate exercise of all or any of these faculties in others." Such a conceptualization applauded liberty, notably in the sense guaranteed by the limits which the Bill of Rights set on official power. It also resembled that of liberal Democrats. Jefferson, for instance, used the term "liberty" to include the conditions which make possible the emergence of a natural aristocracy of virtue and talent by encouraging the development of each man's intellectual and moral faculties. Sanguine prophets of America's millennial future similarly attributed spiraling progress to liberty, which permitted the full growth and development of man's faculties. The *Democratic Review* for July 1840 promises that the "exercise and discipline [of] these faculties" results in "a perfect man."[20]

The concept of happiness also implied more to this generation, as it did to the phrenologists, than it did to Locke. Garry Wills shows in *Inventing America* that the most popular usage of the term "happiness" derived from Jefferson's readings in the political thought of the moral-sense philosophers, most notably Hutcheson and, to a lesser degree, Hume and Ferguson. These writers argued that happiness exists when man, responding to the promptings of the moral sense, commits himself to promoting the well-being of his fellow citizens.[21] Judge Hurlbut's use of the term similarly conveys a concern with moral and communal conduct: "Now the man of the highest mental endowment and culture naturally perceives and adopts the mode of moral and intellectual action which best subserves human happiness. His conduct is approved by reason and natural morality."[22] Hurlbut also included a predictable aside to allay conservative fears—that government must restrain those few who, formed with a defective organization or training, are guided by low instincts. In the main, however, he seems prepared to trust in the inherent intelligence and morality of the majority of republicans.

Not so Combe. Less interested in specifically vindicating the wisdom of the American founding fathers, Combe studied instead the theory and practical workings of American democracy. He marshaled but a faint hurrah. While he and Spurzheim were quick to deplore the uniformity of European populations constricted along artificial class lines, they also deplored the shrill American pursuit of an imperfectly conceived idea of liberty: "If ever knowledge of what is right, self-control to pursue it, and high moral resolve to sacrifice every motive of self-interest and individual ambition, to the dictates of benevolence and justice, were needed in any people, they are wanted in the citizens of the United States."[23] Combe felt American society too sanguine about giving its citizens the free play of all their faculties and sounded a stern admonitory note: optimism over America's future was unwarranted, he cautioned, if its citizens continued to mistake the pursuit of license for true happiness.[24] Spurzheim similarly warned millennially expectant Americans: "Union and morality alone can save the future happiness of the United States of America. Being divided or without morality, they will have the fate of the ancient and modern nations of the old world. Intellectual education alone cannot produce the desired effect."

Clearly, this represented a conservative view. The defeat of Edward Everett for reelection by a majority of one vote for governor of Massachusetts in 1839 appalled Combe. That a man of such "great talents and accomplishments" should go down to defeat at the hands of a populace guided by "their faults, foibles, and imperfections," haunted him.[25] To avoid such debacles in the future, Combe proposed a typically Whiggish solution—that the enlightened classes raise "the mental condition of the people...which will enable them to understand the moral and political principles on which the welfare of nations is founded." Otherwise, Combe predicted an uncontrolled development of the faculties of Acquisitiveness (greed), Self-Esteem (excessive self-confidence), and Love of Approbation (vanity), which could destroy the Union.[26] Citing the existence of lynch mobs, wild money speculation, impulsive changes in laws and policy, and an appalling self-complacency, he also recommended the strengthening of those civil laws already in existence.[27] As a good over-all moral tonic for the masses, he even urged the publication of a paper "composed partly on the principles of Addison's Spectator—taking cognizance of manners and minor morals, and partly on those of Chambers's Journal—combining didactic instruction with a reasonable amount of entertaining reading."[28]

Combe's moralistic and prescriptive tone when speaking about American democracy is no different from that pervading his most influential work, *The Constitution of Man,* which he once described as "an attempt...to arrive, by the aid of phrenology, at a demonstration of morality as a science." Under his aegis phrenology came to resemble a secularized version of his childhood Calvinism. Retaining a distrust of human nature and a borderline deterministic view of man's innate faculties, he shaped phrenology into a science of morality based on the moral precepts said to be embedded in natural law. In translating the doctrine of obedience to natural law into practical behavior, Combe extolled virtues that were bound to cheer the heart of any conservative; he upheld everything from temperance and cleanliness to regular habits and family life. He anticipated the day when the laboring classes would "recognize Phrenology" and "devote themselves to improvement, with a zeal and earnestness that in a few generations will change the aspect of their class."[29]

Surely the conservative sponsors of Combe's American tour must have been pleased with such sentiments. Combe publicly praised his "philanthropic" sponsors for promoting a system of instruction in superior citizenship. Clearly, the officers of the many phrenological committees in each city where Combe spoke belonged overwhelmingly to the educated classes. That Combe mingled with and assiduously sounded the upper classes for their views is evident from the description of his data-gathering methods: "I found no cause of enquiry so instructive in the United States as conversations with persons of different professions, such as proprietors of land, merchants, lawyers, bankers, ministers of the Gospel, teachers, doctors in medicine, as well as common working men," the latter group occupying a symbolic position, one senses, in his catalogue.[30] In an anniversary address delivered before the Boston Phrenological Society, Elisha Bartlett, M.D., probably represented the political persuasions of Combe's own audiences when he warned that mere "education of the intellect" was "a broken reed" on which popular government cannot rest for security, prosperity, and social cohesion. Neither is security to be found, he asserted, "in that other misnamed rock of safety,—the democracy of numbers,—the mere preponderance, ever changing, of numerical strength." For him security rested rather in a combination of revelation and phrenology, which teach men to subordinate "the animal appetites and selfish desires to the moral and religious powers."[31]

Others, however, felt differently. Recognizing phrenology's epistemological malleability, Judge E.P. Hurlbut and O.S. Fowler gave it a more liberal shape. Using the language and logic of phrenology, they endorsed the kinds of extravagant claims and visions that normally comprise heady Fourth of July orations. In so doing they ignored history and denied human nature, celebrating instead the excellence of the American Constitution and the professed transforming effect of free institutions on individuals.

While Combe might have expected far-fetched political theories from a mountebank like Fowler, the so-called "practical" phrenologist, he must have found Judge Hurlbut's views as expressed in *Essays on Human Rights and their Political Guaranties*[32] disconcerting. Strange to say, Combe once publicly expressed admiration for the judge; stranger yet, he also wrote notes and commentary on this very volume. The former event occurred on March 23, 1840, when Combe accepted a gift vase presented to him by a committee comprised of officers of the New York Phrenological Society. The chairman of that committee was Hurlbut. Named "the champion of truth" by Hurlbut in his presentation speech, Combe responded in kind by declaring his admiration of "the enlightened minds" of various Americans he had met during his stay in America; he named Horace Mann ("a gifted individual") and Hurlbut (who "penetrated to the core with his last and best of human sciences," phrenology). He also recommended Hurlbut's recent volume *Civil Office and Political Ethics* (1844) as "a valuable work," no doubt because its ethical content was specifically aimed at raising the patriotism and virtue of the American populace.[33] *Essays on Human Rights,* however, he must have found considerably less salutary.

So radical are its views that even the American historian Benjamin Fletcher Wright justly wonders "whether a more extremely individualistic interpretation of natural rights has ever been written" than Hurlbut's *Essays.* In discoursing on the origins of natural rights as conceptualized in the American Constitution and the Bill of Rights, Hurlbut offers a theoretical justification for "negative government" that would have satisfied even the most ardent Jacksonian. He begins by taking issue with Blackstone's contention that a legislator's duty involves ruling on issues to which no natural laws apply. Arguing instead that natural laws exist for every issue, Hurlbut finds Blackstone's view pernicious because it invites tyranny, encouraging governments to elevate impiously man-made laws above those of nature. True justice and safety occur only when laws reflect man's constitution and its adaptation to external nature such as described by phrenology. Hurlbut next asserts the commonplace that man's fundamental right includes the gratification of all of his faculties. But he soon slips into an uncommon view when he maintains that governments are constituted exclusively to protect these rights, and he denies the right of government to place any restraints on citizens which are incompatible with their own moral natures and intellectual faculties. Further, he insists, government is passive, existing only to obey voters' directives. His proposals for witnessing a true democracy in America, uncontaminated by borrowings from defective British precedents, grow naturally out of the logic of his views on natural rights. These include disallowing executive appointments, permitting the direct election of every office from president to constable, and removing property qualifications from suffrage.

Combe's "Notes" to *Essays on Human Rights* were surprisingly restrained and even gracious, considering the extremity of Hurlbut's theory of natural rights. He prudently ignored Hurlbut's definition of happiness (the full exercise of all the faculties), contextually using the term to imply obedience to natural laws. To this end he proposed that government should actively promote happiness through education and other measures necessary to raise the nation's moral level. Combe stood firm in his conservatism and Hurlbut, from his published reply to Combe in the appendix, stood firm in his radicalism. Combe's other notes are rather perfunctory; in the main he simply quotes from other political discourses in support of Hurlbut's views. Perhaps Combe felt that the ideological gap separating him from Hurlbut was too vast, making extensive commentary pointless.[34]

Perhaps, too, Combe guessed that other Americans were bound to take up Hurlbut's sentiments anyway. He guessed right. The first two chapters of Hurlbut's book provide the theoretical groundwork, if not the direct source, for O.S. Fowler's twelve-part series on "Republicanism the True Form of Government: Its Destined Influence, and Improvement" that appeared in the *American Phrenological Journal* between September 1846 and August 1849. Here Fowler, like Hurlbut, signaled his sympathy with a program of total democratization that the Jeffersonians originally envisioned and the Jacksonians later attempted. This included the direct election of the president and the federal judiciary, general white suffrage, the accountability of all officials to the electorate, and the removal of residential requirements for elective office. Simiarly, Fowler subscribed to the view that men in masses are sound logicians, confidently defining republicanism as "the rule of the majority in every thing."[35] He urged eliminating all Federalist contaminations from the Constitution—checks and balances, the electoral college, and executive privilege—and viewed elected officials as passive agents of their constituents. Government was to be the "union of the many for the good of all."[36]

Both he and Hurlbut saved their bitterest denunciations for those few who attempted to circumvent the operation of a true democracy in petitioning legislatures for special privileges. Duties, monopolies, and charters, Fowler asserted, were residues of kingcraft and threatened to corrupt a natural democracy.[37] For Hurlbut, "A just government will confer no special privileges; its powers will be exerted only in the vindication and defence of human rights. Privilege conferred upon one man implies a derogation from the rights of others."[38] In the logic of phrenology, the unjust advantages special interests gained were felt to play havoc with the faculty of Self-Esteem and to violate natural equality as revealed in natural law. Hurlbut and Fowler would have seen Jackson's attacks on the "hydra-headed monsters"—the United States Bank and the American System, and his handling of the Charles River Bridge case—as they were seen by the Jacksonians, as measures necessary to ensure the operation of natural law.

Predictably, their commitment to disestablishing special privilege made Fowler and Hurlbut sympathetic to a laissez-faire concept of political economy popularized in America by William Gouge, William Leggett, and Theodore Sedgwick as well as by Frances Wayland and other academics. However impractical such a policy might appear to political theorists in our own age of political and economic engineering, the phrenologists viewed laissez-faire as something akin to "an act of moral communion."[39] To them, as to liberal democrats, it represented the extension of natural rights into economics. Hurlbut sounds like O'Sullivan in urging government to permit business and the interests of society to find their own balance. Clearly, Fowler and Hurlbut advocated a form of negative or hidden government that had its origins in eighteenth-century Enlightenment thought. In response to this romantic primitivism, conservatives charged that laissez-faire encouraged an unchecked and unprincipled individualism. Phrenologists responded in turn, arguing that the very nature of democratic society, by compelling its members to participate in human affairs, checked extreme individualism. They were also prepared to tune to their highest pitch the activity of sentiments such as Justice, Benevolence, and Morality, and to shape individualism to serve a higher law.

While Fowler approved of Jackson's campaign to remove as much government as possible, he remained somewhat cautious. He urged more education of the intellect and moral sentiments during the period when established authority slowly relinquished its power. (He estimated the year 1900 for the unfolding of the Great Republic.[40]) This stands in sharp contrast to Combe, who recommended more government and more education aimed at instructing the populace in their proper duties as citizens. Whereas Combe believed education could merely influence a person's faculties and sentiments regarding their proper use, Fowler optimistically asserted that education could overhaul and restructure a person's mental constitution. With many of his contemporaries, particularly champions of public school education, he viewed education as a tool to shape malleable human nature into a work of virtue and intelligence.[41]

Fowler's correctives had a special urgency about them. They combined, as they did for many, with a faith in the law of progress that would witness the unfolding of an enlightened society of free men guided only by the checks of their own natural morality. This was to be the secular millennium. Never doubting the divine origin of democracy's mandate, Fowler was as mystical as any passionate patriot. In such a society the spontaneous impulses of enlightened men would be to do right, the state existing only to provide a resplendent intellectual and cultural atmosphere to aid in each man's apotheosis. Hurlbut envisioned not merely the absence of government restraints or the Lockean submission to rational laws, but the complete supremacy of men's will over lower desires and propensities.[42] For O.S. Fowler the stimulation of the higher faculties by spiritual love was needed: "Then superadd that good, pure, moral, normal action of all the Faculties imparted by 'love pure and undefiled,' and we *have a millennium,* individual and universal."[43] While the revivalists of the period anticipated the creation of a millennial society founded on the fatherhood of God and the brotherhood of man, the phrenologists promised the unfolding of the Great Republic founded on the laws of human and external nature and the brotherhood of man.

By his adherence to millennialistic thought, Fowler committed the science of phrenology to a complex of prewar liberal humanitarian crusades, all of which were manifestations of the larger pattern of American perfectionist aspirations. The condition of liberty constituted a necessary prerequisite for men to learn to govern themselves and to establish a collective moral order. Temperance, women's rights, public education, and penal reform, in which the phrenologists took a decisive role, were its first stirrings. They offered the empirical intelligence of their science in mapping out this new and dazzling country hovering just over the horizon.

For some, phrenology's authority helped quell the unquietness that Major Wilson asserts characterized the first half of the nineteenth century. To radicals and conservatives alike, this science promised an orderly movement from the present toward a sublimely perfect future according to familiar beliefs about America's national destiny that many came to regard as truths. But in the wake of vast postwar social and economic changes, men grew impatient with fine questions about liberty and equal rights and natural laws. The scientific and philosophical paradigm of beliefs, values, and techniques of eighteenth-century nature philosophy that the phrenologists used as a point of departure for their own speculations had slipped into quaint anachronism. Their conflation of political theory and natural law was no less delusive.

Now men concerned themselves with the threat of infringements on personal liberty brought about by an increasingly complex industrial society. More government was needed, not less; simplicity and economy in government were not feasible any more. The only agency of redress against the powerful and wealthy was a strong federal government, one that would safeguard the very liberties Jefferson and Jackson insisted resided naturally in the people. Laissez-faire abandoned the belief (in Jackson's words) that a government should "shower its favors alike on the high and low, the rich and the poor" in order to ensure the greatest amount of liberty to all men. In too many instances it became a rationale for ruthlessly defending monopolies and protective tariffs.

Phrenology's remarkable compatibility with the major currents of mid-nineteenth-century thought was not calculating.[44] Rather, it reminds us that scientific discovery, for all its much vaunted objectivity, is seldom value-free or uncontaminated by the prevailing political and social ideology of the age in which it appears. The message of Darwin's *Origin* and particularly Spencer's popularization, may be convincingly viewed as a corollary expression of the Victorian social structure no less than Lysenko's genetic experiments were of Soviet social theory. Similarly, John McLoughlin has taught us the impossibility of properly understanding nineteenth-century pietism without studying its secular expression in Jacksonian faiths.[45] Herein lies phrenology's greatest value to the scholar. Because it addressed a wide range of issues and committed itself to many of the premises regarding the nature of man and of human society held during this period, phrenology's rise, flourishing, and eventual decline describe in miniature the fate of so many segments of nineteenth-century thought and idealisms.

NOTES

Epigraph: Johann G. Spurzheim, *The Physiognomical System of Drs. Gall and Spurzheim,* 2nd ed. (London: Baldwin, Cardock and Joy, 1815), p. 345.

1. George Combe, *Notes on the United States of North America during a Phrenological Visit in 1838-9-40* (Philadelphia: Carey and Hart, 1841) 2:321-54; John D. Davies, *Phrenology: Fad and Science* (New Haven: Yale Univ. Press, 1955), p. 21.

2. Combe, *Notes* 2:104.

3. "Literary Reviews," *Ladies' Companion* 15 (May 1841): 48, cited in Davies, *Phrenology,* p. 22n; Combe, *Notes* 1:361-62.

4. "Combe on Phrenology," *Philadelphia Journal of the Medical*

and Physical Sciences 5 (1822): 398-424; "Phrenology Made Easy," *Knickerbocker Magazine* 2 (June 1838): 523-27; "Combe's Lectures on Phrenology," *Eclectic Journal of Medicine* 3 (Nov. 1838): 32-34; [Park Benjamin], "The Late Dr. Spurzheim," *New England Magazine* 4 (Jan. 1833): 40-47.

5. Gall's concept of the mind was not new; a faculty psychology based on localized brain functions had been proposed as early as Galen and as recently as Scottish common sense philosophy. But Gall stressed the functional role of the mind, and, more importantly, removed the study of the mind from the province of theology and metaphysics and placed it among the biological and medical sciences. Gall's work also challenged the two major epistemological philosophies: the rationalistic view of innate ideas as the sources of man's knowledge (Plato and Descartes) and the sensationalistic (Locke, Condillac, and Hume). Robert M. Young, *Mind, Brain and Adaptation in the Nineteenth Century* (Oxford: Clarendon Press, 1970), p. 15.

6. Owsei Temkin, "Gall and the Phrenological Movement," *Bulletin of the History of Medicine* 21 (1947): 276-81, 307-12; Davies, *Phrenology,* pp. 5-11; Anthony A. Walsh, "Phrenology and the Boston Medical Community in the 1830s," *Bulletin of the History of Medicine* 50 (1976): 261-73.

7. Douglas Adair, " 'That Politics May be Reduced to a Science': David Hume, James Madison, and the Tenth Federalist," *Fame and the Founding Fathers,* ed. Trevor Colbourn (New York: Norton, 1974), pp. 94-95; Bernard Crick, *The American Science of Politics: Its Origins and Conditions* (London: Routledge & Kegan Paul, 1959), pp. 4-6. The study of political science at the unviersity was a poor affair. Included under the rubric of moral philosophy in the curriculum, its texts never influenced the development of an American science of politics. Francis Wayland's *The Elements of Moral Science* (New York, 1835) and William Whewell's *Elements of Morality, Including Polity* (London, 1845; New York, 1856) were suffused with homilies about the relation of liberty to order and overlaid with didacticism. Crick, *American Politics,* p. 12.

8. Quoted in Adair, "Politics Reduced," pp. 95, 94.

9. Arthur Wrobel, "Orthodoxy and Respectability in Nineteenth-Century Phrenology," *Journal of Popular Culture* 9 (summer 1975): 38-50.

10. Garry Wills, *Inventing America: Jefferson's Declaration of Independence* (Garden City, N.Y.: Doubleday, 1978) argues that the Scottish philosophers influenced Jefferson's formulation of major ideas that he

wrote into the Declaration. See part 3. In minimizing the influence of John Locke, Wills challenges Carl L. Becker's study *The Declaration of Independence: A Study in the History of Political Ideas* (1922; rpt. New York: Vintage-Knopf, 1942). Other valuable discussions of the background of early American political thought include: Yehoshua Arieli, *Individualism and Nationalism in American Ideology* (Cambridge: Harvard Univ. Press, 1964); and Gordon S. Wood, *The Creation of the American Republic, 1776-1787* (Chapel Hill: Univ. of North Carolina Press,1969), especially Part 1 and chapter 15.

11. John Adams, *A Defence of the Constitution of Government of the United States of America,* in *The Works of John Adams* (Boston: Charles C. Little and James Brown, 1851), 4: 292; idem, *Four Letters,* ibid., 6: 483; Johann Gaspar Spurzheim, *Education: Its Elementary Principles Founded on the Nature of Man,* 12th American ed. (New York: Fowler & Wells, 1854), p. 271.

12. Temkin, "Gall," pp. 86-87, 306-7, 302-3; [Orson Squire Fowler], "Republicanism the True Form of Government: Its Destined Influence, and Improvement," *American Phrenological Journal* 8 (Sept. 1846): 271. This last is the first in a series of twelve articles that extends over three years. See also Combe, *Notes* 2:322-33.

13. [Elisha P. Hurlbut], "On Rights and Government," *United States Magazine and Democratic Review* 9 (Nov. 1841): 462. For a discussion of Shaftsbury's presence in early American political thought, see Arieli, *Individualism and Nationalism,* pp. 57-59.

14. Spurzheim, *Education,* p. 262; [Fowler], "Republicanism," 8 (Sept. 1846): 271-73; Combe, *Notes* 2:322-33.

15. [Fowler], "Republicanism," 8 (Nov. 1846): 339.

16. "The Course of Civilization," *United States Magazine and Democratic Review* 6 (Sept. 1839): 213; [Hurlbut], "On Rights," 9 (Nov. 1841): 464.

17. Combe, *Notes* 2:322.

18. Ibid., pp. 322-24.

19. Walt Whitman, "American Democracy," *The Gathering of the Forces,* Cleveland Rogers and John Black, eds. (New York: Putnam, 1920), 1:4; Samuel Gridley Howe, *A Discourse on the Social Relations of Man* (Boston: Marsh, Capen & Lyon, 1837), p. 7.

20. George Lyon, "Essay on the Phrenological Causes of the Different Degrees of Liberty Enjoyed by Different Nations," *Edinburgh Phrenological Journal* 2 (1824): 599-600; Don M. Wolfe, *The Image of Man in America,* 2d ed. (New York: Thomas Y. Crowell, 1950), p. 33; "The Progress of Society," *United States Magazine and Democratic*

Review 8 (July 1840): 68. For a background discussion about liberty, see Major L. Wilson, *Space, Time and Freedom: The Quest for Nationality and the Irrepressible Conflict, 1815-1861* (Westport, Conn.: Greenwood Press, 1974).

21. Wills, *Inventing America*, pp. 216-17, 149-54.

22. [Hurlbut], "On Rights," 9 (Dec. 1841): 570.

23. Combe, *Notes* 2:244.

24. Ibid., p. 333.

25. Spurzheim, *Education*, p. 262; Combe, *Notes* 1:xi-xii.

26. Combe, *Notes* 2:109; George Combe, *Lectures on Phrenology*, introduction and notes by Andrew Boardman (New York: Fowler & Wells, 1839), pp. 360-61.

27. Combe, *Notes* 2:341-43.

28. Ibid., p. 273.

29. George Combe, *The Constitution of Man Considered in Relation to External Objects*, 9th American ed. (Boston: William D. Ticknor, 1839), p. 200; Roger Cooter, *The Cultural Meaning of Popular Science: Phrenology and the Organization of Consent in Nineteenth-Century Britain* (Cambridge: Cambridge Univ. Press, 1984), p. 121; Combe, *Constitution*, p. 232. How Combe's rigid conservatism resembled a secular Calvinism constitutes but one motif in Roger Cooter's rich and exciting study. Cooter's study challenges the conventional view that phrenology, through Combe, contributed toward shaping positivist social philosophy and an intellectual climate receptive to socialist experiments and freethinking among English artisans. Phrenology did, and Cooter shows this, but not with Combe's blessings so much as through the efforts of others who chose to interpret Combe's doctrines according to their own ideological bent.

30. Combe, *Notes* 1:xii.

31. Elisha Bartlett, M.D., *An Address Delivered at the Anniversary Celebration of... the Organization of the Boston Phrenological Society, January 1, 1838* (Boston: Marsh, Capen & Lyon, 1838), pp. 17, 21, 22.

32. E[lisha] P. Hurlbut, *Essays on Human Rights and Their Political Guaranties*, with a preface and notes by George Combe (New York, 1845; Edinburgh: Maclachlan, Stewart, 1847). The first two chapters appeared as the two-part series "On Rights and Government" in the *Democratic Review*, as cited earlier. Hurlbut added another title to his list much later in the century: *A Secular View of Religion in the State, and the Bible in the Public Schools* (Albany, N.Y., 1870).

33. Combe, *Notes* 2:400.

34. Benjamin Fletcher Wright, Jr., *American Interpretations of Nat-*

ural Law (Cambridge: Harvard Univ. Press, 1931), p. 257; Hurlbut, *Essays,* pp. 221-22.

35. See Arieli, *Individualism,* p. 166; Rush Welter, *The Mind of America* (New York: Columbia Univ. Press, 1974), p. 173. See also [Fowler], "Republicanism," 9 (July 1847): 206-10; 9 (Dec. 1847): 370-73; 10 (Oct. 1848): 308.

36. [Fowler], "Republicanism," 11 (July 1849): 214.

37. Ibid., 9 (Dec. 1847): 371.

38. [Hurlbut], "On Rights," 9 (Dec. 1841): 576.

39. Arthur M. Schlesinger, *The Age of Jackson* (Boston: Little, Brown, 1945), pp. 314-17; Harold Kaplan, *Democratic Humanism and American Literature* (Chicago: Univ. of Chicago Press, 1972), p. 5.

40. Carl Becker, "What Is Still Living in Jefferson's Philosophy?" *The National Temper,* ed. Lawrence W. Levine and Robert Middlekauff (New York: Harcourt Brace & World, 1968), p. 106; Schlesinger, *Age of Jackson,* pp. 314-17; [Fowler], "Republicanism," 9 (Feb. 1847): 73.

41. [Fowler,] "Republicanism," 10 (Oct. 1848): 309-10.

42. [Hurlbut], "On Rights," 9 (Dec. 1841): 572-73.

43. H.R. Schetterly, "The Millennium," with notes by the editor [O.S. Fowler], *American Phrenological Journal* 8 (July 1846): 199-210. For other instances of Fowler's millennial thought see: "Progression a Law of Nature: Its Application to Human Improvement," *American Phrenological Journal,* 7 (March 1844): 73-77; June 1845: 161-66; O[rson] S[quire] Fowler and L[orenzo] N[iles] Fowler, *Phrenology: Proved, Illustrated and Applied* (New York: Fowler & Wells, 1836), p. 425; O[rson] S[quire] Fowler, *Creative and Sexual Science, or Manhood, Womanhood and Their Mutual Inter-Relations* (n.p., n.d.), p. 55.

44. John Higham, *From Boundlessness to Consolidation: The Transformation of American Culture, 1848-1860* repr. in Bobbs-Merrill Reprint Series in American History (New York: Bobbs-Merrill, 1969), pp. 15-21. See also Richard Hofstadter, *The American Political Tradition and the Men Who Made It* (New York: Knopf, 1973), pp. 162-82.

45. William G. McLoughlin, introduction to Charles Grandison Finney, *Lectures on Revivals of Religion* (Cambridge, Mass.: Belknap Press of Harvard Univ. Press, 1960).

HAROLD ASPIZ

7. Sexuality and the Pseudo-Sciences

In 1862 Eliza Farnham named the established "truths of the age ...in their chronological order" as "Reformed Medical Practice, Phrenology, Magnetism, Woman's Rights, [and] Spiritualism."[1] To this list I would add the "truth" of evolutionary eugenics, which, like all pseudo-sciences, formulated supposedly immutable "laws" of personal and racial improvement by combining scientific fact, millennial optimism, and a mechanistic approach to change. Formulas to perfect body and spirit through sexual means co-existed with the other pseudo-sciences and were a common denominator in many of them. Obsessed with health and generally assuming that one's bodily condition reflected one's spiritual state, Victorian reformers often lamented a perceived physical decline among their contemporaries when compared to the supposedly superior condition of their ancestors; and they interpreted this falling off as a sign of moral decay. To halt racial deterioration and to upgrade the population, reformers and pseudo-scientists advocated the selection of the best qualified parents who would breed according to prescribed "laws."

Victorian America articulated its concerns in sexual prescriptions and proscriptions. In this context, eugenic pseudo-scientists and reformers generally represented a liberating force, helping to demystify the sexual processes and enabling women to demand at least minimal control of their own sexuality. They fueled the pervasive faith in the improvability of the species and of the individual. They defended and broadened the limits of free speech and helped to bring about a respect for sexuality as a fundamental element in the human character. Their equation of success with being well begotten and well sexed contributed to the myth of the strongly sexed personality, so prominent in American culture from Whitman to Mailer, and beyond. Their conviction that sexual intercourse had a sanctifying spiritual element and that mutually orgasmic intercourse was productive of the most splendid offspring have etched themselves into our folklore. Their insistence that sex must be studied as a science has helped to spur the modern study of the subject.

The faith that the healthy body could be a moral force, an agent of progress, was deeply rooted in nineteenth-century thought. Catharine Beecher, the mother of physical education in America, Horace Greeley, and Walt Whitman were among the many sympathizers with the pseudo-sciences who considered physical regeneration to be the indispensable first step toward personal and national greatness.[2] Typically, Whitman decried the "pale, dissipated, 'used up' " American young men and the young women incapable of becoming the sort of healthy mothers that their grandmothers had been. Whitman's essay on moral and esthetic reforms, *Democratic Vistas* (1870), formulated a sexual-eugenic program for an America whose youth lacked the "magnetism of sex," were "puny, impudent, foppish, prematurely ripe, and characterized by an abnormal libidinousness" and a diminished "capacity for good motherhood." His language is that of the eugenic pseudo-sciences: "magnetism" alludes to the supposedly electrical basis of the sexual functions; premature ripeness to the inadequate development of the sexual powers, said to result in "green" children; "abnormal libidinousness" to the corruption of the body's capacity to reproduce. Whitman's suggested remedy—planting "crops of fine youths" who would, in turn, become America's best breeders—is based on the eugenic premise that the physiological upgrading of the American citizenry must precede, and form the basis of, political and moral advancement. He was convinced that America's "great common stock" (*i.e.*, a birthstock of vigorous young native-born Americans emerging from among the common people) could produce "copious supplies" of "healthy, acute, handsome individualities, modernized and fully adapted to our soil, our days, city and country."[3]

Like many of the pseudo-scientists, Whitman believed in what has been called the "procreative dream" of nineteenth-century eugenic reformers—"a renewed and more desperate attempt to control and shape procreative powers as if the American body politic were really a body"—to "have Anglo-Saxon parents reproduce on stock-breeding principles" in order to preserve "the blood of strong races in our veins" and reestablish a sound national health.[4] Among Whitman's contemporaries the famed anti-masturbation campaigner John Todd warned in 1867 that only sweeping physiological reforms could "prevent the rapid extinction of the American people." America's most prominent gynecologists, Drs. J. Marion Sims and Augustus Kinsley Gardner, maintained that by instituting physiological reforms and managing the reproductive process America could produce superior offspring: "There has never been a people with larger opportunities for building up a fine national physique, than we Americans enjoy," Gardner said. On the other hand, by neglecting the "laws" of scientific breeding and "the rules of health [America] may rapidly degenerate, or even disappear, as the poor Indians are doing." Conservative eugenic reformers like Gardner viewed the control of the parenting process as a means to alter the race without changing the social system; but many radical reformers saw sexual reform as the key to all social improvement.[5]

An important eugenic passage in Whitman's *Democratic Vistas* asserts that America's future greatness depends on scientific breeding. Whitman proposes that parents capable of transmitting the best hereditary traits should create a "clear-blooded" progeny of nordic Americans. Brashly identifying himself as an "ethnologist,"[6] he proposes a "new ethnology" grounded on the recognizable principles of sexual reformism:

Parentage must consider itself in advance. (Will the time hasten when fatherhood and motherhood shall become a science—and the noblest science?) To our model, a clear-blooded, strong-fibred physique is indispensable, the questions of food, drink, exercise, assimilation, digestion, can never be intermitted. Out of these we descry a well-begotten selfhood—its youth, fresh, ardent, emotional, aspiring, full of adventure; at maturity, brave, perceptive,...and a general presence that holds its own in the company of the highest. (For it is native personality, and that alone, that endows a man to stand before presidents and generals, or in any distinguish'd collection, with *aplomb*—and *not* culture, or any knowledge or intellect whatever.)[7]

Whitman's goal of scientific begetting—a process which would endow children with desirable native qualities and thus inaugurate a new American race—was shared by two generations of eugenic pseudo-scientists.

Reformers tried to synthesize the antithetical Victorian attitudes toward sexuality: that sex was an animalistic attribute which must be curbed and that sex was a sacred gift designed to produce superb children. With few exceptions, their sexual theories were tinged with an advocacy of sexual continence or abstinence (although these terms were given a broad latitude of interpretation), as if to say that orgasmic intercourse was sanctified only when it was intended to produce children. At its extreme, the attitude that sex was inherently vile was represented by Thomas Lake Harris, a spiritualist whose program of sexless monogamy was designed to thwart sexual desire altogether ("Monogamists who enter into union with me rise, by changes of life, *into a desire for the death of natural sexuality*") and by the followers of George Rapp, the mystic communitarian, who advocated total celibacy as a means to restore God's kingdom on earth: "Since man's fall, the sexual organs have become bestial and separated, contrary to God's design...all intercourse of the sexes, both in and out of marriage [is] pollution [an act of unredeemed man]. After his fall Adam no longer begat a son in the image of God but in his own sexual likeness. All men and women born since Adam are his sinful posterity, all have the bestial sexual organs, and all, because they represent only a half, and that the fallen half, of the original Adam, are living symbols of the disharmony brought into the world by Adam's sin." After the cessation of all sexual intercourse, the truly celibate would be reborn as saints.[8] (In this light, we may appreciate the profound eugenic meaning of Whitman's *Democratic Vistas* and of the new Adam in his poems, whose being reconciles the natural and divine halves of the original Adam into one noble creature, the very ideal of American sexual reformers.)

One of the many reformers who tried to accommodate the revulsion against sexuality to the ubiquitous evidence that Victorians had strong sexual drives was A. J. Ingersoll, who operated a marriage and sex "cure" in Corning, New York. Ingersoll, a conservative mind curist, made two assumptions: first, that the repression of women's naturally powerful sexual drives leads to a broad range of "female" diseases, malfunctions, and hysteria; second, that these problems can be remedied by a faith in Jesus Christ and by women's cheerful submission to the rule of their husbands in all matters. Such compliance, he said, would cure menstrual ailments, which, in turn, are manifestations of the wife's resistance to her husband's marital prerogatives. A nation of submissive Christian women would find, in Ingersoll's phrase, that they had been "born again sexually," that their husbands had become loving and devoted but at the same time less insistent on frequent sexual intercourse, and (in a notion that runs through most of these eugenic formulations) that their sexual relations had become much more pleasurable. Ingersoll intended his restrictive system to bring about higher levels of chastity and morality and, at the same time, to produce better children. Children born as a consequence of the infrequent and reverential, but decidedly ardent, matings of enlightened parents were sure to be superior beings.[9]

The pseudo-scientific formulas for attaining an improved progeny which were published between 1830 and 1900 generally involved several tenets. Most important of these was an obligation to analyze the traits inherited from one's parents and those inherited by one's prospective spouse. Because ancestral strengths and infirmities were thought to be transmitted to one's offspring, the coupling of persons with similar natural flaws would result in inferior children. These formulas generally forbade "premature marriages, especially of delicate females, and persons strongly disposed to hereditary disease"; "marriage between partners too nearly allied in blood, particularly when either of them is descended from an unhealthy race"; and "great disproportion in age between parents." Prospective bridegrooms were told to find mates endowed with the "vital" temperament—robust, strongly sexed, well-muscled, large-breasted, wide-hipped, large in the pelvis, fair complexioned (as best suited to childbearing), and to avoid corseted, wasp-waisted women. At the beginning of our century, Bernarr Macfadden, the impresario of the physical culture industry, could still counsel men to "Marry a Woman, not a Corseted Sexless Nonentity," and warn them that if they married a wife who lacked a vigorous sex drive their marriages were sure to fail. Macfadden also instructed men that they must be powerfully sexed if they would succeed as husbands, businessmen, or artists: "The sexual power of a man indicates with marvelous accuracy his general physical and mental condition." These formulas also specified a long abstinence from sexual indulgence when children were not desired; a period of preparation and self-enlightenment preceding the decisive coitus which created the child; sexual consummation only when both of the partners are ready, with particular emphasis on the woman's passionate readiness for sexual congress; heroically vigorous copulations to engender the child; prolonged abstinence from sexual indulgence following impregnation; and the proper nurture both in the womb and during the child's formative years. The formulas were based on the premise that a child's character and constitution are determined by "the state of the parents at the time of conception" and by "the state of health and conduct of the mother during pregnancy."[10]

Among the most prolific American preceptors of eugenic sexual reform during the four decades commencing in the 1830s were the Fowler brothers, phrenologists, whose periodical pieces, pamphlets, and books collectively totaled thousands of pages and possibly reached millions of readers. Like most eugenic reformers, their work was repetitious, humorless, dogmatic, and constantly changing to meet the encroachment of new scientific knowledge. Lorenzo Niles Fowler's little volume

The Principles of Phrenology and Physiology, Applied to Man's Moral Nature, appropriating the phrenological ideas of Johann Gaspar Spurzheim and George Combe, told readers how to evaluate each of the forty or so of their phrenological organs (or "faculties") located in the brain in order to determine the sort of children they would, or could, bring into the world. Lorenzo Fowler saw phrenology as a handmaiden of conventional monogamy. Thus he described a phrenological organ of Philoprogenitiveness, governing the conduct of tender parenthood; an organ of Union for Life; an organ of Inhabitiveness, governing both patriotism and loyalty within the marriage relationship; and an organ of Amativeness, governing the sex drive, whose powerful development in both parents he deemed essential for the soundest mating. He voiced what was to become an operative principle among eugenic reformers: that sexual intercourse transmits the parents' weakest traits with the same precision as it does their best traits; therefore they must strengthen their good qualities and temper their weaker ones if they wish to improve the "product" of their lovemaking, paying careful attention to their physical and mental states at the time of the fateful insemination.[11]

Lorenzo Fowler's best-seller *Marriage: Its History and Ceremonies* expressed another eugenic principle: desired natal traits are transmitted to the unborn child during intercourse by means of a sort of science of the mind which raises the will power of the parents to a veritable biological force. "As is the *mental condition* of the parents, particularly the mother, before the birth of the child—so is the state of the mind after birth; and this principle also extends to an influence on bodily conditions." He also endorsed the venerable notion that an individual's body affords accurate data (derived from the reading of the physiognomic features or the phrenological "head bumps," say)—clues that may be used to diagnose the prospective parents and improve the results of their matings. Quite typically, he insisted that his method of analyzing the physiques and pseudoscientific indicators, then modifying the physical and mental states in order to bring about the production of better children, was in keeping with God's plan and nature's laws.[12]

But it was Orson Squire Fowler, America's premier phrenological ideologue, who developed the most elaborate formulations of phrenology, sex, marriage, and nurture. His manual on heredity and sex, *Love and Parentage*, a self-styled "missionary volume from God," prescribed the means for realizing "the boundless capabilities and perfections of our God-like nature" and eliminating "the scape-goats of humanity which infest our earth," thus repairing the damage done by Adam's fall. Bringing about the Christian millennium by the scientific management of the birth processes was a tenet of the eugenic pseudo-sciences. The premise of Fowler's book was that each aspect of human existence is governed by combinations of the forty or more phrenological faculties, all of which can be modified during one's lifetime and even in the midst of sexual intercourse, when they are "*temporarily* excited"; that all human traits are sexually transmissible; and that copulation is an instrumentality of human control and betterment. Even the most transitory condition—the result of an inflammation or of an exhilarated mood—is passed on in the "sub-magnetic fluid," which seems to be produced by the twin magnetic poles (located in the brain and in the chest of each parent). Sexual intercourse, thus defined, is a "reciprocity" of life-giving and life-supporting magnetism, or electricity, in which each phrenological faculty emits an electrical charge corresponding precisely to its condition and strength. These electrical emanations are blended in the brain of the child, thus patterning the child's personality. When the parents' traits are complementary or dissimilar, they become "balanced" in the character of the child; when the parents' traits are similar, they become intensified in the child.[13]

The electrical nature of the sex act was imaginatively described by the Fowler and Wells staffer Daniel Harrison Jacques, a specialist in the pseudo-science of the temperaments. Jacques identified electricity as a "subtile fluid" which "seems to form the connecting link between the soul and the body, and to be the instrument by means of which the former builds, rebuilds, or shapes the latter. It is generally supposed to be electric or magnetic in nature. The ancient Magians called it *living fire*." Although this magnetic essence is a distillation of our basic selfhood, he claimed, we can purposefully modify it by training our faculties. As each faculty is exercised, it stimulates a corresponding element of the brain's magnetic current. And, expressing a concept that became an article of faith among eugenic pseudo-scientists and reformers, Jacques argued that the magnetic fluid when not expended during sexual activity but chastely conserved and stored up within the body, "rebuilds," strengthens, and beautifies the individual. Variations of this electromagnetic theory of sexual intercourse were widespread in the literature of sexual reform, even among such "scientific" expositors as Dr. Edward Bliss Foote.[14]

Desirable hereditary traits can be bestowed and superior offspring created, the thrice-married Orson Fowler urged, only by married lovers engaged in a "spiritual banquet of love." Like many eugenic reformers, he enunciated a "law" of heroic copulation, reasoning "that the *product* of any given function is more or less perfect in proportion to the perfection of the *function itself*" and that "the health or disease, vigor or feebleness, &c., of *offspring*" varies with "the energy or tameness of that function which gives them being and capability." (Were he less circumspect, Fowler would certainly have added the widely credited belief—as expressed in an 1839 marriage manual—that "an immediate [orgasmic] response of the female at the moment of emission" is "indispensable to accomplish a healthy impregnation.") As though describing a manufacturing process, Fowler argued that the "*quantity*" and intensity of sexual intercourse are critical: "Other things being equal, the more powerful this function and intense its action at the time it stamps the impress of life and character on its products, the more highly endowed such products. Hence, at those occasions every means consistent with its healthy action should be employed to augment its intensity. Indeed, those who incur the liability of becoming parents EXCEPT when this function is wrought up to its highest pitch of intensity, are BAD CITIZENS, and deserve the curse of their posterity." (Small wonder that Victorians were familiar with so many substances and concoctions intended to arouse tumescence and female passion.)[15]

Responsible parents, Fowler said, should bottle up their sexual passions prior to marriage and, to a large extent, during marriage in order to release them, as planned, in a volcanic baby-begetting session. Love "heightens the ardor of the parental embrace, and thereby improves the offspring" by creating "a spiritual communion promotive of parental pleasure, and so indispensable to the mental endowment of offspring." Healthy parents produce prime children; enfeebled parents "violate the laws of matrimony" and produce weaklings. Regulated copulation enjoyed when woman's sexual passion has crested in an irrepressible urge to become pregnant and when the actions of both parents are controlled by the noblest aspirations for the child-to-be can assure optimum results. To accommodate the Victorian cliché that women were less "passional" and that they take much longer to reach their sexual peak, reformers assumed that the flaring up of woman's dormant sexual desire signaled her readiness for impregnation. Hence she should never be compelled to have intercourse. Narrow-minded as was this male version of female self-determination, Fowler had asserted a principle of nineteenth and twentieth-century feminism: the right of women to control their sexuality and, in a measure, their own bodies.[16]

Henry C. Wright, who touted his "Law of Reproduction" as the means to expel disease, regenerate human nature, and reform society, affirmed that "higher types of Humanity" cannot be produced "till the passional intercourse is brought into subjection to marriage-love." "The *perpetuation and perfection of the race* are the two great objects of sexual intercourse," declared Wright, a well-known reformer, abolitionist, lecturer on marriage, and sex "clinician." "Progress, not pleasure, is our aim," he declared. "The purest enjoyment is indeed designed to be experienced in intercourse when prompted solely by love and a desire for offspring. But unless such pleasure is mutual, the offspring of such a union must be imperfect and distorted in its constitutional tendencies." In the intervals between the sessions of lovemaking, the unexpended "sexual element" becomes a reservoir of "magnetic power" between the sexes. Attempting to reconcile reformist eugenics and conventional religion, Wright explained that the magnetism of sex is fully awakened only during "passional intercourse" in an ecstatic union of two souls—"the hour of highest spiritual communion, when heart and soul are merged in the consciousness of but one existence, one life, one eternity." Like other reformers, he cautioned against the wasting of the vital element (semen) in the marriage bed when children were not desired. He, too, insisted that the wife must not be compelled to sexual intercourse "till she demands it, and is ready cheerfully to receive, nourish, and develop...a living, healthy, perfect child." He expressed an idea that became an article of faith among feminist reformers, that woman is a "maternal" creature rather than a "sexual" one; hence a good husband must accord his wife complete authority in sexual matters: "It is woman's *right*, not her privilege, to control the surrender of her person...of all woman's rights, this is the most sacred and inalienable."[17]

Orson Fowler's *Hereditary Descent* makes clear why the upgrading of future generations depends on skillful copulation. Put simply, a child's traits of body and mind are not acquired but inborn. "The physical and mental capacities of mankind are INNATE, not created by education—have a CONSTITUTIONAL character inherited from parents, instead of being a blank on which education and circumstances write ALL they contain." All is transmissible; "all is hereditary." But even those with defective organisms should strive to improve themselves to their biological limits—even if the improvement is only temporary—in order to transmit the best traits to their offspring. According to this vulgar biological determinism, good qualities in a child come from good qualities in the parents. "Our primary mental powers must be CREATED before education can have any data on which to operate. Education can only DEVELOP AND DIRECT what is born in and with us." By way of illustration (and a point not lost on Walt Whitman, who owned a copy of this book), Fowler insisted that "Poetry is INHERITED, not educational," that the "poetic TEMPERAMENT...is transmitted," particularly from the right sort of mother. "What son of genius was ever born of dolts?" he scoffed. "And when, in fact, the proper attention is paid to HEREDITARY influences," and people learn "to regulate their matrimonial choice as to produce offspring endowed with WHATEVER qualities may be desired," a new and unblemished race will people the earth "and earth become a perfect paradise."[18]

Because the quality of a child was deemed to be regulated by the condition of its parents, the production of genius could be treated as a technology. The process involved the timing of the fateful copulation at that moment when the man and the woman, having hoarded their sexual reserves, were most intensely "passional," the fixation of the parents' minds on the material and spiritual attributes with which their offspring was to be endowed, the electrical transfer of their cherished desires through their will power and the sexual-magnetic fluid, and the obedience to countless "laws." Dante, Petrarch, Goldsmith, Coleridge, and Schiller were all descendants of mature, spiritually minded parents, explained an obscure author, whereas Cesare Borgia and Boccaccio were bastards, children of lust, so that the one grew up to be a dissolute tyrant, the other a dissolute author. Orson Fowler cited other illustrative case histories: a girl who conceived out of wedlock while in a drunken stupor gave birth to an idiot, a judge who was mirthful during his lovemaking fathered a jolly child, and a whaleman who had been gored amidships begot a child with a weak groin.[19]

John Cowan's "Law of Genius," intended to upgrade the "mediocre" quality of mankind, enunciates this principle: "That in its plastic state, during ante-natal life, like clay in the hands of the potter, it [the child] *can be molded into absolutely any form of body and soul its parents may knowingly desire*." "The reformation of the world can never be accomplished," Cowan claimed, "the millennium of purity, chastity, and intense happiness can never reach this earth, except through cheerful obedience to pre-natal laws." According to Cowan's phrenologically tinged *The Science of a New Life*, the first step toward a perfect marriage ("The Law of Choice") requires couples to marry when they attain physiological ripeness, when their "life-power" matures—the man at thirty years of age, sober, moral, and masculine; the woman "at twenty-four, perfectly developed, ripe and lovable," and well sexed. A spouse should not be chosen because of affection or romance but because an analysis of the temperaments and phrenological faculties reveals a well-matched pairing of parental traits. When traits are too much alike, they generate insufficient magnetic attraction and inhibit the production of children.[20]

The core of Cowan's program was his "law of continence," which, with certain variations, was echoed by many reformers: "The noble army of the continent of mankind" is made up of those who don't drink, smoke, wear corsets, dress ostentatiously, overeat, or live sedentary lives. They practice "voluntary and entire abstinence except when used for procreation," and they do not misuse the marriage bed for the "perverted amativeness" of physical pleasure or sexual relief. Since Amativeness, the phrenological organ of the sex drive, is located at the rear of the lower skull along with other animal faculties, it may become an organ of animal lust. But coitus that occurs when Amativeness has been subordinated to Spirituality, the organ of reverence located at the top of the head, permits the highest sexual-magnetic impulses to be telegraphed from the brain of the parents to the brain of their child. The "law of continence" mandates one heroic procreative session every two years during a sunny August or September morn, so that the child may be born in springtime. Following a four-week period in which the prospective parents, in a spiritual mood, have been focusing their will powers on those qualities with which they want to endow their child, their copulation generates an electrical transference of these very qualities to the child. The act of mating should occur in a pleasant room between 11 a.m. and noon, when the sun, the electrical heart of the universe, is at its zenith, reinforcing the parents' electricity, the interchange of which is the essence of begetting and conceiving. (Parents should copulate "in active exercise when the sun is up in the heaven, so as to furnish electrical states of body," affirmed a distinguished physician.) Prior to this "interview" the couple have been sleeping apart in separate bedrooms in order to store up the mysterious sexual-magnetic fluid; and following the conception the continent couple resume sleeping apart during pregnancy, "natural childbirth," lactation, and until the much awaited August morn two years later when they are again ready to begin the mating cycle.[21]

Even those reformers who challenged institutionalized marriage affirmed most of the eugenic principles heretofore discussed, including the need for sexual continence and chastity in relation to creating children. John Humphrey Noyes composed a scandalous and widely read tract, "Male Continence," which outlined his celebrated formula to allow a broad latitude of pleasurable sexual experiences, including the female orgasm, while at the same time retaining the precious semen for the sacred purpose of propagation. His scheme of "Bible communism" was essentially a perfectionist eugenic science. His method of *coitus reservatus* (penetration without male orgasm), permitting "*scientific* procreation" in which men saved up their sexual powers for the union that would engender the superior child—a child sanctioned by the community's eugenic planners—was said to conform to the principles of physiology and to the divine law, and to elevate and ennoble society. Noyes's most distinctive contribution to sexual reform, however, may have been his teaching that pleasurable and varied sexual intercourse helps to develop social skills, morality, and humane sentiment, even while the precious semen is being hoarded until such time as the community may sanction the impregnation of a selected woman by a selected man. To offset criticism that intercourse intended for mere pleasure was controlled by the baser instincts,[22] Noyes revised phrenological dogma, contending that "strictly speaking, the [phrenological] organs of propagation are *physiologically* distinct from the [phrenological] organs of union in both sexes"; the "propagative" organs may be animalistic, but what he calls the "amative" organs are distinctly spiritual. Noyes, too, defined intercourse as "a medium of magnetic and spiritual interchange, an exercise in social magnetism," a "vital element" in the well-being of men and women. While raising recreational sex to one of the social graces, Noyes insisted on the strictest control of the *birth* process by enforcing the same sort of "laws" advocated by Fowler and Cowan. Only the fittest parents would be chosen by the community to propagate and only when they were deemed ready to do so. In the performance of this sacred and civic duty the male would finally expend the semen that he had so carefully hoarded.[23]

Sexual "laws" were also espoused by advocates of "free love."

Although he denounced traditional monogamy and believed that men and women are promiscuous by nature, Ezra Heywood insisted that love is itself sacred. An anarchist, civil libertarian, and feminist, he defended "sexual thought and experiment," maintaining that the divine mission of liberated lovers is to be "students in the laboratories of their own bodies." Invoking the pseudo-scientific notions of electrical biology and Francis Liebig's equation of bodily heat and the life force, he defended sexual intercourse for its own sake: "Health, Temperance, Self-Control, and native grace are developed by intimate exchange of Heat and Magnetism, while both sexes are thereby fitted for Parentage." The stronger and more practiced the sexual art, Heywood insisted, the better one is qualified for successful parenthood. Heywood rejected abstinence, abortion, and contraception as harmful and unnatural; to avoid unwanted impregnation, he prescribed *coitus reservatus* and the rhythm method. Like Noyes, Heywood distinguished between sociable intercourse and the act of begetting children. And like all eugenic reformers, he insisted that the engendering of children was a momentous act that must be performed subject to immutable "laws." Heywood's feisty little book of sexual criticism, *Cupid's Yokes*, became the special target of Anthony Comstock and his retinue of smut hunters, I suspect, because Heywood was perceived by them as the subverter of two sacrosanct Victorian institutions: monogamous marriage and the spending of semen solely for begetting.[24]

The feminization of sexual reform built upon the same eugenic "laws." Alice Stockham, a Chicago-based physician, drew from Noyes's pamphlet (without crediting him) to propose her own combination of continence and sexual enjoyment, which she called Karezza. Like Noyes and like several of her contemporary women and men sexual reformers, she advocated a sexual embrace not climaxed by orgasm but controlled by the concentrated will power of both lovers. She, too, insisted on the spirituality of the sex act whether it was intended for propagation or for loving togetherness. But she made a breakthrough toward twentieth-century mysticism by asserting that sexual intercourse can culminate in an exalted mental state. She envisioned a sexual embrace which would reconcile sex and spirit, traditional Christianity and an orgiastic Bacchic transcendence, physical and spiritual ecstasy. The prolonged but restrained physical pleasure of Karezza could become an epiphany: "In the course of an hour the physical tension subsides, the spiritual exaltation increases, and not uncommonly visions of a transcendent life are seen and consciousness of new powers experienced." These are magic moments of "spiritual truth," when the soul rules the body and the harmony of the universe vibrates through men and women to be expressed in their reproductive powers.

Karezza could also become the vehicle of spiritual growth:

> In the physical union of male and female there may be a soul communion giving not only supreme happiness, but in turn conducing to soul growth and development. There may, also, be a purpose and power in this communion, when rightly understood, not less significant than the begetting of children. Creative energy in man is manifold in its manifestations, and can be trained into channels of usefulness. Consciously it may be utilized in every activity, devising, inventing, constructing. It may be directed to building bodily tissue and permeating every cell with health and vigor. Sex in nature is universal, progressing from lower to higher manifestations of life.[25]

But these ideas did not lessen Stockham's regard for the careful production of children or for the holy function of maternity. Like Margaret Fuller, Eliza Farnham, and a host of male and female reformers, she defined motherhood as "a divinely appointed mission," in conformity "with nature's plan, a law of spirit," obedience to which will "lessen or entirely overcome the usual sufferings of pregnancy and parturition."[26]

Dr. Stockham had touched upon two themes whose importance seemed to increase in the course of the century: that the procreative substance retained in the body can strengthen and inspire the psyche, and that sexuality is the basis of artistic creativity. Earlier reformers had often quoted the precept that "*totus homo semen est,*" that semen was man's microcosm, the vehicle of his immortality. The conservative sexual reformer Eliza Duffey had named semen as "an important constituent of manhood...the very essence of life. It is necessary for the proper development of a man, that this should be secreted, and then reabsorbed into his system, adding vigor and tone to his whole being." Dr. Gardner defined sperm as "the purest extract of the blood," which, when not spent in begetting, could be reabsorbed to "nourish" the male system with "an entirely new energy and a virility which contributes to the prolongation of life."[27] In this context, one is perhaps prepared for Dr. Stockham's declaration that semen, "when retained in the system may be coined into new thoughts, perhaps new inventions, grand conceptions of the true, the beautiful, the useful; or into fresh emotions of joy and impulses of kindness and blessing all around." Retained semen, which facilitates "procreation on the mental and spiritual planes, instead of the physical," is as much "a part of the generative function as is the begetting of offspring." This "virile principle" can add to "man's magnetic, mental, and spiritual form," and it can bring "signs of this creative power...throbbing and pulsating through every fibre"—a power that can be devoted to "the world's interests and development."[28]

Here, somewhat refined, was Orson Fowler's notion that potent sexuality so "sexes" creative persons that their "ideas and feelings...impregnate the mentality" of others and that all great artists are well-sexed, "while the ideas of the poorly sexed are tame, insipid, emasculated, and utterly fail to awaken enthusiasm."[29] Here, too, we may recognize Whitman's self-advertisements as a spermatic "brawny embracer" whose sexual superfluity qualified him to become America's greatest poet and who illustrated, in a number of his poems, the way that the Whitman persona's sexual arousal (with and without climax) coincided and merged with his magic moments of sexual-creative exaltation. (As a Whitmanite, Dr. Stockham should have understood the poet's intent.) Here, also, lay the point of Herman Melville's humorous contrast between the "spermatic" Lord Byron, who was both horny and artistically creative, and the woebegone Bartleby, a character devoid of any trace of the virile principle. Melville symbolically equated stored-up sperm and worldly success in *Moby-Dick*, when he described the whaling ship *Bachelor*, its hold brimming with accumulated sperm oil, cheerily returning to its home port after a profitable whale-hunting expedition. And as late as 1922 these tenacious ideas stirred the imagination of Ezra Pound, who shouldered a heavy burden of pseudo-scientific baggage, identifying the semen with brain fluid, making "a certain connection between complete and profound copulation and cerebral development"; finding a close relation in the spiritual and phallic religions; defining semen as a creative reservoir, the conservation of which enables one to "super-think"; locating the center of creativity in the male sexual element; and reviving the pseudo-scientific dogma that to control the semen is somehow to control personal and racial destiny.[30]

As documented in the exemplary studies of Hal D. Sears and Taylor Stoehr, the movement for social reform in the nineteenth century was large, fluid, even amorphous. Sexual reform was often linked to social, spiritualist, and scientific causes in schemes to ameliorate the lot of mankind and, most particularly, of womankind. Given the Victorian constraints on free speech, and specifically the prosecutions and persecutions that Anthony Comstock and his minions directed toward the dissemination of information relating to sexual practice and birth control, most reformers necessarily developed a kind of obscure and reticent language. Surely much of the century's advocacy of chastity and continence amounted to a tacit call for efficacious birth control rather than a moral appeal for fundamental abstinence from sexual intercourse. Particularly, there seems to have been an obscuring of the idea of continence and that of *coitus reservatus* in the formulations of Noyes, Robert Dale Owen, the Dianists, and many other reformers. Nor should one overlook the fact that the eugenic reformers, whose programs ranged from the conservative to the anarchistic, represented a wide range of ideologies and were themselves a most varied group. And despite what may now be perceived as some rather strange views on their part, many of them were ardent defenders of free thought and heroes and heroines in the causes which they espoused.

In the century and a half since pseudo-scientific eugenics first became a part of American thought, we have become much more sophisticated concerning the physiology and psychology of sex. Yet much remains mysterious. To speak charitably, the Fowlers, Cowan, Stockham, and dozens of others were not altogether unworthy predecessors of Havelock Ellis, Alfred Kinsey, and Shere Hite. However flawed, their works are indispensable to those who seek to understand the sexual attitudes of the last century and to explore the roots of our present-day interpretations of sexuality.

Notes

1. Mrs. Eliza W. Farnham, "A Lecture on the Philosophy of Spiritual Growth," pamphlet (San Francisco: Valentin & Co., 1862), p. 62.

2. Catharine E. Beecher, *Physiology and Calisthenics for Schools and Families* (New York: Harper & Brothers, 1856); Horace Greeley, *Hints towards Reforms* (New York: Fowler & Wells, 1853). See also T.W. Higginson, *Out-Door Papers* (Boston: Ticknor & Fields, 1863). Dozens of authors reached similar conclusions.

3. Walt Whitman, "What Are We Coming To?" *Brooklyn Daily Times*, Aug. 5, 1857; idem *Democratic Vistas*, in *Prose Works 1892*, ed. Floyd Stovall (New York: New York Univ. Press, 1964), pp. 369-72, 377-79; *The Correspondence of Walt Whitman*, ed. Edwin H. Miller (New York: New York Univ. Press, 1961): 2:18-19.

4. Ben [*sic*] Barker-Benfield, "The Spermatic Economy: A Nineteenth-Century View of Sexuality," in *The American Family in Social-Historical Perspective*, ed. Michael Gordon (New York: St. Martin's, 1973), pp. 351-52.

5. G.J. Barker-Benfield, *The Horrors of the Half-Known Life: Male Attitudes toward Women and Sexuality in the Nineteenth Century* (New York: Harper & Row, 1976), pp. 222, 293-98, 109-10, 301; Taylor Stoehr, *Free Love in America: A Documentary History* (New York: AMS Press, 1979), p. 125. On theories of racial improvability, see John S. Haller, Jr., *Outcasts from Evolution: Scientific Attitudes of Racial Inferiority, 1859-1901* (Urbana: Univ. of Illinois Press, 1971); Harold Aspiz, *Walt Whitman and the Body Beautiful* (Urbana: Univ. of Illinois Press, 1980), pp. 183-209. In a spirit of chauvinism reformers expressed the fear that healthy German and Irish immigrant women might become prize breeders because native white girls were physically unfit.

6. Whitman, "Passage to India," *Leaves of Grass: Comprehensive Reader's Edition*, ed. Harold W. Blodgett and Sculley Bradley (New York: New York Univ. Press, 1965), pp. 415-16.

7. Whitman, *Democratic Vistas*, pp. 395-97.

8. "Letter of Thomas Lake Harris" (1877), in *American Utopianism*, ed. Robert S. Fogarty (Itasca, Ill.: F. E. Peacock, 1972), pp. 105, 107; Karl J.R. Arndt, *George Rapp's Successors and Material Heirs* (Rutherford, N.J.: Fairleigh Dickinson Univ. Press, 1971), pp. 149-50. The quoted words are Arndt's.

9. Andrew J. Ingersoll, *In Health* (1899; rpt. New York: Arno Press, 1974), pp. 8, 15, 39, 110, 143-44, 249, and passim. The earliest edition in the Library of Congress is dated 1877.

10. Orson S. Fowler, "Laws of Hereditary Descent from 'Combe on Infancy,' " *American Phrenological Journal* 3 (Oct. 1840): 36-37; D.H. Jacques, *Hints toward Physical Perfection* (New York: Fowler & Wells, 1859), pp. 44-50; Bernarr A. Macfadden, *The Virile Powers: How Developed, How Lost, How Regained* (New York: Physical Culture Pub. Co., 1900), pp. 95-97.

Macfadden's *The Power and Beauty of Superb Womanhood* (New York: Physical Culture Pub. Co., 1901), a companion volume to *The Virile Powers*, lacks sexual details but is illustrated by photographs of women clad only in panties. Macfadden, whose physical culture magazines circulated in the millions of copies in the first four decades of our century and whose advertisements guaranteeing to transform every "97-pound weakling" into a muscleman graced hundreds of Sunday supplements, had hit upon a sure-fire formula for making money: combining nineteenth-century physiological "laws" with provocative photographs of half-clad athletic bodies.

11. Lorenzo Niles Fowler, *The Principles of Phrenology and Physiology* (1842; rpt. New York: Arno Press, 1974), pp. 12-14, 20-21, 36-37, 90-91, and passim.

12. Lorenzo Fowler, *Marriage: Its History and Ceremonies* (1889; [first ed. ca. 1841]; rpt., New York: Arno Press, 1974), pp. 193, 196-97.

13. Orson S. Fowler, *Love and Parentage, Applied to the Improvement of Offspring*...(New York: Fowler & Wells, 1846), pp. viii-ix, 20-29, 47-48, 81-82, and passim. Typically, in Orson S. Fowler's *Creative and Sexual Science* (Philadelphia: National Pub. Co., 1870), pp. 85-86, the theories are updated to accommodate more recent physiological discoveries.

Pseudo-scientists were vague about electricity, some attributing it to the male, some to both sexes. Margaret Fuller hinted that electricity is associated with sex and that women may have a greater supply of it: "The special genius of Woman I believe to be electrical in movement, intuitive in function, spiritual in tendency"; see her *Woman in the Nineteenth Century* (New York: Norton, 1971), p. 115.

14. Jacques, *Hints*, pp. 53-63; Hal D. Sears, *The Sex Radicals: Free Love in High Victorian America* (Lawrence: Regents Press of Kansas, 1977), p. 187.

15. Orson S. Fowler, *Love and Parentage*, pp. 39, 47-48, 106, 133-35; Orson S. Fowler, *Amativeness* (1889 [original ca. 1840]; rpt. New York: Arno Press, 1974), pp. 71-72; John Dubois, *Marriage Physiologically Discussed*, trans. William Greenfield (1839; rpt. New York: Arno Press, 1974), p. 101. Dubois cites a number of sexual stimulants (pp. 105-10); see also John S. Haller, Jr., *American Medicine in Transition, 1840-1910* (Urbana: Univ. of Illinois Press, 1981), pp. 112-15.

16. O.S. Fowler, *Love and Parentage*, pp. 118, 128-30. Fowler claimed that he had refuted Malthus and found the cure for overpopulation (pp. 143-44).

17. Henry C. Wright, *Marriage and Parentage: or, The Reproductive Element in Man* (1855; rpt. New York: Arno Press, 1974), pp. 237-39, 246-51, 257, 265, 271; Lewis Perry, *Childhood, Marriage, and Reform: Henry Clarke Wright, 1797-1870* (Chicago and London: Univ. of Chicago Press, 1980), pp. 231-38. Perry conjectures that Wright's version of continence and spiritual love may be another veiled reference to intercourse without ejaculation (pp. 239-41).

18. O.S. Fowler, *Hereditary Descent: Its Laws and Facts Applied to Human Improvement* (New York: Fowler & Wells, 1847), pp. 5, 34, 89-92, 130-31, 203-10, 280-81, and passim.

19. L.A. Hink, "The Relation of Marriage to Greatness," *American Phrenological Journal* 12 (1850): 60-66; O.S. Fowler, *Love and Parentage*, p. 32.

20. John Cowan, *The Science of a New Life* (1874; rpt. New York: Source Book Press, n.d.), pp. 137-39, 40-63, 32-33, and passim.

21. Cowan, *Science*, pp. 122, 169-72, 95-97, 394-95; A.K. Gardner, quoted in Barker-Benfield, *Horrors of the Half-Known Life*, p. 297.

22. Cowan, *Science*, pp. 109-10, rejects Noyes's method on these grounds and because accidental insemination is bound to occur.

23. John Humphrey Noyes, *Male Continence* (1872 [original ca. 1840]; rpt. New York: Arno Press, 1974), pp. 11-20.

Charles Knowlton's pioneering *Fruits of Philosophy* (1839; rpt. with intro. by Norman E. Himes, Mount Vernon, N.Y.: Peter Pauper, 1937) became notorious during the Bradlaugh-Besant trials of 1877-78. Combining utilitarianism and Spurzheim's phrenological eugenic laws of "hereditary descent," Knowlton argued in favor of early marriages combined with birth control in order to improve the breed and to avoid social disgrace, weaklings, and sexual frustration. He also cautioned against the psychological harm inflicted by zealous anti-masturbation and abstinence propagandists.

24. Ezra H. Heywood, *Cupid's Yokes: or, The Binding Force of the Conjugal Life* (1876; rpt. New York: Arno Press, 1974), pp. 5-23; Sears, *The Sex Radicals*, pp. 159, 162.

25. Alice B. Stockham, *Karezza: Ethics of Marriage* (1896; rpt. New York: Arno Press, 1974), pp. 13-14.

26. Ibid., 60-62, 108-11. On sexual ecstasy, see Wayland Young, *Eros Denied: Sex in Western Society* (New York: Grove Press, 1966), pp. 169-70.

27. Stockham, *Karezza*, pp. 21, 99-100; Augustus K. Gardner, *Conjugal Sins against the Laws of Life and Health* (1870; rpt. New York: Arno Press, 1974), pp. 162-63. For similar statements on sperm, see Dio Lewis, *Chastity: or, Our Secret Life* (1874; rpt. New York: Arno Press, 1974), p. 25; Eliza B. Duffey, *The Relation of the Sexes* (1876; rpt. New York: Arno Press, 1974), pp. 179-81. The volumes by Sears and Stoehr contain many versions of sexual theory and practice.

28. Stockham, *Karezza*, pp. 100, 16, 21.

29. O.S. Fowler, *Creative and Sexual Science*, pp. 220-21.

30. Ezra Pound, postscript to Rémy de Gourmont, *The Natural Philosophy of Love* (New York: Boni & Liveright, 1922), pp. 206, 218.

GEORGE HENDRICK

8. Washington Irving and Homoeopathy

Homoeopathy was "significant in its faddish popularity among the upper classes," notes John S. Haller, Jr., in *American Medicine in Transition, 1840-1910*, and "it also represented the last of the major systems to flourish before the onrush of extensive advances in germ theory, treatment of infection, pathology, and pharmaco-therapeutics."[1] Homoeopathy was, however, only one of several systems opposed to traditional medicine: water-cures, Mesmerism, faith cures, fads, and other isms proliferated in the United States and Europe in the nineteenth century. The battles among the various schools of medicine were bitter and protracted. Patients were often unable to evaluate the charges and counter-charges and made use of several of the systems of medicine.

This essay explores Washington Irving's conversion to homoeopathy and the controversies that developed after he embraced this "irregular" medical practice. Irving (1783-1859) was the first internationally known American writer, acclaimed for his fiction, histories, biographies, and travel books. He often worked when he was in ill health, for during his long and active diplomatic and creative life he suffered from a multitude of illnesses, some brought on, no doubt, by poor sanitation in America and Europe and others by his exposure to contagious diseases during his many travels, while still others were seemingly psychosomatic in origin.

When he was "taking the waters" in Mayence, he wrote to his sister on September 2, 1822, about one episode of poor health:

> I am now convinced, though reluctantly, that this malady has an internal origin, and arises from the derangement of the system, and particularly of the stomach. The anxieties that I suffered for three or four years in England used frequently to affect my stomach, and the fits of study and literary application, and the disuse of exercise to which I frequently subjected myself, and to which I had not previously been accustomed, all gradually prepared the way for some malady, and perhaps the one under which I at present suffer has prevented one of the more dangerous nature. I now foresee that it will take me some time, and patience, and care to restore my system to a healthful tone; all these external applications are but palliative; they relieve me from present pain and inconvenience, but it must be by diet, by gentle and slowly operating remedies, by easy recreation and tranquility, and moderate exercise of mind, that I must gradually bring my constitution once more into vigorous activity, and eradicate every lurking evil.[2]

Irving recognized the element of stress in his illness and also the curative powers of rest and change of scenery, and he often chose water-cures, which were usually painless. While he was at the spa at Mayence, he said, his mind was having a "complete holiday."

Irving did not dramatize his frequent illnesses when he wrote friends and relatives. On his trip West in 1832, writing from Independence, Missouri, on September 26, he noted only that he had "been much affected by the change of climate, diet & water" since he had been on his trip.[3] The implication is that he was suffering from intestinal complaints, but Irving, a veteran traveler, was obviously accustomed to such illnesses.

When it was necessary, Irving saw whatever doctors were available, and in his early life, before he turned to homoeopathy, he certainly had no prejudices against recommending a physician who used "heroic" measures. He wrote on August 29, 1842, from Madrid, where he was envoy extraordinary and minister plenipotentiary, that his major domo Benjamin had come down with pleurisy, "one of the most dangerous maladies of this place. I put him immediately in the doctors [*sic*] hands; had him bled and leeched and succeeded in checking the complaint which had got under alarming head way."[4]

During his last years, however, Irving turned against such heroic practices and sought relief through an unorthodox school of medicine, homoeopathy, founded by the German physician Samuel Hahnemann (1755-1843). Instead of such measures as bleeding and purging, favored by many orthodox physicians, Dr. Hahnemann proposed quite different approaches. A patient with specific symptoms was, in Hahnemann's system, to be treated with a drug which caused the same symptoms in a healthy person (*let likes be cured by likes*), and the patient was to be given highly diluted doses of the prescribed medicine. Dr. Hahnemann believed that during illness the body was more sensitive to drugs, and he used minute amounts of the active agent: 1/500,000 or 1/1,000,000 of a grain.[5] These dilutions were then *dynamized* by being struck against a leather pad. Dr. Hahnemann said of this procedure: "Homeopathic *dynamizations* are processes by which the medicinal properties of drugs, which are in a latent state in the crude substance, are excited and enabled to act spiritually (dynamically) upon the vital forces."[6] This spiritual medical theory, painless in practice, was to appeal in America to a wide variety of people: radical thinkers, Transcendentalists, religious groups such as Swedenborgians, German immigrants, women, parents with small children, writers, and intellectuals.

Homoeopathy was introduced into the United States in 1825 and began to develop a significant following after 1840; but this new school of medicine was from the first a subject of controversy. One of the most famous attacks was Dr. Oliver Wendell Holmes's amusing and scathing "Homoeopathy and Its Kindred Delusions," two lectures delivered in Boston in 1842 and soon published. Dr. Holmes believed that nine out of ten patients would recover from their illnesses under *any* medical system then in use; therefore, medical charlatans could easily point to their great number of miraculous cures.[7]

Using all his literary skills, Dr. Holmes analyzed four earlier medical delusions, beginning with the belief from the time of Edward the Confessor to the reign of Queen Anne that the touch of the English monarch would cure scrofula, and ending with the quackery of Dr. Perkins, whose tractors (two pieces of metal), when drawn over the afflicted part for a third of an hour, were believed by many to cure rheumatic and other complaints.

Homoeopathy, Dr. Holmes noted, "began with an attempt to show the insignificance of all existing medical knowledge. It not only laid claim to wonderful powers of its own, but it declared the common practice to be attended with the most positively injurious effects, that by it acute diseases are aggravated, and chronic diseases rendered incurable. It has at various times brought forward collections of figures having the air of statistical documents, pretending to show a great proportional mortality among the patients of the Medical Profession, as compared with those treated according to its own rules."[8] Dr. Holmes went on to attack the very basis of this new system and was sharply satirical in his analyses of Dr. Hahnemann's theories. He was methodical in his demolition of homoeopathic tenets, building his case slowly and with frequent traces of biting wit. The published essay was answered almost immediately by Hahnemann's true believers, who were unwilling to be branded quacks and charlatans.

Attacks such as Holmes's upon homoeopathy by "regular" physicians were not particularly successful. Many patients were more interested in the ability of the doctor to bring about a cure (especially a painless cure), and in his personality and bedside manner, than in the quarrel between rival schools of medicine.[9] The homoeopaths spent a great deal of time with patients, and this certainly contributed to their popularity.

There is no indication of just when and how Irving first learned of Hahnemann's system of medicine. Perhaps it was during Irving's travels in central Europe in 1822-23, for he took water-cures at Aix-la-Chapelle, Wiesbaden, and Mayence, where he could well have heard of Hahnemann. Irving himself was vague about his actual embracing of this "irregular" medical theory, and it may be that he had no real interest in homoeopathy until late in life. On December 20, 1853, he wrote his friend John P. Kennedy jocularly that his "homeopathic physician, who has my head in his hands, and is poisoning me into a healthy state of the brain by drachms and scruples," would not allow him to attend the dinner of the Maryland Historical Society.[10] Irving wrote Mrs. Kennedy on February 21, 1854, "I have found, in my own case, great relief from Homeopathy, to which I had recourse almost accidentally; for I am rather slow at adopting new theories." Irving went on to remark that after homoeopathic treatment he was able to apply himself to his literary labors.[11] Later in 1854, on August 31, Irving again wrote Mrs. Kennedy on the same subject: "You ask me whether the homeopathics still keep me quite well. I really begin to have a great faith in them. The complaint of the head especially, which troubled me last year, and obliged me to throw by my pen, has been completely vanquished by them."[12] By 1852 Irving had become a patient of Dr. J. C. Peters, in whom he had great confidence. Dr. Peters contended that Irving gave "cordial approval"[13] to homoeopathic principles, and that statement seems to be true, though it should be stressed that Irving did not see himself as a special pleader for homoeopathy as William Cullen Bryant did, did not himself make public statements about his medical preferences, and did not incorporate ideas from homoeopathy into his writing.

Dr. Peters (1819-93), this physician in whom Irving had such confidence, was a New Yorker who had studied medicine in Berlin, Vienna, and Leipzig. Upon his return from study abroad, Peters was examined in 1842 by the Comitia Minora of the Medical Society of the County of New York and was duly licensed to practice medicine. Perhaps influenced by his study in Germany, where there were many followers of Hahnemann, Dr. Peters was drawn to homoeopathy, developed a large practice, and became one of the editors of the *North American Journal of Homoeopathy*. He wrote widely on medical subjects, read avidly the literature of both schools of medicine, and counted nervous diseases among his medical specialties.[14]

According to Dr. Peters, Irving was suffering from dizziness but otherwise in good physical health in February of 1852, when the doctor first began seeing him. Dr. Peters described the state of mind of his patient who was at that time at work on the massive *Life of Washington*: Irving, he wrote, "had lately begun to be troubled with vertigo, suggesting the fear of apoplexy, more from the overtaxed condition of his brain than from any signs of failure of his general health."[15] For the vertigo, Dr. Peters prescribed Cocculus (Indian Berries), a specific homoeopathic treatment for the symptoms described by Irving. It seems obvious that Dr. Peters believed that many of Irving's problems were caused by mental strain. During the next few years Dr. Peters treated Irving's minor complaints, but it was one of Irving's self-treatments, Dr. Peters believed, that helped bring about a severe attack of asthma. During one of Irving's frequent catarrhal attacks Dr. Peters wrote that Irving was "over-persuaded to use Goodale's Catarrh Remedy by snuffing it up into the nostrils. The discharge was quickly dried up, and, ere long, some previous tightness of the chest was steadily developed into severe paroxysms of catarrhal and intensely spasmodic asthma."[16] Even before the severe asthma attack, Dr. Peters, concerned about Irving's difficulty in breathing, had found that his patient's heart was affected, but the doctor hoped that the heart disease might be "kept in abeyance."[17]

During the years that Irving's health began to deteriorate, the author clearly had great faith in the professional abilities of Dr. Peters and consulted him frequently. Though some of Irving's relatives had qualms about homoeopathy,[18] in the last seven years of his life he and his family consulted the doctor 598 times, and Dr. Peters often spent the night at Irving's home, "Sunnyside," when he made house calls. The relationship of doctor and patient was particularly cordial, as this letter of Irving's dated June 22, 1857, would indicate:

> "My Dear Dr. Peters:—I wish, before you embark on your short trip to Europe, you will have put up for me a few of those powders which proved so efficacious before. I hope you will be able to come up on Thursday, and stay over night with us, and expect you to put us all in such condition that we will need no physician while you are gone. Do not fail to come on Thursday, for my nieces would be disappointed not to see you before you leave."[19]

By the winter of 1858-59, as Irving was coming to the end of the fifth and last volume of his biography of George Washington, his health was much worse. He suffered, Dr. Peters wrote, "from loss of sleep, attacks of asthma, obstinate coughs, indigestion, feebleness, and nervousness." Dr. Peters went on to say that the heart problem was not valvular but an enlargement of the heart—"its sounds were muffled, occasionally it would falter in its beating, and, at times, manifest itself in a different kind of oppressed breathing from that which attended his severe and open attacks of asthma."[20] Irving's physical and emotional suffering was apparently great during his restless, sleepless nights. His nephew, Pierre M. Irving, described one night in January of 1859 when Irving, unable to sleep, was "haunted with the idea that he could not sleep." The nephew speculated about this "strange disease, which seemed to want reality, and yet the most distressing." That night Irving refused to go to his own bedroom but slept on a couch in the parlor; Dr. Peters occupied another couch until four o'clock, when he was relieved by Irving's nephew.[21] A pattern was beginning to develop: Irving, restless at night and afraid to stay alone, and Dr. Peters often staying with him. Whatever psychological factors were at work, Irving was obviously a sick man physically, seemingly suffering from congestive heart failure. Dr. Peters described one of his bedside watches: there would be signs of "impending dissolution," then "after many sudden gasps, and starts, and awakenings from this troubled and dangerous condition, his breathing would slowly and steadily become gentle and regular."[22]

In spite of these restless, troubled nights, Irving, during the day, continued his steady work on the final volume of the *Life of Washington*. On January 15, 1859, Dr. Peters paid Irving a visit at 5 p.m., intending to return to New York at 8, but Irving prevailed upon the doctor to spend the night. Pierre M. Irving commented, "The faithful Doctor still encourages us and himself with the hope that this is only a morbid condition of the nervous system, which may pass off, but I have at times an ominous feeling as if we were watching his decline. He also has, no doubt, his misgivings."[23] It must have been about this time that Dr. Peters told Irving about the enlargement of the heart. Almost twenty-five years after Irving's death Dr. Peters in an interview, recalled the scene in which he informed Irving of the seriousness of his illness:

I remember as if it were only yesterday the day I first told him his heart was affected....I explained to him my hopes and fears. I hoped by care to ward off any evil result, but I was in duty bound to tell him that there was danger to his life being brought to a close suddenly at any time. He looked me straight in the eye without a quiver or a change of color, and the first words he said were, 'Very well, Doctor, but let me beg you to mention it to nobody.'...He had a repugnance to being an object of sympathy to any one, and he shrank from the idea of having people watch for the moment when he should fall dead. However, he broke the intelligence himself to his nephew and secretary.[24]

Irving's declining health caused considerable alarm among his friends and admirers. One indication of this concern can be seen in the reaction of Dr. Oliver Wendell Holmes to Irving's health problems. Dr. Holmes, renowned as physician and author, visited Irving at "Sunnyside" on December 20, 1858. The two famous men had never before met. At the end of their social conversation Dr. Holmes made two suggestions to alleviate Irving's asthma and cough—medicated cigarettes and "Jonas Whitcomb's Cough Remedy." When Dr. Holmes wrote Irving thanking him for his hospitality, he sent along supplies of these medications.[25] In addition, Dr. Holmes wrote Dr. Peters to make suggestions about treating Irving. Dr. Peters, upon receiving this letter from an avowed enemy of homoeopathy, replied with restraint. In his article about Irving Dr. Peters quoted this section of his reply: "You were kind enough to make a few suggestions for Mr. Irving's benefit; unfortunately, all his friends mistake his case, and he is overwhelmed with remedies for asthma alone; but, it is right to say to you that Mr. Irving has enlargement of the heart in addition, and that much of his difficulty of breathing, and apparent catarrhal trouble, arises from obstructed circulation....If you can make any further suggestion for his benefit, I can assure you that it will be most faithfully tried, and with a most earnest desire that it may relieve one whom I love inexpressibly."[26] Dr. Peters did not point out in his article that he had treated the patient for several years and that Dr. Holmes had prescribed after seeing, not examining, Irving, but readers could hardly miss the point.

Dr. Peters quoted only a brief portion of this letter to Dr. Holmes, but the letter was a long one, with many clinical details, including an extended account of Irving's sleeplessness. One section of the unpublished portion of the letter is particularly pertinent: "He [Irving] often gets almost frightfully uneasy, nervous, and unhappy while awake at night—an undefined horror and apprehension seems to possess him—he is not afraid of death, & the hereafter, but occasionally he dreads an attack of paralysis, & perhaps insanity, altho he has never hinted at the latter—still, I am confident he broods about it —."[27] Dr. Peters did enumerate some of the remedies he had used to alleviate various symptoms: "musk & asafoetida," "Cypripedium," Coffea cruda, cannabis, and dulcamara. The effectiveness of the drugs was erratic; one might work one night, then fail the next. Pierre Irving gave his uncle cannabis one night to no avail, then followed that drug with dulcamara, which also failed to relax the patient. Brandy and water finally helped Irving to fall asleep.[28]

In his article on Irving Dr. Peters did not print Dr. Holmes's rather vague apology in his letter of reply: "I suppose we all do pretty much the same thing in cases like this, feel our way along, heave the lead, watch the currents, throw over cargo if we must, keep the pumps going, the flag flying and trim to the wind of every day. To speak more literally we all try, as you have done, all safe means which promise better than mere inactivity seems to provide."[29] Vague as this was, it is a far cry from Dr. Holmes's condemning comments in *Homoeopathy and Its Kindred Delusions* on this "irregular" practice and its practitioners.

Dr. Peters did follow Dr. Holmes's suggestion, however, and prescribed "Jonas Whitcomb's Remedy for Asthma" on February 1, 1859. Pierre Irving reported that his uncle had a good night after that treatment, but two days later he suffered another nervous attack.[30] Dr. Peters undoubtedly returned to his homoeopathic treatments after the remedy suggested by Dr. Holmes failed. Dr. Peters did report, however, that Irving was grateful that Peters "had studied both schools of medicine, and unhesitatingly used those parts of each which seemed safe and truly useful."[31]

The biography of Washington was completed, and for a time in the spring of 1859 Washington Irving, free from his writing, seemed to improve physically. In March of 1859 Dr. Peters was able to call less often, making professional visits only twice a week during most of that month, while Pierre M. Irving watched his uncle's health carefully and made frequent reports to the doctor.[32] Dr. Peters did continue to spend nights and weekends at "Sunnyside" when necessary. Unfortunately, he himself become ill in the fall of 1859; he contracted "intermittent fever" and was confined to bed. Since he was unable to visit "Sunnyside," Pierre M. Irving came to his sickroom to consult about the elder Irving. Dr. Peters's own physician, Dr. Alexander Mott, also a follower of Hahnemann, was in attendance during one of those visits. Dr. Peters requested Dr. Mott to remain during the consultation, for in case a doctor was needed to visit Irving at "Sunnyside," he wanted Dr. Mott to be informed about the case.[33]

The last weeks and months of Irving's life were obviously dreadful ones. He called out at one time, "Good God! What shall I do—how shall I get through this day—What is to become of me?"[34] How much of this misery was the result of his physical illness, how much the result of his psychological state, it is not now possible to know. Dr. Peters, given the state of medicine in 1859, undoubtedly did the best he could. Some of his prescriptions were effective for a short time in alleviating Irving's sleeplessness and his feelings of distress. Perhaps of more importance, Dr. Peters also gave psychological support to the ailing writer, seeing him constantly, spending the night when needed. Unfortunately, Dr. Peters was not with Irving during his last hours, for death came suddenly and unexpectedly: as Irving was preparing for bed on November 28, 1859, he clutched his side and said, "If this could only end" or "When will this end"[35] and fell backward onto the floor. By the time a local doctor arrived, Irving was dead. Dr. Peters arrived the next morning and pronounced the cause of death as heart disease.

The cause of death came as a surprise to most people. Pierre M. Irving later wrote in *The Life and Letters of Washington Irving* (1863-64) that he had known of his uncle's enlarged heart for eleven months, but that the doctor had not expressed "serious apprehension." Pierre M. Irving did praise the doctor for his attention and skill, "but the difficulty lay too deep for remedy. No skill could have averted or delayed the castastrophe."[36] Curiously enough, though, Dr. Peters was not identified by Pierre M. Irving as a homoeopathic physician; it was as if Irving's nephew did not wish Irving, in death, to be drawn into the controversy between two schools of medicine, a controversy even then becoming acrimonious.

Dr. Peters, on the other hand, wanted to claim Irving as a believer in this "irregular" school of medicine. The English homoeopathic physicians made much of their royal and aristocratic patients, and Dr. Peters obviously wanted to help the homoeopathic cause by showing that Washington Irving, a writer of great fame, was a true believer in the new medicine. He also had to defend himself, for many people, including Irving's friends, thought that the writer had been suffering from asthma and were unaware of his heart disease. Dr. Peters attempted to set the record straight in a letter written to a relative of his on December 2, 1859, a letter soon published, pointing out that Irving did not want his heart condition known, for the author did not wish pity from those around him. Dr. Peters respected those wishes, and concluded in his letter, "I never for a moment thought of my reputation when his wishes and welfare pointed out a line of conduct as agreeable to him and wise in his eyes."[37]

Dr. Peters turned immediately to writing the long article "The Illnesses of Washington Irving"; it was published, he said, because he had been asked to write on the subject and because he "ought to satisfy the wishes of his [Irving's] distant admirers in this respect."[38] It is obvious, though, that he also wanted to help the cause of homoeopathy. He presented himself as a wise homoeopathic physician who had the complete confidence of his famous patient, as one devoted to the well-being of Irving, willing to sacrifice his nights at his own home in order to treat his patient. He showed that Dr. Holmes, one of the best known "regular" physicians in the country, prescribed for Irving after a social visit and without making a proper examination. Embarrassingly enough for "regulars," Dr. Holmes's diagnosis was seemingly incorrect, and even after he was informed of Irving's enlarged heart he did not suggest the use of digitalis. (It should be noted, however, that an autopsy was not performed and that it was Dr. Peters who listed "enlarged heart" as the cause of death. Modern readers may well question the ethical conduct of Dr. Peters in revealing intimate details gained from consultations with Washington Irving and also the professional conduct of Dr. Holmes in prescribing remedies without thoroughly examining a patient.) Nineteenth-century readers who came upon "The Illnesses of Washington Irving" were undoubtedly impressed, for Dr. Peters presented his case effectively. General readers, however, did not see the article in the *North American Journal of Homoeopathy*, since it was a professional journal for homoeopathic physicians. Most readers learned about Irving's last illnesses in *The Life and Letters of Washington Irving* by his nephew Pierre M. Irving. In this four-volume biography published by G. P. Putnam in 1863-64, Dr. Peters is mentioned favorably but is not identified as an "irregular" physician. Since some of Irving's relatives had not been enthusiastic about homoeopathy, and since many people regarded homoeopathic physicians as quacks and charlatans, it is likely that Irving's nephew in the 1863 biography was attempting to ensure his uncle's respectability by wiping his slate virtually clean of involvement with what many thought to be a pseudo-medical science.

Notes

1. John S. Haller, Jr., *American Medicine in Transition, 1840-1910* (Urbana: Univ. of Illinois Press, 1981), p. 106. I have used the spelling *homoeopathy* in the text of this essay, but another accepted spelling, *homeopathy*, is often found in titles and in quotations.

2. *Washington Irving Letters*, ed. by Ralph M. Aderman, Herbert L. Kleinfield, and Jenifer S. Banks (Boston: Twayne Publishers, 1978-82), 1:703. For accounts of Washington Irving's many health problems, see Stanley T. Williams, *The Life of Washington Irving*, 2 vols. (New York: Oxford Univ. Press, 1935).

3. *Washington Irving Letters*, 2:725.

4. Ibid., 3:304.

5. For an excellent discussion of homoeopathic principles see Martin Kaufman, *Homeopathy in America* (Baltimore: Johns Hopkins Univ. Press, 1971), pp. 23-27.

6. Ibid., p. 26.

7. Oliver Wendell Holmes, *Works* (Boston: Houghton Mifflin, 1904), 9:75.

8. Ibid., pp. 39-40.

9. Kaufman, *Homeopathy*, pp. 28-47, is particularly good on Dr. Holmes's "Homoeopathy and Its Kindred Delusions" and its attackers and defenders.

10. *Washington Irving Letters*, 4:457.

11. Ibid., p. 464.

12. Ibid., p. 494.

13. J.C. Peters, "The Illnesses of Washington Irving," *North American Journal of Homoeopathy* 8 (February 1860): 451-73.

14. For a biographical account of John Charles Peters see *Dictionary of American Biography* (New York: Scribner's, 1934), 14:505-6.

15. Peters, "Illnesses," p. 452.

16. Ibid., pp. 454-55.

17. Ibid., p. 455.

18. Wayne R. Kime, *Pierre M. Irving and Washington Irving: A Collaboration in Life and Letters* (Waterloo, Ont.: Wilfrid Laurier Univ. Press, 1977), pp. 175-76, notes: "Despite a few of their relatives' misgivings touching Peters' ideas, all the Irvings at Sunnyside eventually made him their regular attendant." Irving's niece wanted to know if Dr. Peters were "a man of eminence." She had little faith in homoeopathy. See Kime's notes, *Pierre M.*, pp. 175-76, for this discussion.

19. Peters, "Illnesses," p. 454.

20. Ibid., p. 458.

21. Pierre M. Irving, *The Life and Letters of Washington Irving* (New York: Putnam, 1863), 4:267.

22. Peters, "Illnesses," p. 458. The discussion of congestive heart failure in *The Merck Manual of Diagnosis and Therapy* (Rahway, N.J.: Merck Sharp & Dohme Research Laboratories, 1977) includes the following statements, pp. 409-10: "In some patients the major manifestation is marked bronchospasm or wheezing, termed *cardiac asthma*." "In advanced failure severe cough is a prominent symptom." Patients may experience "restlessness" and "anxiety with a sense of suffocation."

23. Pierre M. Irving, *Life*, 4:268.

24. "Washington Irving's Family," *New York Herald*, March 30, 1884, p. 8.

25. Kime, *Pierre M.*, p. 176.

26. Peters, "Illnesses," p. 455.

27. Quoted in Kime, *Pierre M.*, pp. 177-78. The letter is in the Berg Collection, New York Public Library.

28. I am indebted to Wayne R. Kime for this information, drawn from an unpublished letter by Dr. Peters.

29. Quoted in Kime, *Pierre M.*, p. 178.

30. Pierre M. Irving, *Life*, 4:272.

31. Peters, "Illnesses," p. 460.

32. Kime, *Pierre M.*, pp. 173-240.

33. Peters, "Illnesses," p. 463.

34. Williams, *Life*, 2:239.

35. Kime, *Pierre M.*, p. 239. Irving's niece Sarah was not certain which sentence he spoke.

36. Pierre M. Irving, *Life*, 4:327-28.

37. "A Letter from the Physician of the late Washington Irving," undated clipping, Berg Collection, New York Public Library.

38. Peters, "Illnesses," p. 451.

CHARLES THOMAS WALTERS

9. Sculpture and the Expressive Mechanism

Writing in the *American Phrenological Journal*, Orson S. Fowler predicted in 1846 that the "genial rays of truth" would soon replace the errors and prejudices of the past.[1] Fowler's confident prognostication reflected his age's certainty that triumphant advances in fields ranging from technology and the pure sciences to poetry, philosophy, and the arts would soon transform American life and culture. American sculpture was no less expectant and, for a brief time, its theory and practice did indeed keep pace with advances in science. To enhance the validity of their work, American sculptors experimented with the disciplines of mathematics, phrenology, and comparative anatomy. The spirit of scientific inquiry transformed sculpture, esthetically and analytically, from an art of experience to an art of process and reduced creativity to a measurable quantity that could consequently be judged on moral grounds. During this time artists and critics viewed the attempt at such a synthesis of science and technology with sculpture as a legitimate means for explicating the mysteries of creativity and making the artistic impulse more understandable for an American audience. It also provided an excellent method of evaluating the success or failure of a work of art. Because sculpture itself was viewed as a highly specialized form of artistic expression, the successful sculptor was expected to perfect two skills, one conceptual, the other technical. He was to be a poet in stone, yet someone

Fig. 9.1. Henry Dexter's "Apparatus for Sculptors to be Employed in Copying Busts," patented March 28, 1842.

equally gifted in the skills of the mechanic, the inventor, and the mathematician.

Sculptural technology might be enhanced with a mechanical contrivance or a philosophical system as simple as Henry Dexter's sculptural apparatus or as complex as William Wetmore Story's historic revision of the measurement of the human body. Henry Dexter (1806-76), appropriately enough, began his career as a blacksmith. After completing an unsuccessful apprenticeship in painting, he began his career as a sculptor in 1838 with a bust of Samuel Elliot. During the winter of 1843-44 he repaired Thomas Crawford's *Orpheus*, damaged in transit from Italy to the Boston Athenaeum. Dexter's most remarkable achievement, however, lay in his efforts to combine the exactitude of technology with sculptural creativity. On March 28, 1843, Dexter applied for and was granted a patent (the first, I believe, given to an American artist) for what he described as an "apparatus for sculptors" (figure 9.1). A mechanism for the transposition of proportions, Dexter's machine required a considerable amount of manual skill to construct and to operate. Yet his apparatus made the sculptor's task considerably easier. The device simplified the process of carving. Making a piece of sculpture usually required three steps: the artist made a clay model which was cast in plaster; the plaster was then pointed; and, finally, small pieces of metal called points were driven into the plaster model at regular intervals. The distances between the points were punched into the final block of marble by craftsmen using an instrument that looked like an ice pick. Studio assistants roughed up the final composition, while the artist himself supplied the finishing touches. The holes were then polished away.[2] Dexter's device made it possible to transfer the clay image directly to the final block of marble by using a series of calibrated metal rods. Dexter's mechanism also made it feasible to reproduce works of art for the general public. Because of Dexter's invention, it now became possible for the average American to purchase a work of art for display in his home, above his fireplace, or on a table in his library.[3]

To measure the beauty of the human frame, William Wetmore Story (1819-95), on the other hand, developed an involved literary method founded on heavy doses of philosophy and history. Divided into four sections, Story's *Proportions of the Human Figure According to a New Canon for Practical Use* (1866) argues that scientific measurement could be combined with numerical symbolism. Story firmly believed that numbers themselves were based upon philosophical connotations. In the first two chapters Story discusses the ancient prototypes for his own theories, including the Cabala, a system of ancient Jewish mysticism, and the canon of Polyclitus. In the third chapter he dissects the flaws of modern anatomical quantification, drawing on the work of Johann Lavater. And in the final section of the book Story demonstrates his own practical solutions to the problem of proportion.

He devised a simple module consisting of three perfect forms—an equilateral triangle and a square set within the circumference of a circle (figure 9.2). Story's system was practical

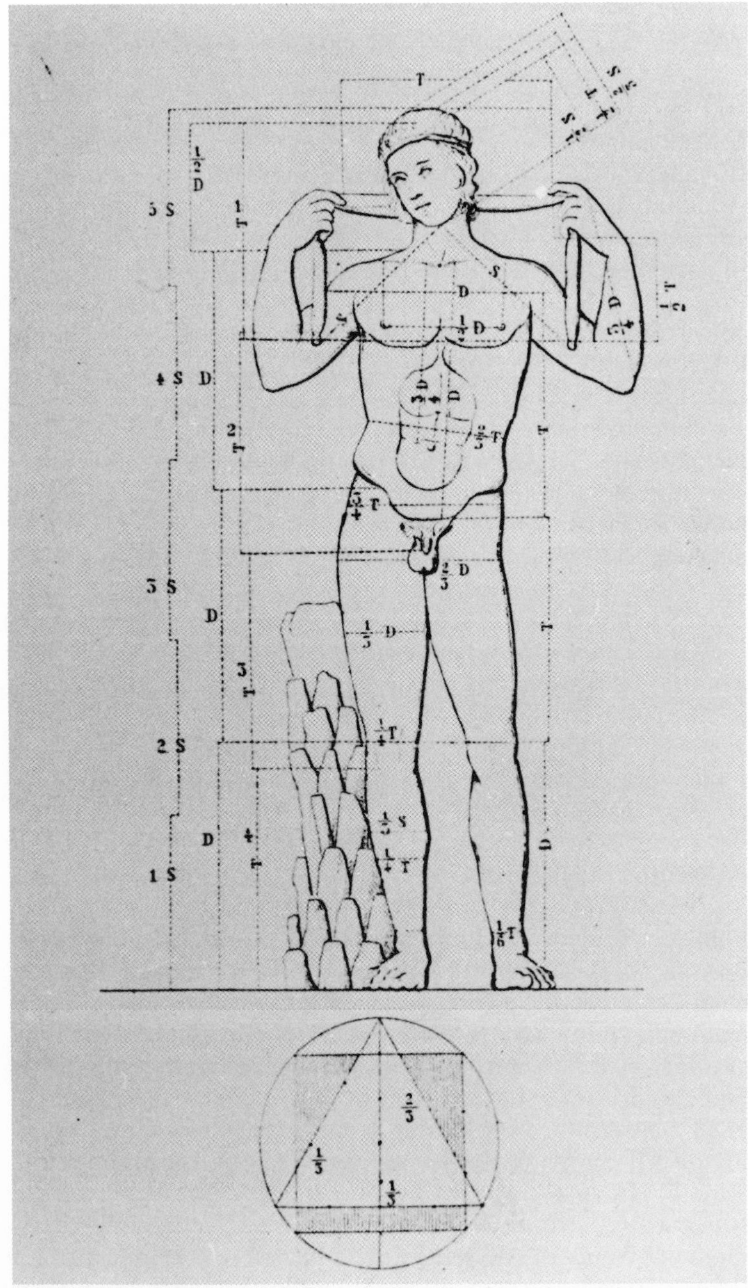

Fig. 9.2. William Wetmore Story's module of three perfect forms (bottom) and illustration of the ideal proportions of the human form. From Story's *Proportions of the Human Figure According to a New Canon for Practical Use* (London, 1866).

and philosophically valid. The module, Story wrote, symbolized all mankind. The circle exemplified the world; the triangle, the Trinity; and the square, man's existence according to divine law. The human figure was measured in terms of circles, squares, and triangles. The height of the figure, Story indicated, equaled four times the base of the triangle or five times the side of the square. An artist could measure every anatomical fragment by applying Story's canon. Story's most famous statue, *Cleopatra* (after 1860), illustrates the perfect equilibrium between poetry and science, between science and symbolism. Story even wrote a poem for his statue in which he compares his heroine to a velvety tigress who broods upon her fate among an "aromatic pastille" of crushed flowers.[4] Composed of a set of equilateral triangles, the statue exhibits a whole host of philosophical considerations. According to Story's theories, *Cleopatra* demonstrated the divine nature of human existence. She represented the soul, the intellect, and the body.[5]

A most important scientific event was the discovery by American sculptors and painters that phrenology could be applied to art. The Scotsman George Combe (1788-1858) introduced phrenology to the artistic community in America. As a system of human psychology that purported to explain human behavior, based upon the study of cranial topography, phrenology's study of the skull's surface (figure 9.3) could provide insight into a subject's character that could then be incorporated into a work of art. From 1838 to 1840 Combe made a phrenological tour of the United States, lecturing in New York, Boston, New Haven, and Philadelphia. After visiting Mt. Auburn Cemetery and paying his respects at the sarcophagus of Johann Spurzheim, one of phrenology's founding fathers, Combe journeyed to the Capitol in Boston, where he took notes on Sir Francis Chantry's statue of George Washington. On October 23, 1838, he examined a painting in a private collection by Washington Allston known today as *Jeremiah Dictating to the Scribe Baruch*. The sparkling eyes of Jeremiah, he wrote, expressed the supernatural, a sentiment attributable specifically to the sentiment of "Wonder." Allston, he believed, succeeded in painting a figure that exhibited as well the phrenological faculties of Firmness, Conscientiousness, and Self-Esteem.[6]

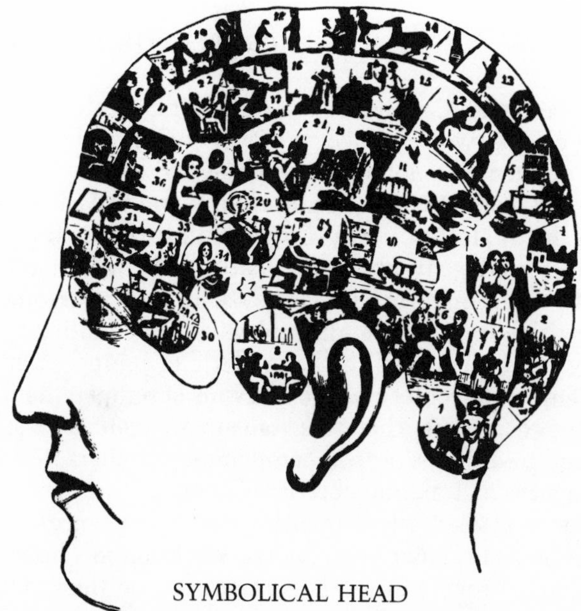

Definitions of Organs as Numbered Above

1—Amativeness, Sexual love
2—Philoprogenitiveness, Love offspring
3—Adhesiveness, Friendship
A—Matrimony, Desire to marry
4—Inhabitiveness, Love of home
5—Continuity, Aversion to change
6—Combativeness, Energy
7—Destructiveness, Executiveness
8—Alimentiveness, Appetite
9—Acquisitiveness, Accumulation
10—Secretiveness, Reserve, policy
11—Cautiousness, Prudence
12—Approbativeness, Love of praise
13—Self Esteem, Independence, dignity
14—Firmness, Stability
15—Conscientiousness, Love of right
16—Hope, Anticipation
17—Spirituality, Love of spiritual things
18—Veneration, Deference
19—Benevolence, Kindness
20—Constructiveness, Ability to do
21—Ideality, Love of Niceness
B—Sublimity, Love of Grandeur
22—Imitation, Ability to pattern
23—Mirthfulness, Love of fun
24—Individuality, Observation
25—Form, Remembrance of shape
26—Size, Cognizance of Bulk
27—Weight, Balancing, walking
28—Color, Perception of shades
29—Order, Arrangement
30—Calculation, Counting
31—Locality, Ability to determine points of compass
32—Eventuality, Memory of facts
33—Time, Recollection of dates
34—Tune, Harmony of sound
35—Language, Expression of idea
36—Causality, Desire to know why
37—Comparison, Perception of resemblance
C—Human Nature, reading Man
D—Agreeableness, Easiness of manner

Fig. 9.3. Frontispiece from C.H. Burrows, *Phrenological Description* (Lincoln, Illinois, 1870), with each mental faculty illustrated by an appropriate tableau.

In Philadelphia Combe visited Rembrandt Peale's studio, an experience that would prove to be beneficial for both parties. Combe applied phrenological principles to a large equestrian portrait of George Washington that he found in Peale's studio. Inspired by Peale's portrait, Combe informally wrote in his notebooks a lengthy phrenological profile which reflected favorably on the historical image of Washington's personality. In choosing the appropriate phrenological personality type for Washington, he rejected the Lymphatic (a temperament that was languid and feeble) and the Nervous (a temperament more applicable to an artist than to a statesman). Instead he selected the Sanguine-Bilious profile temperaments characterized by vivaciousness and mental activity.[7]

Combe next mentally "superimposed," so to speak, a series of phrenological plates over George Washington's head. From the evidence provided by this comparison, he then identified the general's most prominent faculties, or bumps: Secretiveness, Firmness, and Caution. The three faculties formed a chart of characteristics worthy of Washington, "one of these rare specimens of humanity," he concluded, "in whom nearly all of the mental elements [were] largely developed in harmonious proportion." The process that Combe used was tedious and laborious, but, in his estimation, a triumphant success. After all, he vindicated the popular American myth about George Washington's character and demonstrated unequivocally the possibility of measuring the scientific accuracy of a sculpture.

Shortly after Combe and his wife returned to Scotland, they went abroad again. Inspired by his growing awareness of phrenology's applicability to art, he visited the major cultural cities of Italy. In Milan, Genoa, Lucca, Florence, and Pisa Combe studied pictures and sculpture in public galleries and in artists' studios. After this tour Combe and his wife settled for the winter in Florence. Here, under the tutelage of an all but forgotten artist, Lawrence MacDonald, Combe made his first attempt to identify artistic genius by subjecting the masters of the Italian Renaissance to phrenological analysis. A letter written during this period of study gives some indication of Combe's procedure. He analyzed the temperaments of three Italian Renaissance painters—Leonardo, Raphael, and Michelangelo—from portraits of them he had seen during his trip. Leonardo and Raphael, he concluded, had the most appropriate temperaments for artists as well as the finest combinations of organs. Michelangelo did not fare as well. When compared to his compatriots, Michelangelo's temperament was judged inferior. He had a large head, a dark Bilious and Nervous temperament, and a distorted set of organs, particularly those of Combativeness, Self-Esteem, and Firmness.[8] Combe concluded that the shape of Michelangelo's skull detrimentally influenced the work that he produced. Although Michelangelo's sculpture may have been energetic and intense, it lacked the finer qualities of "grace," "purity," and "sentiment" that Combe found in Raphael's work.

From his study of the history of art, Combe concluded that being an artist required certain natural gifts that were, in turn, complemented by certain practical skills.[9] To succeed, the artist had to be of a Nervous temperament and had to be gifted with the innate faculties of Form, Size, Coloring, Constructiveness, and Ideality. He then had to combine these with the appropriate technical skills.

Combe published his conclusions in a subsequent book, *Phrenology Applied to Painting and Sculpture* (1855), which provoked all sorts of articles, including reviews in the *Zoist, Christian Examiner,* and the *Crayon.*[10] The essay that appeared in the *Crayon*, entitled "What Makes an Artist?" argued the relationship between the practice of art and the theory of phrenology, each position in this hypothetical debate being defended by an appropriate spokesman: the artist, Professor Hart; and the scientist, George Combe. The point of this dispute was to discover "how near alike were the results which each method attained." The article asked a single question whose answer had multiple overtones. What were the mechanical and mental prerequisites of a masterpiece? Each participant agreed on the necessity of technical excellence and that the element of genius distinguished mere mechanical reconstruction from sublime creativity. But the question remained, what constituted "genius"? Professor Hart argued that genius depends upon discipline, visual analysis, and manual dexterity. Combe emphasized that genius depended not upon intuition, but upon certain measurable

Fig. 9.4. Thomas Crawford, *Beethoven*, 1855. Bronze. New England Conservatory of Music, Boston. Reproduced by permission.

faculties. While Hart attributed genius merely to an "invisible power," Combe, through phrenological analysis, insisted he could calibrate every facet of this mysterious power: that is to say, he could measure and describe the very temperaments and faculties constituting genius. Because of the configuration of the artist's head, a genius sculpted or painted in a particular way. The results of genius could then be analyzed. Guided by such phrenological criteria, he proposed that the critic appraise a work of art not simply because it demonstrated poetic sentiment, but because its intellectual, moral, and physical attributes were grounded in a science.

A measure of the influence that phrenological criteria exerted in esthetic circles is the reception accorded Thomas Crawford's statue of Beethoven (figure 9.4). Before the statue was installed in Symphony Hall amidst appropriate pomp and circumstances—flowers and poems—it was placed on exhibition in the sculpture gallery of the Boston Athenaeum. One of the many admirers who viewed the statue wrote a carefully worded description of his impressions for *Dwight's Journal of Music.*[11] He described the statue to its last detail, from its golden bronze color to Beethoven's fanciful dress. The composer held under his left arm a sheet of music inscribed with the opening lines of Schiller's "Ode to Joy," the theme for the Choral Symphony. Sublime and majestical, Crawford's Beethoven was never considered by his contemporaries to be a realistic portrait. It did not portray Beethoven the man with his warts, lines, and creases, but Beethoven the creative genius. In Crawford's conception, the sublime beauty of the composer's music superseded his personal eccentricities and physical defects. Yet for all of Crawford's creative liberties, his statue was still believed to be a precise representation. Beethoven's forehead was marked with ridges, the external disclosure of the phrenological organ of Tune, the psychological prerequisite for success as a musician.

The most distinguished sculptor of the age, Hiram Powers, (1805-73), best demonstrated the applicability of Combe's theories. Powers's most famous statue, *The Greek Slave,* met esthetic standards according to those propounded by the latest science. Stripped to the waist, bound in chains, and destined for a seraglio, she stood upon a pedestal to declare the virtues of chastity and perseverance. Despite her obvious nudity, *The Greek Slave* was nonetheless pronounced morally acceptable because she was judged to be scientifically accurate. The features of her face conveyed radiance, beauty, and dignity; her head exhibited, it was thought, the "beau ideal" of phrenology.[12] Clearly, Powers arranged the bumps on her forehead perfectly to express the spirituality of her mind.

Powers's familiarity with the vocabulary and concepts of phrenology was such that he even used them outside the studio in a variety of other creative and serious ways. He made them part of his conversational idiom. Phrenology's insights into human nature helped Powers to understand his own character.[13] Powers also applied his knowledge of phrenology to a critical reading of the two standards of female beauty dear to nineteenth-century sculptors, the *Venus de Medici* and Antonio Canova's revision, the *Venus Italica*.[14] He analyzed these works of art to discover their flaws according to the esthetic dictates of phrenology. To explain why the image of Venus had such widespread acceptance, Powers drew on the insights provided by phrenology. The sculptor attributed the overwhelming historic significance of the Venus not to the statue's intrinsic merit, but rather to the viewer's own phrenological deficiencies. The viewer who worshipped the Venus, he conjectured, did so because of a distortion in the organ of Veneration, a deformity that produced irrational respect for objects and opinions which had nothing to recommend them but their antiquity.

He also applied the phrenological gauge to the Venus itself, as well as to its modern adaptation. Of the Canovan Venus, Powers made the following criticism: "The distance between the organ of self-esteem and the chin is extravagant and without parallel in any head of a great statue of the same size." What Powers meant was that the distance between the faculty of Self-Esteem and the chin was distorted. According to the logic of phrenology, this particular angle also reflected poorly on the artist, to whom Powers attributed an enlarged organ of Self-Esteem. He accused Canova of mistakingly thinking himself a transcendent genius. When Powers judged the original version of the *Venus de Medici*, he still retained the meticulous logic of phrenology. He praised the beautifully shaped head of the original Venus, yet concluded there was room for improvement since the constituent fragments of the skull were either malformed or misplaced. The eyes, for example, were much too small for the rest of the face; the forehead was much too angular; the ears were totally inaccurate. Powers's tedious analysis produced positive results. He developed new standards of perception and proportion and implemented them in his own work.

Hiram Powers used the principles of phrenology in his portrait busts to capture the illusive qualities of likeness. He looked for specific visual manifestations or "signs" of character to support his thesis that cranial shapes reflected personality. Powers himself insisted that there was a striking coincidence between the "signs" and those who bore them. To support this hypothesis, Powers drew his evidence from prominent American statesmen, each of whom he thought succeeded or failed because of a particular phrenological attribute. Powers maintained that Jackson, Clay, and Calhoun were all successful politicians because of "marked perceptive organs." At the same time, the artist belittled Webster and Everett because of a craniological deficiency in each man. According to Powers, Webster and Everett had failed to carry the sympathies of the common man because they lacked development of the perceptive organs. Therefore, neither man was able to address himself to the immediate expectations of the popular will.[15]

Despite Hiram Powers's prononcements, Daniel Webster's countenance was prized both for its physical dimensions and for its intellectual dynamics. In a text written on comparative physiognomy, for example, James W. Redfield likened Webster's bodily and mental processes to those of a bear. Webster's countenance and the phrenological characteristics that it revealed provided an important inspiration for Powers's sculpture. Between 1835 and 1837 Powers sculpted the *Athenaeum Webster*; and later, between 1855 and 1859, Powers made a monumental bronze statue of Webster for the city of Boston. This latter statue was met with ridicule as an inaccurate image of a great American hero. Powers felt slighted and offended. He had sculpted in accordance with the principles of phrenology, yet he had failed. In 1860, shortly after this setback, he invited the great American phrenologist Lorenzo Niles Fowler to apply the phrenological gauge to a plaster cast made from the *Athenaeum Webster*. He did so in order to settle in his own mind whether he had sculpted according to phrenological standards. Fowler judged the bust to be a success and pronounced Powers's understanding of phrenology and its application to sculpture without flaw. For Powers, Fowler's reading represented an esthetic professional vindication; he concluded that the general public's versing in scientific theory was deficient. Fowler's analysis of the bust of Daniel Webster reaffirmed Hiram Powers's belief in phrenology.

So highly did Powers value phrenology that he submitted himself to a head reading during this visit with Fowler in London. Lorenzo Fowler's extensive reading of Powers's cranium is now housed at the Archives of American Art. According to Fowler, Powers's brain was unusually large—a particularly propitious indication since size reflected intelligence. Fowler next identified the appropriate temperament for his subject. He judged Powers to have a well-balanced temperament, indicative of a "nervous susceptibility, with a full degree of vital powers and animal life, [and] no excess of the vital element." In his written analysis Fowler mentioned thirteen prominent faculties, beginning with individuality and ending with cautiousness. He implied others as well, including Sublimity, Ideality, Alimentiveness, Constructiveness, and Philoprogenitiveness.

Fowler's perceptiveness regarding his client's ego was uncanny. His vignette exactly matched his subject's personality. According to Fowler, Powers was tenacious, "vivid, distinct, [and] direct." He was plain and frank, his speech temperate, his habits uniform. He was "hopeful, buoyant, sanguine." And he was blessed with a good sense of humor. He was also, Fowler maintained, gifted with the talent of construction, the ability to construct, invent, and measure—an analysis that fit Powers, the Yankee Mechanic, like a well-tailored glove.

Fowler's evaluation of Powers's constructive dexterity was not quite as accurate as it might have been. "Your constructive talent is good, but as an artist and mechanic, your forte lies in your intellectual perceptions, knowledge of proportions, and power to plan and adapt means to ends, more than in the dexterous use of tools."

Powers held two United States patents, one for a file, the other for a punching machine. The inventor's interest in construction extended to the "knowledge of proportions," as Fowler described it. Like William Wetmore Story, Powers was fascinated by the mathematical measurement of the human figure. In an undated "studio memorandum," Powers wrote of dividing the human figure into halves. "From the *os pubis*," he wrote, [equals] "one half the entire length of the figure." The memo reads as follows:

From the *os pubis* to the top of the head—one half of the entire length. There are equal divisions from the acromion of the scapula to the bottom of the inner ankle. From the bottom of the pubis to the bottom of the patella is the same length as from the bottom of the patella to the sole of the foot two thirds each, but we must observe the ancients generally allowed half a nose or more to the length of the lower limbs exceeding the length of the body and the head. Second from thence to the top of the patella, first from the acromion to the point in the spine of the illium from which the [illegible] the sectus and the sartonius begin.[16]

Hiram Powers's art expressed the aspirations of his age. His portrait busts immortalized the American hero, his idealized statues' moral and physical beauty. Science helped Powers to deal with the intangibles of human character. Hiram Powers's contemporary William Rimmer, however, rejected phrenology and instead chose Darwin as his source of inspiration. The connection between Hiram Powers and William Rimmer, artists who differed radically from one another, particularly in the realm of scientific theory, can be precisely documented. On May 3, 1861, Stephen Higginson Perkins (1804-77), Rimmer's patron, initiated correspondence with Hiram Powers, then residing in Florence. Perkins opened his correspondence by describing a sculpture of a "male figure, life size, perfectly made in violent action." He then questioned Powers on the expense of copying a full-sized statue (later to be called *The Falling Gladiator*) in marble. He also enclosed a photograph of a head of St. Stephen made in what he described as a "curious manner." According to Perkins, the artist responsible, Dr. William Rimmer, selected a block of granite, set it upon a barrel in the woodshed behind his home in East Milton, Massachusetts, and cut the bust, recording the time required in chalk. Rimmer expended more than two hundred hours in carving the bust.

Within three weeks, on May 27, Hiram Powers responded. Not known for his generosity to his colleagues, Powers surprisingly voiced approval of Rimmer's achievement. Powers praised the St. Stephen for its expressiveness and attention to detail. "Rimmer," Powers wrote, "deserves the highest encouragement." On November 2nd Perkins forwarded a final letter that included a photograph of *The Falling Gladiator*. He reported that Rimmer was "much pleased" by Powers's interest in his sculpture.[17]

William Rimmer (1816-79) was as gifted as he was eclectic. A sculptor and a painter, a trained physician, and a gifted teacher, he held positions at Harvard and Cooper Union at various times during his life. Rimmer's career culminated with the publication in 1877 of *Art Anatomy*. One of the most intriguing of nineteenth-century drawing books, Rimmer's *Art Anatomy* remains a remarkable testament to the creative possibilities of science, particularly the study and categorization of human emotions and their physical expression in the human frame. Rimmer's book is a consolidation of many different sources. To make his point that emotions can be reduced to a visible formula, Rimmer used an iconography that is decidedly neoclassic. The illustrations for the book abound with broad-chested gods and beautifully refined goddesses. The style of his drawings, however, is intensely romantic, indeed almost frighteningly so. Some of the heads he constructs evolve as grotesque masks of fear, pain, anger, and disgust.

According to Rimmer's most distinguished biographer, Lincoln Kirstein, Rimmer used as sources for his *Art Anatomy* works by Charles Darwin, Johann Spurzheim (1776-1832), and Johann Kaspar Lavater (1741-1825).[18] All the systems that Rimmer assimilated in his sculpture and his writings, however, shared one element. Each attempted to define human personality within the perimeters of comparative anatomy. George Combe, for instance, attempted in *Elements of Phrenology* to compare the organ of Constructiveness in the beaver and the bee to that of man.[19] Lavater's definition of comparative anatomy was even more flexible.[20] For Lavater it was possible to couple man with a frog, man with an elephant, or man with any other fauna that moved beneath the arch of nature. The flexibility of Lavater's thesis becomes apparent if we examine a plate within his work (figure 9.5). In one instance he compared two human faces with their bestial counterparts: an ox and a monkey. The results of the pairing with an ox are not particularly convincing. The only signs of compatibility are the shape and focus of the eyes and the relationship of the head to the shoulders. The comparison with the monkey is more conclusive because the monkey is the creature who most resembles man. The only

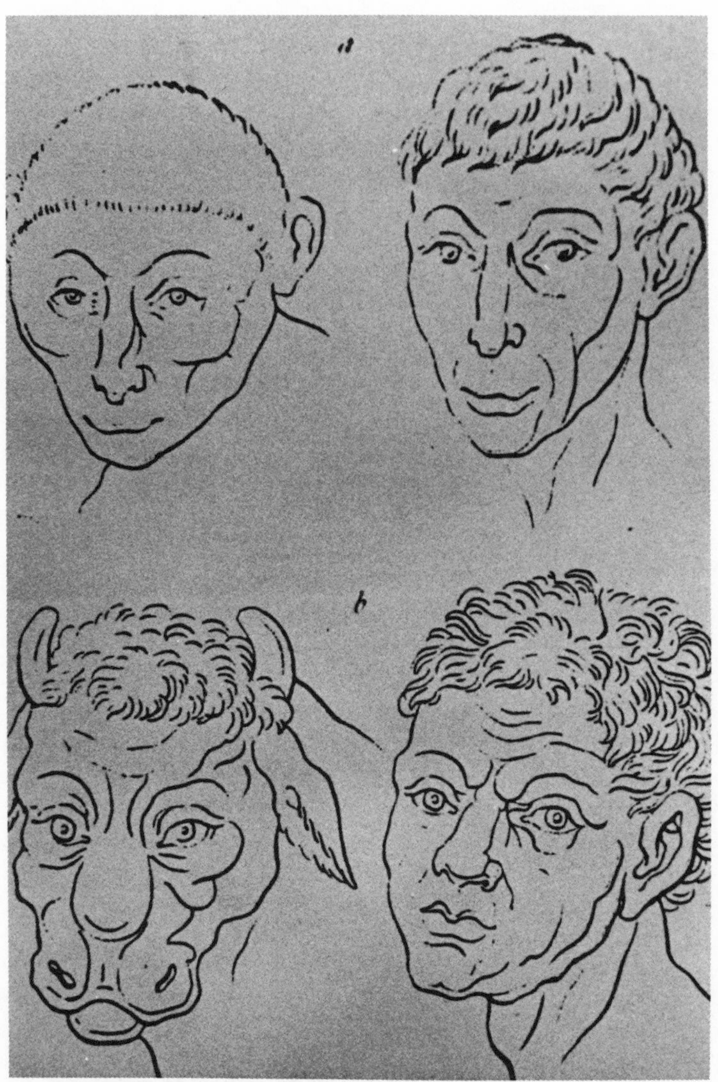

Fig. 9.5. Johann Lavater's comparison of human faces with those of a monkey and an ox. From his *Essays on Physiognomy* (London, 1804), 3:138.

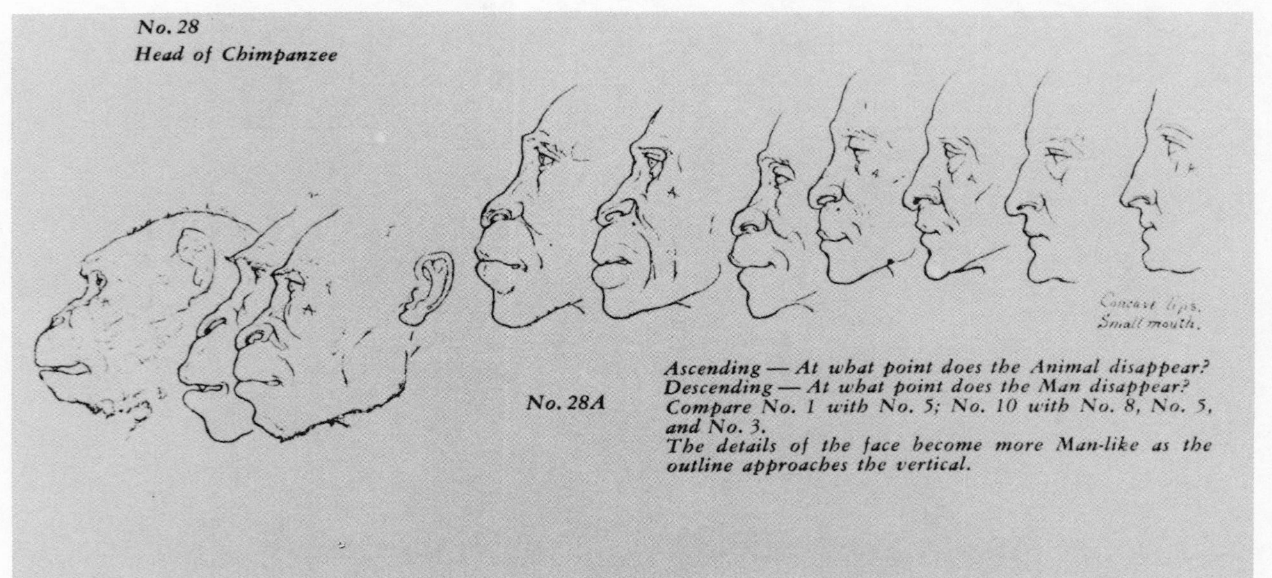

No. 28
Head of Chimpanzee
Concave lips.
Small mouth.
No. 28A
Ascending — At what point does the Animal disappear?
Descending — At what point does the Man disappear?
Compare No. 1 with No. 5; No. 10 with No. 8, No. 5, and No. 3.
The details of the face become more Man-like as the outline approaches the vertical.

Fig. 9.6. Rimmer's evolutionary scale comparing human and ape profiles. From his *Art Anatomy* (Boston, 1877), p. 8.

difference is that the ape's skull is more compressed than the angular visage of the human face.

Rimmer's specific interpretation of comparative anatomy, adapted largely from Darwin's theory of evolution, is to be found in his *Art Anatomy*, a pictorial statement of profound artistic significance that challenged the refinement, perfection, and delicacy of Hiram Powers's sculpture. Powers's art was an art of concealment. His statues are precise and succinct. His achievement can be reconstructed only through the eyes of nineteenth-century scientists and writers. Rimmer's drawings for *Art Anatomy*, however, are vigorous, energetic visualizations of human emotions in which every tissue, every fragment, every feature is clearly displayed. What Powers hid beneath the surface of his work, William Rimmer now revealed to student and critic alike. Rimmer's skill as a draftsman matched his curiosity as a scientist. For example, under the heading of "Skulls of Men and Apes Compared," Rimmer produced an evolutionary scale like that of Darwin's (figure 9.6). To trace the progressive development of ape into man, Rimmer defined ten separate steps. At one end of the scale he placed an ape, at the other a fully developed Caucasian. Moving up the scale, from left to right, the animal disappears completely. Moving in the opposite direction, man is totally subsumed by the ape. When dealing with what he labeled "mixed types of heads," Rimmer altered any suggestions of linear progression to demonstrate that man was simultaneously human and bestial. By altering what he called the planes of the face—the section in front and back of the ears—Rimmer was able to combine man with ape in the same human profile (figure 9.7). Within the creative context of his *Art Anatomy*, Rimmer was not content with the obvious or the simplistic. Under the heading "Expression—Resistant" (p. 50), Rimmer listed three separate profiles: the profile of a classical head, that of an ape, and that of a lion. The classical head epitomized an aura of emotional restraint; the head of the ape, man's anthropological ancestor; the head of the lion, man's nobility.

Rimmer's illustrations dissect the origins and physical manifestations of the human psyche. The plates for his *Art Anatomy* represented a revolution in thinking about art and man. His drawings questioned the assumptions of nineteenth-century sculpture, which was stylistically placid, calm, and composed. They challenged the naive moralism that previously lay at the heart of scientific inquiry—that man was perfectible and that science could prove his divinity. Nineteenth-century audiences viewed phrenologically inspired sculpture, for instance, with the same piousness that they once studied the landscapes of Asher B. Durand. God, the Great Designer, planned everything from trees and leaves to temperaments and personality. Influenced by recent advances in science, Rimmer, on the other hand, suggested that man was no longer a divine creature. He was no longer noble, like a lion; he was morally fallible, simply another species in the long evolutionary process.

Rimmer acquired his radical theories from Darwin and used them creatively to enhance both his writing and his sculpture. In his epic poem *Phillip and Stephen* William Rimmer wrote of the human condition by utilizing the metaphor of comparative anatomy.[21] A long, rambling discourse similar to Edgar Allan Poe's "The Conversation of Eiros and Charmion," *Phillip and Stephen* is a virtual bestiary in which Phillip represents the ideal life and Stephen, the grotesque. The unpublished manuscript is filled with characters that combine the human with the bestial. Rimmer labeled one of his characters a "troglodyte" (p. 157). The hero of the tale, Phillip, confronts a beast, a Chimeran Shadow, an animal with the agility and grace of a tiger (pp. 47-49). Victimized by his own lust, another hapless creature rises like a lion with "shaggy front [to] rend the lightning with his savage claws" (p. 77). Gazing into the vacuity of his soul, a fallen angel assumes the guise of a "lion in human form" (p. 139).

Similarly, Rimmer's sculpture reflects the human savagery that is contained in his writing. His sculpture *Fighting Lions* visually paraphrases his writing (figure 9.8). Two dynamic forces are locked in a life and death struggle, the results of which are never fully resolved. And in his *Dying Centaur* (ca. 1871) Rimmer combined the human element with the body of an animal, thus creating an intense muscular knot of reciprocal

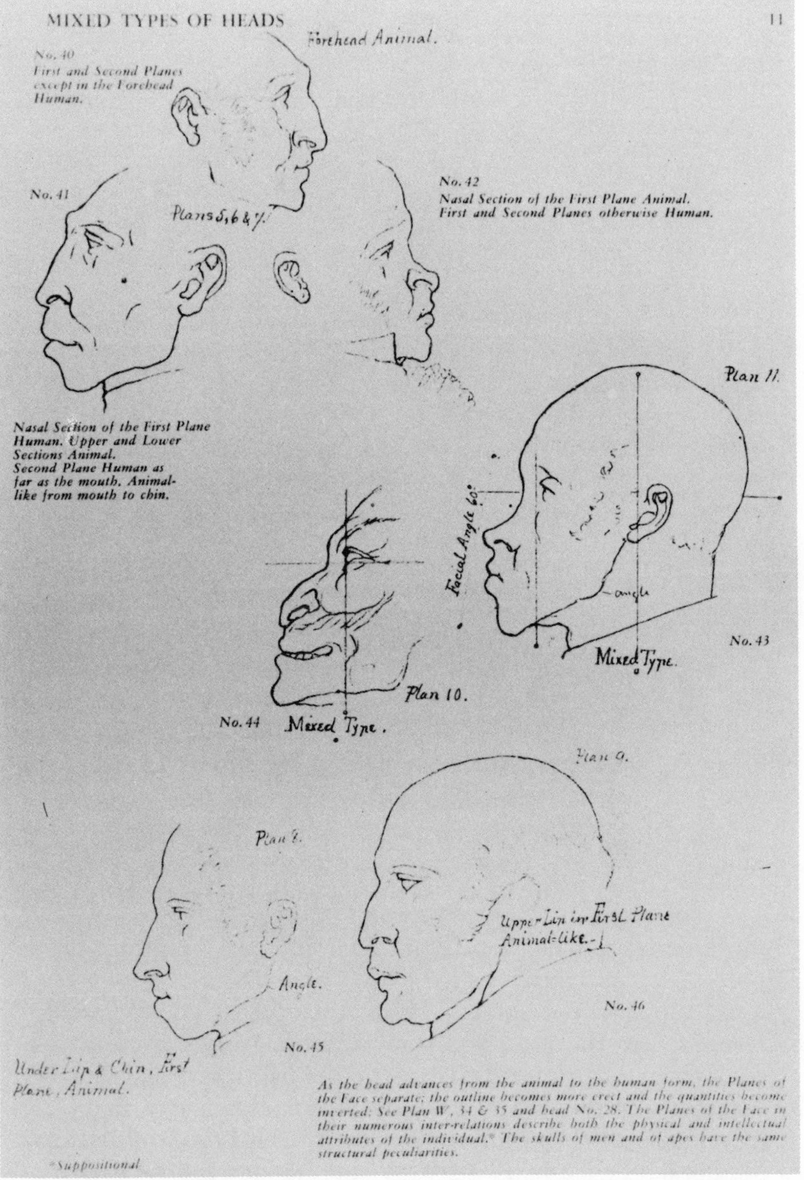

Fig. 9.7. Rimmer's illustration of heads combining human and animal characteristics. From *Art Anatomy* (Boston, 1877), p. 11.

Fig. 9.8. William Rimmer, *Fighting Lions,* ca. 1871. Bronze. Metropolitan Museum of Art, gift of Daniel Chester French.

movement and complementary anatomy that functions on a poetic level as a study on the pathos of death.

As the spiritual values of the nineteenth century quickly receded into the past, William Wetmore Story reminded his readers that all American art, whether painting, sculpture, or literature, conformed to a precise model, a paradigm that was simultaneously beautiful and practical. In his *Conversations in a Studio,* published in 1890, Story summarized the view, dominant in nineteenth-century America, that art expressed a union between "the mechanical and the poetic."[22] Inspired by the claims of science, American sculptors widely accepted views such as Story's. Sculpture was poetic and scientific and didactic. This paradigm, however, was collapsing just about the time Story stated it.

The ideal of achieving a balance between poetic exuberance and scientific discipline proved short-lived. After seeing *The Greek Slave* in the Lyceum in New York City during the autumn of 1849, an unnamed critic seemed to sense that Hiram Powers's perfect fusion of poetic inspiration with scientific craft represented a rapidly fading ideal. An era in American culture was coming to an end. The correspondent concluded his remarks on a note of poignancy: "*Tempora mutant et nos mutamur in illis*."[23] Times change and we must change with them. Times did indeed change, and with them so did American sculptural theory.

Science, which was once welcomed as the handmaiden of sculpture, was soon even seen as a threat. Edward Augustus Brackett (1818-1908), whose bust of Washington Allston (1843-44) remains an exquisite testimony to the Romantic Age, wrote a poem toward the end of his life entitled "Pseudo-Science." Brackett did not mean phrenology, physiognomy, or spiritualism, which he himself practiced. Instead, he meant Charles Darwin and his American followers. Brackett felt that Darwin had destroyed the secrets of Divine Creation and thereby threatened the hope of mankind. He even feared that the light of the radium tube would supersede the rays of the sun. He ended his poem on a dire warning of the consequences of scientific research. Science, he lamented, produced not enlightenment, but instead gloom and fear:

> Far way in Life's mid-ocean
>   Where the waves have ceased their motion
>
> . . . .
>
> Freighted with its speculations,—
>   Dreary, gloomy speculations,
> That have cursed the life of nations,—
>   Drifts this scientific bark,
> Crumbling, rotting, in the dark.[24]

By the dawn of the twentieth century the forces of progress had forever altered the delicate balance between science and morality. The study of science became a specialized discipline, no longer accessible to the amateur. The artist responded by developing painting and sculpture not so much as an expressive mechanism, but as a self-contained entity defined according to its own intrinsic rules. In the modern esthetic world the symbiosis between sculpture and science no longer existed, because it was no longer relevant.

Notes

1. Editorial note on H.R. Schetterly, "The Millenium," *American Phrenological Journal* 8 (1846): 202-3.

2. For Nathaniel Hawthorne's discussion of this process, see "Kenyon's Studio," *The Marble Faun* (New York: Modern Library, 1937), pp. 655-56.

3. Multiples of popular pieces of sculpture were quite common. It has been estimated that seventy busts of *The Greek Slave* were made. Fifty copies of Randolph Rogers's *Nydia* (1856) were also constructed.

4. W.W. Story, *Dwight's Journal of Music* 25 (Sept. 16, 1865): 97.

5. In Story's *Proportions of the Human Figure* (London: Chapman and Hall, 1866); see particularly pp. 3 and 42-56.

6. George Combe, *Notes on the United States of North America during a Phrenological Visit in 1839-40* (Edinburgh: Maclachlan Stewart, 1841) 1:122-23.

7. Ibid., pp. 341-43.

8. Charles Gibbon, *The Life of George Combe* (London: Macmillan, 1879), 2:167-74.

9. My remarks in this instance have been summarized from "On the Application of Phrenology to the Fine Arts," *Phrenological Journal* (Edinburgh), n.s. 79, no. 26 (April 1844): 113-245, no. 27 (July 1844): 225-45. Combe published these articles in book form. The final results of his research were encyclopedic. The book itself was divided into eleven chapters covering such topics as the "Constituent Element of Expression in Painting and Sculpture," and the "Cerebral Development and Genius of Raphael." The analysis of Raphael's character marked a rather macabre episode in Combe's life. According to Combe's biographer Charles Gibbon, Raphael's tomb in the Pantheon was opened and a number of plaster casts were taken from his remains including

casts of his skull and his hands. It was from these artifacts that Combe devised his phrenological reading.

10. J.W. Jackson, review of *Phrenology Applied to Painting and Sculpture*, by George Combe, *Zoist* 12 (April 1855-Jan. 1856): 406-12; *Christian Examiner* 70 (July, Sept., Nov. 1858): 87-95; "What Makes an Artist," *Crayon* 3 (July 1856): 218-19, 298-300.

11. The information on Crawford's statue is located in *Dwight's Journal of Music* 7 (June 23, 1855): 94.

12. The information on phrenology and *The Greek Slave* has been adapted from the Hiram Powers Papers, a compendium of approximately 3,000 newspaper clippings in the collection of the Cincinnati Historical Society. The specific selection can be identified only as "For the *American*; Powers' *Greek Slave.*"

13. Powers described himself as an incorrigible child who had once paddled a Canadian goose to death. He attributed his behavior to a large organ of Destructiveness, a deficiency that in later life he successfully overcame. C. Edward Lester, *The Artist, the Merchant, and the Statesman* (New York: Paine & Burgess, 1845), 2:193-96.

14. Ibid., 197-99, 200-202.

15. Henry Bellows, "Sittings with Powers, the Sculptor," *Appleton's Journal* 1 (1869): 471 (Sitting No. 4).

16. Hiram Powers' Papers, Archives of American Art, Washington, D.C.

17. Stephen H. Perkins, May 3, 1861; Hiram Powers, May 27, 1861; Perkins, Nov. 2, 1861; Archives of American Art.

18. Lincoln Kirstein, *William Rimmer* (New York: Whitney Museum of Art, 1946), p. 11. It should be noted, however, that Rimmer in his *Art Anatomy* (p. 140) more or less dismissed phrenology as an effective source: "There can be no such thing as fineness of proportions in any person in whom the head is too large, especially in those in whom there is that exaggerated protrusion of the frontal portion of the brain so much admired by phrenologists." Rimmer probably read copies of these books in the collection of the Boston Athenaeum. According to the Fine Arts Committee Report, January 4, 1864: "A class of students under the instruction of Dr. Rimmer has been admitted to draw from the fine collection of casts." Archives of the Boston Athenaeum.

19. George Combe, *Elements of Phrenology* (New York: William H. Colyer, 1843), pp. 206-8.

20. Johann Kaspar Lavater, *Essays on Physiognomy* (London: C. Whittingham, 1804), 2:146-203; see particularly pp. 147-48, and 154.

21. In its present form, written in a blue-lined ledger book, the unpublished manuscript of *Phillip and Stephen* measures 8 by 12 inches. The book is numbered on alternate pages from 5 to 381. The numbering is not consistent since some of the pages are missing. The manuscript contains two small illustrations: one, a Civil War battle scene between pages 128 and 129; the other, an illustration of an Apollo figure between pages 264 and 265. The manuscript is in the collection of the Countway Library, Harvard University.

22. W.W. Story, *Conversations in a Studio* (Boston: Houghton Mifflin, 1890), 2:311.

23. "Powers' Statue of 'The Greek Slave,' " unidentified newspaper clipping, Hiram Powers' Papers.

24. Edward A. Brackett, *My House, Chips the Builder Threw Away* (Boston: Gorham Press, 1904), p. 121.

ROBERT C. FULLER

10. Mesmerism and the Birth of Psychology

Mesmerism is undoubtedly the least studied of the many nineteenth-century "sciences of human nature." Derived from the healing techniques and so-called science of animal magnetism employed by the Viennese physician Franz Anton Mesmer, mesmerism developed in American culture in ways that have made it an unlikely candidate for sustained historical analysis. For although evidence suggests that the American mesmerists were remarkably successful healers, few seemed to be interested in establishing a medical science. Instead, most gradually abandoned their mental healing practices to become spokesmen for a metaphysically inclined psychological theory. As a consequence, the actual practice of mesmerism languished through the 1870s and finally expired in the 1880s and 1890s with the emergence of academic psychology. Unlike other nineteenth-century "sciences" such as homoeopathy or spiritualism, which even to this day continue to attract adherents, mesmerism lost its public. It seemed doomed to oblivion, as simply some irrational and decidedly pre-scientific approach to mental healing that appeared to have made no enduring contributions to American culture.

Such, however, could not be further from the case. Mesmerism—precisely because it evolved from a set of healing practices into a philosophy on the mind's latent powers—helped forge the intellectual synthesis which enabled social scientific thought to take root in this country. For whatever mesmerism's theories lacked in terms of the criteria established by modern experimental science, they nonetheless proved capable of stimulating the general public's interest in an entirely new field of intellectual inquiry. Academic departments of psychology at the turn of the century emerged, after all, in no small part because of the popular support generated by the mesmerist-inspired mind-cure or by New Thought philosophy and its message concerning the glorious potentials of the unconscious mind.[1] Thus the story of mesmerism is the story of the culturally ingrained assumptions according to which Americans first turned to psychology in their individual quests for wholeness.

Mesmerism now appears as an intriguing historical phenomenon because it focuses our attention upon the cultural as opposed to the scientific dimension of psychological theories. That is, mesmerism's tenure in popular American culture vividly illustrates the degree to which a "science of human nature" will receive widespread acceptance among the general public. Mesmerism was, after all, the first psychology to filter into the vernacular and to enable the general reading public to take its bearings on life. As such it represented the first in a long line of psychological systems which have attracted followings precisely according to their ability to address problems which arise in everyday life. For this reason, the process whereby the American mesmerists progressively disseminated their insights constitutes an important chapter in the history of American psychology. And, equally important, the story of mesmerism helps supplement and counterbalance extant theories which interpret the emergence of psychology as the triumph of secular rationality over the outmoded supernaturalisms of the nation's religious heritage. A new axiom of modern scholarship asserts that Americans have assimilated psychological ideas into their individual world view in direct proportion to their repudiation of religious beliefs and commitments.[2] Yet, as the case of mesmerism would seem to indicate, those psychological systems that have achieved popular acceptance in this country have done so by rearticulating—not replacing—the religious and metaphysical assumptions at the core of American religious thought.

Mesmerism was, of course, not indigenous to the United States. The German-born physician Franz Anton Mesmer first brought attention to this breakthrough in medical science.[3] Mesmer claimed to have detected the existence of a superfine substance or fluid which had somehow managed to elude scientific notice. Mesmer named this invisible fluid animal magnetism and claimed that it was in fact the most fundamental reality in the physical universe. Mesmer explained that animal magnetism constituted the etheric medium through which sensations of every kind—light, heat, magnetism, electricity—were able to pass from one physical object to another. Every lawful event occurring throughout nature depended upon the fact that animal magnetism linked physical objects together and made the transmission of influences from one to another possible. Mesmer believed that his discovery had removed the basic impediment to scientific progress and that every area of human knowledge would soon undergo rapid transformation and advancement.

Mesmer was naturally most concerned with the application of his discovery to the treatment of sickness and disease. He claimed that animal magnetism was evenly distributed throughout the healthy human body. If for any reason an individual's supply of animal magnetism were to be thrown out of equilibrium, one or more bodily organs would consequently be deprived of sufficient amounts of this vital force and would begin to falter. "There is," Mesmer reasoned, "only one illness and one healing." In other words, since any and all illnesses can ultimately be traced back to a disturbance in the body's supply of animal magnetism, medical science could be reduced to a simple set of procedures aimed at supercharging a patient's nervous system with this mysterious, yet life-giving, energy.

Even before Mesmer's theory reached American shores, his pupils had introduced significant changes which drastically altered the science of animal magnetism; these changes, incidentally, ensured the landing of mesmerism's tenets on receptive Yankee ground. The Marquis de Puységur exerted the most influence upon subsequent interpretations of his teacher's remarkable healing talents. Puységur had faithfully imitated Mesmer's techniques only to have his patients fall into unusual, sleeplike states of consciousness. They had become, so to speak, "mesmerized." This phenomenon was noteworthy because these entranced individuals exhibited the most extraordinary behaviors. Puységur's subjects responded to his questions with more intelligent and nuanced comments than could possibly be expected, given their particular educational and socio-economic backgrounds. Subjects might also suddenly recall long-forgotten memories or become conscious of minute details from an earlier experience. What is more, a select few appeared to have drifted into an even deeper state of consciousness which Puységur described as one of "extraordinary lucidity." These subjects spontaneously performed feats of telepathy, clairvoyance, and recognition. Puységur had stumbled upon the fact that, just below the threshold of ordinary consciousness, there exists a stratum of mental life which had hitherto eluded scientific investigation. In discovering the means of inducing this unconscious mental realm, Puységur placed mesmerism at the cutting edge of a revolution in the study of human nature.

Not until the late 1830s were Americans given any systematic exposure to the science of animal magnetism. Among the first successfully to bring this epoch-making discovery to the attention of American audiences was a Frenchman by the name of Charles Poyen, who had learned the art of mesmerism from the Marquis de Puységur. Arriving in the United States in 1836, Poyen commenced a lecture tour of the New England states in hopes of persuading his audiences to accept the "well-authenticated facts concerning an order of phenomena so important to science and so glorious to human nature."[4] Poyen, however, believed that mesmerism's single most important function lay less in mental healing than in exploring the somnambulic or mesmeric state of consciousness. His public lectures consequently revolved around an actual demonstration of the mesmeric state of consciousness and all of its attendant phenomena which, as he described it, included: "Suspension, more or less complete, of the external sensibility; intimate connexion with the magnetizer and with no other one; influence of the will; communication of thought; clairvoyance, or the faculty of seeing through various parts of the body, the eyes remaining closed; unusual development of sympathy, of memory, and of the power of imagination; faculty for sensing the symptoms of diseases and prescribing proper remedies for them; entire forgetting, after awakening, of what had transpired during the state of somnambulism."[5]

Poyen made a practice of "mesmerizing" volunteers from the audience who came in hope of obtaining a medical cure. Poyen would then proceed to make repeated "passes" with his hands in an effort to direct the flow of animal magnetism to the appropriate part of the body. A large proportion of those receiving this treatment would fall into a sleeplike condition and, upon awakening, claim cure. Poyen's own account, in many cases supported with newspaper reports and letters to the editor, lists successful treatment of such disorders as rheumatism, nervousness, back troubles, and liver ailments.

Roughly ten percent of Poyen's mesmerized subjects were said to have attained the "highest degree" of the magnetic condition. Their behavior went beyond the peculiar to the extraordinary. The formation of an especially intense rapport between the subject and the operator marked the onset of this stage in the mesmerizing process. The crucial ingredient of this rapport was the establishment of some non-verbal means of communication through which the subject could telepathically receive unspoken thoughts from the operator. Most mesmerized individuals attributed this ability to their heightened receptivity to animal magnetism. Some actually reported feeling animal magnetism impinge upon their nervous systems. They felt prickly sensations running up and down their bodies. Others claimed to "see" dazzling bright lights. Nor was it uncommon for subjects who had come into direct contact with these subtle streams of sensation to perform feats of clairvoyance and extrasensory perception. They might locate lost objects, describe events happening in distant locales, or telepathically read the minds of persons in the audience. Yet, upon returning to the waking state, they remembered little of their trance-bound experiences. They seemed to have been existing in another realm altogether. They knew only that they were now more refreshed and energetic; and some even claimed relief from former ailments.

Poyen's efforts attracted a host of newcomers eager to become spokesmen for the science of animal magnetism. According to one estimate, by 1843 more than two hundred "magnetizers" were selling their services in the city of Boston alone.[6] Growing public interest stimulated demand for books and pamphlets, and the American mesmerists willingly complied. Most of the dozens of works to appear over the next twenty years followed a common format: an introductory exhortation of open-mindedness, a short history of Mesmer's discovery, a cataloguing of typical cures, documented reports of clairvoyance and telepathy, and last but not least, a set of do-it-yourself instructions. For example, one widely circulated pamphlet bore the appropriate title *The History and Philosophy of Animal Magnetism, with Practical Instruction for the Exercise of This Power*. Another included in its title the promise to explain "the System of Manipulating Adopted to Produce Ecstasy and Somnambulism."[7]

Poyen had introduced mesmerism to American audiences by heralding it as the "science of the psychological constitution of man."[8] Unfortunately, he was not exactly sure what this actually entailed. While a great deal of attention had been given to validating their observations, mesmerists had as yet offered very little in the way of a scientific rationale. For his own part, Poyen hypothesized that "every human being carries within himself a nervous, magnetic, or vital atmosphere."[9] But beyond that he had little to say.

Only gradually—and with considerable awkwardness—were the American mesmerists able to educe a more fully psychological perspective from the observed phenomena of mesmerized subjects. The first problem they faced was deciding whether intrapersonal or extrapersonal variables produced the mesmeric state. Unable to accept the consequences of either, they took a safer route and chose both. An article that appeared in *Buchanan's Journal of Man* in 1849 registers the confusion:

> The established fact, that imagination may affect the most wonderful cures...seems to have been overlooked by the early magnetizers; they could see nothing in all their experiments but the potency of the wonderful and mysterious "fluid." On the other hand, the anti-mesmeric party, knowing the powers of the imagination, were blind to the existence of any other agent....It is probable that, in this matter, both the mesmerizers and their opponents were wrong in the ultra and exclusive doctrine which each party maintained—but with the lapse of time, we now see that each party had progressed nearer the truth. The opponents of animal magnetism have yielded by thousands to the conviction that there are forces of some kind emitted by the human constitution which had not been recognized in their philosophy; and, on the other hand, many mesmerizers (in the United States at least) have learned that many of their most interesting results are really the product of imagination.[10]

The American mesmerists were awakening to the fact that their experiments attested to an autonomous psychological realm. Well aware of the role that "suggestion" (i.e., the subject's tendency subconsciously to comply with the operator) and prior expectations played in determining the behavior of a person in the magnetic state, mesmerists became the first Americans directly to study the psychodynamic nature of interpersonal relationships.

Most American mesmerists, however, were by no means convinced that the "imagination" or "suggestibility" could account for their data. They feared that without the admission of animal magnetism, however loosely interpreted, their theory quite literally lacked substance. A purely subjective psychological reality was beyond their conceptual horizons. Anyway, it could not be supported on the basis of the data. Mesmerized subjects detected the existence of a discrete and even palpable force impinging upon their nervous systems from without. Thus the American mesmerists could not feel justified in pursuing the phenomenon of suggestion as relentlessly as did their later European counterparts. While Charcot, Breuer, Janet, and, finally, Freud followed the notion of suggestion to a more or less mechanistic view of intraphysic mental processes, the mesmerists remained committed to their belief that an individual's "inner source of feeling" somehow opens the finite mind to transpersonal domains.

Convinced that their observations could be accounted for within a suitably enlarged science, the mesmerists offered as detailed neurophysiological explanations as contemporary medical research permitted. The mesmerists' journals, incidentally, contributed significantly to the study of the physiological structure of the brain. The articles and neurophysiological charts which they circulated throughout the 1840s and 1850s constituted the period's most significant attempt to correlate physiological and psychological perspectives on the nature of consciousness. However, the mesmerists failed to follow a neurophysiological viewpoint to its logical conclusion as they did a psychodynamic one. The phenomena of direct thought transference, clairvoyance, and prevision defied explanation by reference to neural forces constrained within the brain. As one early researcher insisted, the "doctrine of animal magnetism is the connecting link between physiology and psychology...it demonstrates the intimate interconnection between the natural and the spiritual."[11] The mesmerists believed that although it is possible to offer physiological descriptions of any and all mental processes, these descriptions were not themselves final explanations of mesmeric phenomena. According to the mesmerists, mental processes, at least those occurring spontaneously to individuals when in the mesmeric state, demanded an explanation that was at once psychological and metaphysical—that is, one that testified to the existence of animal magnetism.

The mesmerists thus found themselves committed to a psychological perspective which subordinated both physiological and interpersonal perspectives about human nature to metaphysical considerations of the mind's participation in a "higher" psychic realm. Theirs was a "science of the soul considered physiologically and philosophically." And hence, they asserted that the study of mesmerism simultaneously furthered man's scientific and spiritual aims. In the words of Joseph Buchanan, whose career as a midwestern physiology professor led to involvement with a wide range of metaphysical movements, the doctrine of animal magnetism taught that "positive material existence and positive spiritual existence—however far apart they stand and however striking the contrast between their properties—are connected by these fine gradations...both are subject to the same great system of law which each obeys in its own sphere."[12] Mesmerism's discovery of the mind's receptivity to these refined spiritual energies enabled its adherents to speak of ecstatic self-transcendence and mystical illumination as lawful properties of human nature. They affirmed that "the power of disembodied mind and intellectual manifestations...fall within the scope of the fundamental principles of the constitution of man, and spiritual mysteries, too, are beautifully elucidated by the complete correspondence, and mathematical harmony, between the spiritual and material laws of our being."[13]

Unlike Mesmer, who intended to show by his theory how medical and non-medical healings were but variations of the selfsame principle, his Yankee followers focused instead on explaining the commonalities between normal and transcendent states of consciousness. The explanatory model proposed by American investigators did little more than give psychological focus to discussions concerning man's inward participation in a transcendent spiritual order. Which is to say, the American mesmerists had gradually transformed the science of animal magnetism into a psychology whose chief value lay in sanctioning and engineering mystical states of consciousness.

The mesmerists' difficulty in defining the exact nature of their psychological science was compounded by the fact that their work preceded the establishment of the first department of psychology at an American university by fifty years. Their theories consequently lacked the kind of specialized focus which collegiality, corroborative research, and professional associations impart to a theoretical discipline. The audience to which the mesmerists addressed their theories was the general public. It would be inappropriate, then, to expect mesmerist psychology to have developed in accordance with the kinds of criteria identified by disinterested scientific observers. A psychological theory attracts a popular following not by virtue of its formal scientific status, but rather by promising practical solutions to problems which arise in the context of everyday life. In essence this means that it must be able to supply self-help guides for practical living. And perhaps the biggest difference between America's first popular psychology and the twentieth-century ones was the audience itself. In the nineteenth century self-help aspirations were not narrowly focused on specific problems like help with weight reduction or sexual impotence. Rather than merely gaining control over isolated behavioral problems, personality change entailed a thorough transformation. It had to do with reshaping one's entire outlook on life, being inducted into wholly new meanings of human existence. The fact that the American mesmerists won over a large popular constituency ultimately testifies less to the scientific merit of their discipline than to its resonance with the needs and motivations of nineteenth-century American culture.

Poyen, a Frenchman, was all but oblivious to the close connection between mesmerist psychology and the popular American religious climate. Yet as early as February 1837 a letter addressed to the editor of the Boston *Recorder* testified: "George was converted from materialism to Christianity by the facts in Animal Magnetism developed under his [Poyen's] practice....It proves the power of mind over matter...and informs our faith in the spirituality and immortality of our nature, and encourages us to renewed efforts to live up to its transcendent powers.[14] A high school teacher wrote in the Providence *Journal* that God and eternity are the only answer to these mysterious phenomena—these apparitions of the Infinity and the Unknown."[15]

Americans were apparently more disposed to emphasize the religious import of mesmerism than Europeans. An early tract pointed out that mesmerism casts "light on how we are constituted, how nearly we are related to, and how far we resemble our original...God who is a pure spiritual essence."[16] This same author averred that mesmerism "shows that man has within him a spiritual nature, which can live without the body...in the eternal NOW of a future existence."[17]

The act of entering the mesmeric state was thought to be a

decidedly numinous experience. Direct contact with the in-streaming animal magnetic forces momentarily transformed and elevated a person's very being. A fairly typical account of this encounter related how "the whole moral and intellectual character becomes changed from the degraded condition of death to the exalted intelligence of a spiritual state. The external senses are all suspended and the internal sense of spirit acts with its natural power as it will when entirely freed from the body after death. No person, we think, can listen to the revelations of a subject in a magnetic state, respecting the mysteries of our nature, and continue to doubt the existence of a never dying soul and the existence of a future or heavenly life."[18]

Evidently Americans felt mesmerism treated the whole person rather than isolated complaints. They believed that the mesmerizing process helped them to reestablish inner harmony with the very source of physical and emotional well-being. While in the mesmeric state, they learned that disease and even moral confusion were but the unfortunate consequences of having fallen out of rapport with the invisible spiritual workings of the universe. Conversely, health and personal virtue were the automatic rewards of living in accordance with the cosmic order. When patients returned from their ecstatic mental journey, they knew themselves to have been raised to a higher level of participation in the very life power that "activates the whole frame of nature and produces all the phenomena that transpire throughout the realms of unbounded space."[19]

Although mesmerism had no overt connections with religion, many viewed it as a new variation of the religious revivals which had long since become a distinguishing feature of American religious life. Appearing in the mid-1830s, mesmerism was simply swept along in the wake of the progressivist tendencies unleashed by the Second Great Awakening. Charles Finney and others had helped dispose the popular religious climate toward an "alleviated Calvinism" which viewed sin as a function of either ignorance or faulty social institutions rather than as a product of mankind's inherent depravity. Man's "lower nature" was considered potentially correctable through humanly initiated reforms. As a consequence, American religious thought during this period implicitly sanctioned experimental doctrines aimed toward the immediate and total renovation of humanity.

Mesmerism, with its doctrine of the unconscious, recapitulated the themes of the nation's revivalist heritage almost perfectly. Like the revivalists, the mesmerists preached that confusion, self-doubt, and emotional unrest would continue to plague persons so long as they refused to open themselves up to a higher spiritual power. And mesmerism, too, provided inwardly troubled persons with an intense experience thought to restore harmony between themselves and unseen spiritual forces. The mesmeric state, no less than the emotion-laden conversion experience, powerfully and convincingly testified to the belief that man's lower nature could be utterly transformed and elevated when brought under the guiding influence of spirit.

Yet the mesmerists differed from the revivalists in at least one important respect. Instead of reproaching individuals for challenging orthodox religious thinking, they encouraged it. Mesmerism, like so many of the "isms" to appear in the nineteenth century, stood at the far forefront of the liberalizing tendencies spawned by American Protestant culture. Its doctrines appealed to many whose religious sensibilities could not be constrained by scriptural piety and instead yearned for a progressive, co-scientific religious outlook. Mesmerism had, after all, empirically demonstrated the existence of an irreducible spiritual element at the core of the human psyche. The mesmerists were certain that their psychological approach to man's higher spiritual nature would eventually purge Christian theology of its embarrassing irrationalities. By arguing that mesmerism "not only disposes the mind to adopt religious principles, but also tends to free us from the errors of superstition by reducing to natural causes many phenomena," mesmerists provided many who had become intellectually disenfranchised from the churches with a new focus for their religious convictions.[20]

The mesmerists' discovery of the unconscious perfectly expressed nineteenth-century optimism and faith in human progress. Mesmerism, like all other sciences, claimed to be harnessing formerly hidden forces for human use. As the mesmerist John Dods boasted, mesmerism had climbed aboard that "glorious chariot of science with its ever increasing power, magnificence and glory...ever obeying the command of God: ONWARD."[21] Yet mesmerism went all other sciences of the period one better. It showed how human experience potentially extends well beyond the boundaries of the physical senses. Mesmerized subjects proved that the normal waking state of consciousness was neither the only nor even the highest, mental condition. A preeminent spokesman for the Swedenborgian cause asserted that the investigations of the mesmeric state point to "an entirely new class of facts in psychology."[22] For him they provided empirical confirmation of "the grand principle that man is a spirit as to his interiors and that his spiritual nature in the body often manifests itself according to the laws which govern it out of the body."[23] Convinced that mesmerism uncovered the laws which govern the transition between the two, he concluded that it opened "a new chapter in the philosophy of mind and in man's relations to a higher sphere."[24]

The vast amount of literature which Americans produced describing mesmerist psychology reveals that they had found in it more than a key to physical health. Its findings, rather, were lauded on the grounds that "they present a new view of the interior genius of the inspired Word, and of the whole body of Christian doctrine."[25] To those seeking confirmation of the living realities of faith, the mesmerists' concept of the unconscious appeared as a promising pathway by which they might hope to achieve a felt sense of participation in the higher reaches of the cosmos. And, furthermore, mesmerist psychology lent plausibility, legitimacy, and an aura of scientific support to many newly emerging religious groups. American Swedenborgianism, spiritualism, Christian Science, Theosophy, and the mind-cure movement all explicitly drew on mesmerist psychology to substantiate their own claims that men and women had access to higher spiritual realms.

Historical hindsight permits us to view the growth in popularity of these early psychological ideas as following a path hewn by the very needs and interests which they endeavored to satisfy. The mesmerists sold psychology to an American consumer market by first identifying pervasive cultural needs and then demonstrating their product's ability to meet them. Another point is worth noting. In the process of winning popular constituency, mesmerism drew its most enthusiastic support from the ranks of those who were intellectually disenfranchised from religious orthodoxy. Sensitive to the culture lag besetting contemporary religious thought, these individuals had the courage to step outside Christian sources in an effort to reconceptualize the essence of moral and religious living. Since its doctrines were ostensibly those of empirical investigation, mesmerism lent an aura of legitimacy to those seeking reassurance about their spiritual well-being; at the same time, it reflected the progressivist spirit of a dawning modernity. The movement's spokesmen repeatedly underscored the fact that mesmerism represented the nation's first non-evangelical interpretation of human nature and yet did so by focusing upon what one author described as "the point where anthropology weds itself to theology."[26]

As Perry Miller has pointed out, the pragmatic character of the American mind prevented it from ever fully succumbing to Calvinism and its insistence that the ultimate criteria upon which human actions are to be judged lie beyond the grasp of human reason. Instead, the American mind required that "in some fashion the transcendent God had to be chained, made less inscrutable, less mysterious, less unpredictable—He had to be made, again, understandable in human terms."[27] The whole notion of a covenant between God and his creation seemed to imply that He had laid down "the conditions by which Heaven is obtained and he who fulfills the conditions has an incontestable title to glorification."[28] Those willing to be persuaded by the mesmerists' claim that a continuum or orderly hierarchy exists between the lower and higher reaches of human nature found psychology a natural derivative of covenantal conceptions of the good life. Psychological ideas were, so to speak, the lowest common denominator to which America could reduce otherwise hopelessly abstract considerations of how to align themselves with the greater scheme of things.

Mesmerism, as popular psychologies generally do, equivocated the importance of material (e.g., physiological) or efficient (e.g., environmental) cause explanations of human nature. Its postulation of a dimension of psychic reality undetected by the physical senses made it impossible to reduce the ultimate or final cause of psychological processes to empirically verifiable cause and effect relationships. In other words, from a scientific perspective mesmerism was simply bad psychology. Like most popular psychologies, its explanatory power was more properly metaphysical than metaphysiological. Yet mesmerism's inherent inability to specify strictly psychological determinants of human fulfillment permitted nineteenth-century Americans to graft the psychological perspective per se onto culturally ingrained assumptions about the progressive character of human nature. Consequently, they were freed to pursue psychological investigations without experiencing any conflict with the essential postulates of religious commitment. After all, mesmerism's descriptions of latent psychological potentials redefined the details but kept the covenantal bond between the divine and human spheres fully intact. Despite the growing presence of structural inequalities in the socio-economic sphere, psychologically formulated self-help doctrines sustained commitment to the work ethic promising self-respect, success, and eternal happiness to all who asserted and disciplined themselves. Those unsure just how to go to work systematically on the outer world could now go to work on themselves instead. And in all this the nation's first popular psychology resonated almost perfectly with the Puritan-Protestant world view at the core of America cultural thought. That is, it reaffirmed belief in the predetermined harmony of the outwardly disconnected parts of the created universe; in inner adjustment (faith) as prior to good works; and in the essentially religious character of the individual's struggle to seek out and then ascetically order his life in conformity with the ultimate conditions of reality.

Mesmerism successfully entered American intellectual life because it located new experiential moorings for a progressive spirituality. Its psychological terminology transposed the form of personal piety from categories of theological transcendence to those of psychological immanence, thus accommodating the conceptual needs of an increasingly pluralistic culture. To the popular reading public, the mesmerists' descriptions of the structure of human consciousness straddled a fine line between religious myth and scientific psychology. However absurd its references to an etheric energy called animal magnetism might seem to us today, its metapsychological aura seemed eminently plausible to a generation enamored with recent technological discoveries such as the telegraph, photography, and electricity. Dr. Joseph Buchanan offered perhaps the clearest expression of the ideological thrust animating the early growth of American psychology. At the end of a long list of mesmerism's practical applications, he explained that the "function [of the psychologist] is similar to that of the clergyman, and in fact although the anthropologist [psychologist] may not be formally a clergyman, every clergyman should be, for the fulfillment of his own duties, a thoroughgoing anthropologist [psychologist]."[29]

Psychological thought emerged at a time when Americans were beginning to hunger for non-scriptural sources of spiritual edification. The American mesmerists responded by offering an entirely new, and eminently attractive, arena for self-discovery—one's own psychological depths. To the mesmerists' way of thinking, psychological self-adjustment was the ontological equivalent of reconciling oneself with immanent spiritual forces. Simply by cultivating one's innate psychological potentials, anyone, even someone intellectually disenfranchised from churched religion, could feel assured that he was making progress along the line of spiritual development. Mesmerism was, then, but the first in a long line of psychological systems which have attracted popular followings precisely because large segments of the American public are continuously seeking ways to reduce their metaphysical responsibilities to more manageable proportions. Far from functioning in the service of a secular world view, this, the nation's first popular psychology, offered both terminology (myth) and practices (ritual) which neatly transposed the religious dimensions of self-understanding into forms more responsible to the pluralistic character of modern society.

Notes

1. An article by Henry Goddard entitled "The Effect of Mind on Body As Evidenced in Faith Cures," *American Journal of Psychology* 10 (1899): 430-98 is especially helpful in portraying early American psychologists' indebtedness to mesmerism and its various legatees. Related discussions of mesmerism's role in generating Americans' interest in psychology can be found in both Nathan Hale's chapter entitled "Mind Cures and the Mystical Wave: Popular Preparation for Psychoanalysis, 1904-1910" in his *Freud and the Americans* (New York: Oxford Univ. Press, 1971) and my *Mesmerism and the American Cure of Souls* (Philadelphia: Univ. of Pennsylvania Press, 1982).

2. See, for example, Martin Gross, *The Psychological Society* (New York: Random House, 1978), Christopher Lasch, *The Culture of Narcissism* (New York: Warner, 1979), and Phillip Rieff, *The Triumph of the Therapeutic* (New York: Harper & Row, 1966).

3. There are a number of excellent studies of Mesmer and his healing science. The best of these is to be found in the opening chapters of Henri Ellenberger's *The Discovery of the Unconscious* (New York: Basic Books, 1969). Others include Vincent Buranelli's *Franz Anton Mesmer: The Wizard from Vienna* (New York: McCann, Cowan, & Geoghegan, 1975) and Frank Podmore's *From Mesmer to Christian Science* (New York: University Books, 1963).

4. Charles Poyen, *Progress of Animal Magnetism in New England* (Boston: Weeks, Jordan & Co., 1837), p. 10.

5. Ibid., p. 63.

6. A Practical Magnetizer (pseud.), *The History and Philosophy of Animal Magnetism with Practical Instructions for the Exercise of Its Power* (Boston, 1843), p. 8.

7. A Gentleman of Philadelphia (pseud.), *The Philosophy of Animal Magnetism, Together with the System of Manipulating Adopted to Produce Ecstasy and Somnambulism* (Philadelphia: Merrihew & Dunn, 1837).

8. Charles Poyen, *A Letter to Colonel William Stone* (Boston: Weeks, Jordan & Co., 1837), p. 6.

9. Ibid., p. 47.

10. *Buchanan's Journal of Man* 1 (1849): 319.

11. Gentleman of Philadelphia, *Philosophy*, p. 11.

12. James Buchanan, *Neurological System of Anthropology* (Cincinnati, 1854), p. 232.

13. Ibid., appendix I.

14. Poyen, *Progress*, p. 68.

15. Ibid.

16. Gentleman of Philadelphia, *Philosophy*, p. 68.
17. Ibid., p. 71.
18. Practical Magnetizer, *History*, p. 19.
19. John Dods, *The Philosophy of Electrical Psychology* (New York: Fowler & Wells, 1850), p. 57.
20. Theodore Léger, *Animal Magnetism of Psychodynamy* (New York: Appleton, 1846), p. 18.
21. Dods, *Electrical Psychology*, p. 36.
22. George Bush, *Mesmer and Swedenborg* (New York: John Allen, 1847), p. 47.
23. Ibid., p. 127.
24. Ibid., p. 13.
25. Ibid., p. 168.
26. Ibid., p. 15.
27. Perry Miller, *Errand in to the Wilderness* (Cambridge, Mass.: Belknap Press of Harvard Univ. Press, 1975), p. 55.
28. Ibid., p. 71.
29. Buchanan, *Neurological System*, appendix I.

ARTHUR WROBEL

11. Afterword

The hope of Alfred Russell Wallace, the eminent biologist and co-discoverer of evolution—that orthodox science would eventually accord phrenology, mesmerism, and psychical research the status of legitimacy—was never realized. Without denying them their many successes in effecting cures and without impugning the veracity of eye-witnesses and of personal testimonials about psychic encounters or character analyses, new generations found the explanations or theories for these phenomena nothing short of bizarre. Explanations in terms of animal magnetism, or of correlating highly individualized mental capacities with brain architecture, or of explicating the laws of universal correspondence between the lower and upper reaches of the cosmos failed to impress the scientific community. In relying on such explanations, these various pseudo-sciences betrayed their failure to incorporate recent advances in physics, biology, and medicine. But even though these disciplines drifted further and further from the moorings of experimentally derived data, certified laboratory procedures, and statistical methods, orthodox science found it could not entirely ignore them.

They had not only enjoyed considerable popular support but had raised questions, addressed issues, and posed challenges in a wide range of areas that later sciences were forced to confront. Wallace's hope did, in some modest measure, come to be realized: these pseudo-sciences created the environment and prepared the public mind for contemplating theories or research ranging from neurobiology, psychology, parapsychology, evolution, and anthropology to bio-dynamic gardening.

Gall's study of cerebral localization generated such controversy that it forced both his detractors and his defenders to determine the relationship of the brain to the mind. Using ablation or surgical excision, Marie-Jean-Pierre Flourens (1794-1867), François Magendie (1783-1855), founder of the first journal of experimental physiology, and Johannes Müller (1801-58) made discoveries that gave rise to experimental neurophysiology and sensory-motor physiology. In pursuing research on cerebral localization based on the physiology of sensory-motor processes, Pierre Paul Broca (1842-80) discovered the region of the cerebrum that controls the function of speech, while Sir David Ferrier refined the cortical map in various species. Related research on tactile and bodily sensations, aphasia, and on the relationship between the brain, memory, and learning quickly followed. During the 1940s and 1950s Wilder Penfield mapped cortical centers in the brain.[1]

Phrenology also paved the road for the triumphant march of psychology and anthropology. The use of the term "function" as a systematic term in psychology derives from phrenology, as did the important correlation between the operation of the mind and the condition of the brain upon which rests neurophysiology, preventive psychiatry, psychopathology, and psychotherapy. Scientists are even beginning to give limited support to the existence of certain innate functions. Cortical lesions appear to affect numerical, spatial, constructive, and mnemonic functions, while the sociobiologists Edmund O. Wilson and Richard Dawkins believe that various affective, intellectual, and moral powers such as aggression, altruism, religion, language, and sex roles are innate as Gall once argued. These are admittedly of genetic rather than cranial origin, however.[2] Phrenology contributed significantly to the method and theory of physical anthropology, and influenced the mid-nineteenth-century shift away from ethnology. George Combe studied various national skulls including non-Western ones, and actively theorized about the origins of races, evolution, and heredity—all anthropological concerns. The phrenologists also helped establish the cephalic index, the ratio of head length to breadth, which became the mainstay of anthropometry.[3]

Phrenology's interest in racial anthropology had related logically and emotionally both to early hereditarian ideas and to Darwinism. It played a mediating role in the spread of evolution, natural selection, geology, and, later, socialistic thought. As Roger Cooter recently demonstrated, it buttressed the notion of social evolution primarily through the agency of Victorian artisan societies and Owenite socialists, all of whom staunchly supported phrenology. One might also wonder whether phrenology's optimistic views of human progress stand behind works such as B. F. Skinner's *Walden Two*; after all, phrenology similarly proposed that man's mind could be studied objectively and his environment modified to affect various cerebral functions.[4]

Mesmerism's legacy to modern thought is no less impressive. By uncovering the existence of an unconscious that exerted a hitherto unsuspected power on human behavior and thought, it laid the groundwork for dynamic psychotherapy. In a slightly different guise, as spiritual mesmerism, or spiritualism, it contributed to the emergence of various cults, religions, and mindcures from Theosophy to Christian Science and indirectly to several cultlike psychotherapies.

The study of mesmeric trances that eventuated in the scientific study of hypnosis and the development of abnormal psychology began with one of Mesmer's pupils, the Marquis de Puységur (1751-1825). His demonstration of post-hypnotic suggestion and amnesia, somnambulism, and telepathy attracted not only charlatans interested in the stage potential of such phenomena but others with medical credentials. John Elliotson (1791-1868) and James Braid (1795-1860) experimented with mesmerism as a potential therapy for neuroses and as an anesthetic, and amassed an impressive number of cures using magnetic trances.[5]

Related research suggesting that hypnotic effects depend on the susceptibility of patients to auto-suggestion contributed to the rise of a psychotherapy based on persuasion and inspiration. Paul Dubois developed a system of "moral orthopedics"; the

Reverend Elwood Worcester used hypnotism and Christian exhortation in founding the Emmanuel Movement; and Emile Coué based his psychotherapeutics on having patients combine willpower with the daily recitation of a healing mantra: "Day by day, in every way, I am getting better and better."[6]

Hypnotism's uncovering of an accessory consciousness attracted neurologists and psychotherapists, all of whom figure prominently in the emergence of modern medicine: Alfred Binet, Pierre Janet, August Forel, J. Babinski, Krafft-Ebing, Oscar Vogt, and Paul Schilder. Freud jointly published a paper with Joseph Breuer on the effect mental trauma had in precipitating hysterical attacks and the value of having patients relive forgotten or repressed facts under hypnosis. Hypnosis remains an object of psychological inquiry and has its own division in the American Psychological Association.[7]

Americans, however, failed to pursue systematically the role of suggestion in mesmerism that led their European counterparts to the revolutionary discovery of an autonomous psychological realm. Instead, with the Hydesville spirit-rappings in 1848, their attention shifted to the even greater thrill of spiritual mesmerism. Spiritualism's durable legacy can be felt in the current resurgence of interest in unconventional or alternate sources of knowledge, religion, and healing.

Psychical research formally had its beginning in 1882 when a group of professors of philosophy, medicine, and physics, many of them Cambridge educated, and even several Fellows of the Royal Society, founded the Society for Psychical Research. They set out to investigate, systematically and scientifically, reports of spirit and telepathic communication, thought transference, clairvoyant perception, and spontaneous mediumistic trances. Boris Sidis, G. Stanley Hall, and Freud followed closely the society's research.

In this country John Coover at Stanford and William McDougall at Harvard attempted to establish psychical research as a field of university study. J. B. Rhine earned the first doctorate on psychical research awarded by an American university in 1933. Though Rhine never succeeded in proposing a working hypothesis to explain parapsychological phenomena, prominent physicists have noted their affinity to quantum physics. The discoveries of Niels Bohr, Albert Einstein, and Werner Heisenberg prompted many people to call into question the notions of causality, materialism, and determinism in science, thus providing the kind of framework in which psi phenomena might make sense. Although parapsychology currently enjoys but token respectability as legitimate research, the American Association for the Advancement of Science recognizes the Parapsychological Society as a member organization.[8]

While spiritualism offered to many cautious hope that profound psychological depths could be plumbed, it suggested to others the possibility of reconciliation with immanent deity. Sincere spiritualists began forming organizations during the latter part of the nineteenth century; the largest and most conservative of these, the National Spiritualist Association of Churches, now has headquarters in Milwaukee.[9]

Spiritualism represents but one variation on a group of "metaphysical" religious movements. Both Henry Steel Olcott (1832-1907), the first president of the American Theosophical Society, and Helena Petrovna Blavatsky, the co-founder of the Society (1875) and its guiding light, had ties to spiritualism: Olcott when he witnessed spiritualistic displays in Ohio, and Blavatsky as a practicing medium. Between *Isis Unveiled* (1877) and *The Secret Doctrine* (1879) Blavatsky evolved an eclectic synthesis of Eastern and Western religions in order to discover the essential unity of primordial truths in all religions. Theosophical doctrines are typical of most occult religions: the immanence of spirit or life energy that animates the material creation and gives form to matter; the universe's evolution including individual and planetary rebirths; man as a spark of God which evolved into individual consciousness or human ego; and the psychical powers latent in man.[10]

Theosophy has fragmented among various autonomous organizations, less over doctrinal than over personal differences, the predictable outcome of a religion whose leaders claim special and authoritative revelations. Alice Tingley built her Theosophical City at Point Loma in San Diego in 1900, and Dr. Rudolf Steiner, a Goethe authority and leader of the German section of the society, broke with Annie Besant's leadership over the matter of authoritative revelation and founded the Anthroposophical Society in 1912. The Arcane School (1923) teaches students spiritual wisdom, meditation, and discipline through service to mankind as a way of discovering the divinity latent in one's heart; the Astara Foundation (1951) teaches the "ancient wisdom" at the same time that it pursues a ministry of healing using clairvoyance.[11]

These charismatic and metaphysical churches teach, as well, the message of occult schools in earlier centuries—their secret knowledge can engineer the unfolding of perfected millennial society. During the 1920s the Theosophists claimed that the Piscean Age, or the Age of Christianity, was rapidly drawing to a close, seeing among newly returned souls forerunners of a root race that was to develop the Aquarian Age.[12]

Many of these occult beliefs are held by New Thought and its many off-shoots, its popularizers skillfully adding, however, psychological ideas to spiritual or metaphysical matters. In so doing, they have created a new form of religious devotion here in America that teaches the brotherhood of man, the unity of life, the immanence of God, and the power of right thinking to influence health, happiness, and personal success.

Believing that most illnesses were simply the result of people's ideas or beliefs, Phineas P. Quimby (1802-66) healed by psychically implanting images of health in a patient's unconscious mind. His healing triumphs attracted the attention of Warren Felt Evans and Mary Baker Eddy, both of whom were powerfully to shape New Thought. Evans's philosophy linked physical disease to disturbances in man's spiritual being and health to man's recognition of his Christlike nature. Eddy added more metaphysics. For her, health and moral behavior reflect a patient's success in establishing contact with higher spiritual powers, while sin, sickness, and death reflect errors of man's mortal mind and ignorance of his own immortal and spiritual Christlikeness.

Predictably, the freedom of belief and interpretation New Thought encourages, a freedom that has even allowed it to graft onto the body of its beliefs advances in psychology and medicine, has also fostered many branches and sects: The Divine Science Church (1896), the Church of Religious Science (1952), and the Unity School of Christianity.[13]

The distance separating these sects and cultlike psychotherapies such as EST, Scientology, TM, Jungian study groups, and Silva Mind Control is minimal. Similarly fascinated with mystical and altered states of consciousness, all adhere to a belief in the existence of a psychological reality outside the mind-body or normal subject-object relationship; they also encourage people to explore realms beyond the five senses and to control their lives.

These spiritualist offshoots make healing through the mind or spirit a major part of their mission. Their explanation of disease as discord in man's spiritual force which causes an ensuing imbalance in the body manifested as disease, recalls homoeopathic theory. Much as homoeopathy does, recent movements in psychophysiology investigate the relationship between behavioral and physiological functions. Reichian therapy includes analyzing a patient's character structure and dissolving blocks of muscular tension in order to free the flow of orgone energy—a composite of libidinal-muscular and cosmic energy—through the body.[14] Even without such esoteric overtones, the healing doctrines of hydropathy and homoeopathy resemble many of those that holistic medicine or nature pathology currently hold: a comprehensive treatment of the patient, physically and emotionally, and cure through natural means. Such treatments are designed less to attack the disease than to treat the patient and, as in water-cure, to make patients participate in the management of their own disease.

From investigating the nature and dynamics of an ecstatic trance to spearheading the reformation of man's moral life and his institutions, from offering proof of life beyond the physical to the development of a functional psychology and neurophysiology, these pseudo-sciences engaged a range of issues as broad as the legacy they left is rich. During their heyday these pseudo-sciences gave credence to the nineteenth century's compelling dream that all knowledge was unitary and could be ultimately embodied in one grand Science of Man. Whitman termed such a science "omnient," defining it as "nothing less than all sciences comprehending all the known names and many unknown." Such a science would integrate all knowledge, its coherence and orderliness reflecting the harmony and simplicity of the physical creation. In the breadth of their epistemological aims, any one of these pseudo-sciences could lay claim to being such a science.

Such a view implicitly assumed that science is activist, studying man in order to improve human nature. Albert Brisbane sold Fourier's ideas in *The Social Destiny of Man* (1840) on this very basis, as a scientific study of human nature that could engineer the unfolding of a new social order. Many of the utopian communities were experiments in practical social sciences. Brook Farm, for instance, was organized to demonstrate how man's happiness depended on discovering and implementing the scientific laws of human nature and society. Stephen Pearl Andrews, the social activist, reformer, and anarchist, urged the first graduating class of the American Hydropathic Institute on December 6, 1851, to go out into the world and add to "the science of the true social relations of man." He expounded this idea at greater length in *The Science of Society* (1854).[15]

This view, that science contributes certain values—utilitarian, egalitarian, and religious—eventually came in conflict with the new ideal of the scientist and his profession. In the 1870s the new ideal emphasized the pursuit of truth independent of extraneous considerations and even came to regard applied science as a lower enterprise.[16]

This newly emerging triumphant scientism set the rules by which the demarcation debate was to be fought—namely, on the basis of so-called "hard" data and methods of verification inherently incompatible with metaphysical concerns. William James's misgivings—that in rejecting "exceptional occurrences" and mechanically adhering to its mechanistic laws the orthodox scientific view of the world was partial—fell on deaf ears. Science's adherence to objective modes of natural law methodologically made inadmissible the subjective consciousness; it excluded consciousness from both the observer and the observed. While the pseudo-scientists might also speak about experimental proofs and systematic demonstrations, as Mary Baker Eddy did, they nevertheless doubted the adequacy of ordinary sense perception or empirical science to unlock the mysteries of correspondences between the cosmic and mundane worlds. They instead spoke of a "third way" or the use of the "inward eye" to discover a reality lying between faith in the scriptures and naturalistic science.[17]

Despite its efforts, "hard" science has not entirely succeeded in differentiating between occult and clinical matters. This is particularly evident among mentalist self-help movements. For instance, Dr. Arthur Janov's Primal Scream Therapy and Paul Bindrim's Nude Marathon Regression Therapy treat the trauma of childbirth or unhappy childhoods by taking patients back into earlier incarnations. L. Ron Hubbard, a former science fiction writer, founded Dianetics, which has patients relive painful experiences much as Freud, with Joseph Breuer, had subjects relive traumatic experiences under hypnosis in a process called abreaction therapy. With the best of American pragmatism, all can claim that their systems are empirical (they work as therapies) and are secular.[18]

Beyond the fact that pseudo-sciences so often provide the impetus for new research, their study and very presence are valuable for other reasons. No doubt their resiliency and even current proliferation are in no small measure due to the fact that they entertain matters that orthodox science dismisses as unknowable. In its commitment to quantification and objectivity, so its detractors charge, "normal" science ignores the wonder and mystery of the world beyond the material, narrowly confining its investigations to problems that fit only in the puzzle of current methodological paradigms or make sense in terms of "orthodox" data.[19]

But among the pseudo-sciences, as the essays in this book show, man enjoys the reassurance that he constitutes a vital connection between the material and spiritual, and that his investigations need not be confined to the pursuit of mere fact or knowledge but can give him access to meaning and wisdom.

Notes

1. Harry J. Jerison, "Should Phrenology be Rediscovered?" *Current Anthropology* 18 (December 1977): 744-46; Raymond E. Fancher, *Pioneers of Psychology* (New York: Norton, 1979), pp. 53-58; David J. Murray, *A History of Western Psychology* (Englewood Cliffs, N.J.: Prentice-Hall, 1983), p. 144; Thomas H. Leahey, *A History of Psychology: Main Currents in Psychological Thought* (Englewood Cliffs, N.J.: Prentice-Hall, 1980), p. 168; Robert M. Young, *Mind, Brain and Adaptation in the Nineteenth Century: Cerebral Localization and Its Biological Context from Gall to Ferrier* (Oxford: Clarendon Press, 1970), pp. 6-7, 121, 90; Walter Bromberg, *The Mind of Man: A History of Psychotherapy and Psychoanalysis* (New York: Harper & Row, 1963), p. 150; and Murray, *History*, pp. 319-22.

2. Karl M. Dallenbach, "The History and Derivation of the Word 'Function' as a Systematic Term in Psychology," *American Journal of Psychology* 26 (Oct. 1915): 473-84; Eric T. Carlson, "The Influence of Phrenology on Early American Psychiatric Thought," *American Journal of Psychiatry* 127 (1970): 535-38; David Bakan, "Is Phrenology Foolish?" *Psychology Today* 1 (May 1968): 44-50; John McFie, "Recent Advances in Phrenology," *Lancet* 7 (Aug. 12, 1962): 361-62; Richard Dawkins, *The Selfish Gene* (New York: Oxford Univ. Press, 1967); Edward O. Wilson, *Sociobiology: The New Synthesis* (Cambridge: Harvard Univ. Press, 1975); and Edward O. Wilson, *On Human Nature* (New York: Bantam, 1978); as noted in Thomas Hardy Leahey and Grace Evans Leahey, *Psychology's Occult Doubles: Psychology and the Problem of Pseudoscience* (Chicago: Nelson-Hall, 1983), p. 257, n. 59.

3. Ralph Holloway, "The Casts of Fossil Hominid Brains," *Scientific American* 231 (1974): 106-15; Jerison, "Phrenology Rediscovered?" p. 745; Marvin Harris, *The Rise of Anthropological Theory: A History of Theories of Culture* (New York: Crowell, 1968), p. 99; and Paul A. Erickson, "Phrenology and Physical Anthropology: The George Combe Connection," *Current Anthropology* 18 (March 1977): 92-93.

4. Leahey, *History*, p. 65; Charles E. Rosenberg, *No Other Gods: On Science and American Social Thought* (Baltimore: Johns Hopkins Univ. Press, 1976), p. 218 n. 44; Roger J. Cooter, *The Cultural Meaning of Popular Science: Phrenology and the Organization of Consent in Nineteenth Century Britain* (Cambridge: Cambridge Univ. Press, 1984); and Bakan, "Is Phrenology Foolish?" p. 49.

5. Murray, *History*, p. 294; Fancher, *Pioneers*, pp. 182-86; and Bromberg, *Mind of Man*, p. 181.

6. Bromberg, *Mind of Man*, pp. 188, 140, 189.

7. Ibid., pp. 184, 197; and Leahey and Leahey, *Psychology's Doubles*, p. 155.

8. R. Laurence Moore, *In Search of White Crows: Spiritualism, Psychology, and American Culture* (New York: Oxford Univ. Press, 1977), pp. 138-40, 152, 165-66, 169-74, 198, 209.

9. J. Stillson Judah, *The History and Philosophy of the Metaphysical Movements in America* (Philadelphia: Westminster Press, 1967), pp. 63-72 passim.

10. Ibid., p. 12; Robert S. Ellwood, "The American Theosophical Synthesis," in *The Occult in America*, ed. Howard Kerr and Charles Crow (Urbana: Univ. of Illinois Press, 1983), p. 115; Judah, *Metaphysical Movements*, pp. 92-109 passim.

11. Judah, *Metaphysical Movements*, pp. 119-45.

12. J. Stillson Judah, *Hare Krishna and the Counterculture* (New York: Wiley, 1974), p. 192.

13. Robert C. Fuller, *Mesmerism and the American Cure of Souls* (Philadelphia: Univ. of Pennsylvania Press, 1982), pp. 119-43 passim; and Judah, *Metaphysical Movements*, pp. 194-225 passim.

14. Fuller, *Mesmerism*, p. 163; Bromberg, *Mind of Man*, p. 222.

15. Walt Whitman, *The Complete Writings of Walt Whitman*, ed. Richard M. Bucke, Thomas B. Harned, and Horace L. Traubel (New York: Putnam, 1902), 9:96-97; Taylor Stoehr, *Hawthorne's Mad Scientists: Pseudoscience and Social Science in Nineteenth-Century Life and Letters* (Hamden, Conn.: Archon Books, 1978), pp. 139-41.

16. George H. Daniels, *Science in American Society: A Social History* (New York: Knopf, 1971), p. 274.

17. Ellwood, *Theosophical Synthesis*, p. 130; Leahey and Leahey, *Occult Doubles*, p. 190; and R. Laurence Moore, "The Occult Connection? Mormonism, Christian Science, and Spiritualism," in Kerr and Crow, *Occult in America*, p. 140.

18. Leahey and Leahey, *Occult Doubles*, pp. 214-24.

19. Kerr and Crow, *Occult in America*, pp. 5-6; Leahey and Leahey, *Occult Doubles*, pp. 239-40.

Contributors

Harold Aspiz is professor of English at California State University, Long Beach. He is the author of *Walt Whitman and the Body Beautiful* (1980) and has published on nineteenth-century fiction and popular science in journals such as the *Emerson Society Quarterly, American Quarterly,* and *Nineteenth-Century Fiction.*

Robert W. Delp is professor of history at Elon College. He has published extensively on American spiritualism and Andrew Jackson Davis in leading scholarly journals: *Journal of American History, New England Quarterly, Journal of American Culture, New York Historical Society Quarterly,* and *Northwest Ohio Quarterly.* He has also contributed biographical sketches to *The Dictionary of North Carolina Biography* (1979).

Robert C. Fuller is associate professor of religious studies at Bradley University. He is the author of *Mesmerism and the American Cure of Souls* (1982) and numerous articles on religious thought and psychology. His most recent book, *Americans and the Unconscious* (1986), has been published by the Oxford University Press.

John L. Greenway is associate professor of honors and English at the University of Kentucky. He has published on Scandinavian literature, including *The Golden Horns: Mythic Imagination and the Nordic Past.* He is currently researching a book on the importance of energy to the nineteenth-century literary imagination.

George Hendrick, professor of English at the University of Illinois, Urbana-Champaign, is the author of many books ranging from bibliographical guides and checklists to studies and biographies of American writers, reformers, and doctors. Some of his books include: *Katherine Anne Porter* (1965), *Henry Salt: Humanitarian Reformer and Man of Letters* (1977), *Remembrances of Concord and the Thoreaus* (1977), (with Fritz Oehlschlaeger) *Toward the Making of Thoreau's Modern Reputation* (1977), and *On the Illinois Frontier: Dr. Hiram Rutherford* (1981).

Marshall Scott Legan is associate professor and head of the Department of History and Government at Northeast Louisiana University. He has published on medical movements and history in such journals as: *Bulletin of the History of Medicine, Journal of Mississippi History, Journal of the History of Medicine and Allied Sciences, Filson Club Historical Quarterly, Journal of Mississippi History,* and *Louisiana History.*

Taylor Stoehr is professor of English at the University of Massachusetts, Boston. He is the author of *Dickens: The Dreamer's Stance* (1965), *Hawthorne's Mad Scientists* (1978), *Nay-Saying in Concord: Emerson, Alcott, and Thoreau* (1979), and *Free Love in America: A Documentary History* (1979). As literary executor and authorized biographer of Paul Goodman, he has edited nine volumes to date that include Goodman's poetry, political, psychological, and literary essays, collected stories and sketches, and his novel *The Empire City. Words and Deeds: Essays on the Realistic Imagination* (AMS Press, 1986) is Professor Stoehr's most recent book.

C. Thomas Walters is assistant professor of art at Bloomsburg University. He has published articles on film, nineteenth-century American art history, and classic American writers in such journals as *Forum, Winterthur Portfolio, Journal of American Studies,* and the *University of Michigan Museum Handbook.*

Arthur Wrobel is associate professor of English at the University of Kentucky. His articles on Walt Whitman, phrenology, Mark

Twain, and nineteenth-century popular health concerns have appeared in *PMLA*, the *Journal of Popular Culture, American Literature,* and *American Studies*. He has been editor of *American Notes & Queries* since 1982.

Index